The Critic as Advocate

The Critic as Advocate

SELECTED · ESSAYS · 1941 – 1988

BERNARD · SMITH

In my beginning is my end. In succession
Houses rise and fall, crumble, are extended,
Are removed, destroyed, restored, or in their place
Is an open field, or a factory, or a by-pass.
Old stone to new building, old timber to new fires...

T. S. Eliot, 'East Coker'

WITHDRAWN

Melbourne
OXFORD UNIVERSITY PRESS
Auckland   Oxford   New York

OXFORD UNIVERSITY PRESS AUSTRALIA
Oxford New York Toronto
Delhi Bombay Calcutta Madras Karachi
Petaling Jaya Singapore Hong Kong Tokyo
Nairobi Dar es Salaam Cape Town
Melbourne Auckland
and associated companies in
Berlin Ibadan

OXFORD is a trade mark of Oxford University Press

National Library of Australia
Cataloguing-in-Publication data:

Smith, Bernard, 1961–
   The critic as advocate : selected essays
   1941–1988.

   Bibliography.
   Includes index.
   ISBN 0 19 553029 2.

   1. Painting, Australian – History. 2. Painting,
   Modern – 20th century – Australia – History.
   3. Art criticism – Australia – History–
   20th century. I. Title.
759.994

Designed by Pauline McClenahan
Printed in Hong Kong
Published by Oxford University Press,
253 Normanby Road, South Melbourne, Australia

Contents

Part IV   Pluralism in Practice: the 1960s

Part V   Reviews, Revisions and Revisitations:
the 1970s and 1980s

Acknowledgements

Wherever it is appropriate the place and date of original publication of each essay is noted at the foot of the commencing page of the essay. I wish here to express my sincere thanks and appreciation to those editors and publishers who first commissioned the essays in the periodicals and books enumerated below, and have given me permission to republish them here, namely: *Education, Journal of the New South Wales Teachers' Federation*, essay no. 2; *The Australian Quarterly*, no. 3; *Meanjin*, nos. 4, 5, 10, 12, 14, 16, 17, 18, 19, 64, 66, 74; Fine Arts Press, Ltd, nos.7,11; *Arna*, University of Sydney, no. 9; *Hermes*, University of Sydney, no. 13; *The London Magazine*, no. 23; *Age*, Melbourne, nos. 24, 25, 26, 27, 28, 29, 31, 32, 33, 35, 36, 37, 38, 39, 40, 41, 42, 43, 44, 45, 46, 47, 48, 49, 50, 51, 52,53; *The Australian Broadcasting Commission*, nos. 34, 65; *The Bulletin*, Sydney, nos. 54, 56; The Commonwealth Institute, London, no. 57; *Historical Studies*, University of Melbourne, nos. 58, 60, *Hemisphere*, no. 59; *Overland*, no. 61; Secker and Warburg, London, no. 62; *Art in Australia*, no. 63; *Age Monthly Review*, nos. 67, 72; *Island Magazine*, nos. 68, 69.

The following essays are here published for the first time: *Russell Drysdale*, no. 15; *The Antipodean Exhibition, Notes for the Opening Address*, no. 20; *The Antipodean Intervention*, no. 21, *Whither Painting?* no. 55.

List of Illustrations

To the memory of J. Lindsay Gordon
(1912–1988), carillonist, poet and teacher,
who pointed me down this track

Introduction:
Form, Value and Meaning

I have brought together here a selection of essays and reviews
from a larger body of work written between 1940 and 1988. At the
time I began to write there was little interest in Australian art as
an identifiable tradition. My work therefore developed as a kind
of advocacy of the art I admired and as a critique of those
dangers that, it seemed to me, the young and fragile tradition
had to face up to and confront if it were to remain viable. The
selections I have chosen should make this clear. They were written
to make the work of the artists I admired more accessible to the
general public. Those now chosen here may also help to reveal
the development of my own critical practice.

That viewpoint has no doubt changed in response to time and
circumstance; but I do not place a high value upon inconsistency.
I therefore have endeavoured over the years to construct a reasonably consistent critical practice, the dominant components of
which, in retrospect, now seem to be best described as form,
value and meaning. Indeed they could be reduced to the two
components form and meaning, since critical practice implies
evaluation. Some works of art are better than others. Once it
would not have been necessary to say this. Now it seems that
it is.

I take the view that a critic even at the best of times can only
hope to be an effective witness for his or her own generation. I
do not mean that it is impossible to develop a deep interest and
gain enjoyment from later work, but in that case the sense of
personal involvement has departed. A feeling of *déjà vu* sets in.
There is a tendency for the ageing critic too readily to relate what
may be genuinely novel work to the art of the past. What is
original about the new escapes sensibilities formed in earlier
situations.

My own work as a practising critic spans the years between

1942 and 1966, but was discontinuous, since a good deal of time was also taken up with related work in art education and the writing of art history. It seemed best, however, to present this selection chronologically. The result is that the oldest artists whose work is discussed are Sali Herman (b. 1898) and William Dobell (b. 1899), and the youngest Mike Brown (b. 1938) and Gareth Sansom (b. 1939). Although no claim is made that all important artists working in Australia during the 1940s, 1950s and 1960s have been considered I find that this selection does include, despite the contingent nature of my critical practice, comments on the work of just about all the artists I have admired who exhibited in those decades—with the exceptions of Godfrey Miller and John Passmore, two of the most important artists active in Australia during my lifetime.

So far as practical criticism is concerned my work really begins with the second essay in Part I, 'Some Aspects of Contemporary Art in Australia', a review of the fourth exhibition of the Contemporary Art Society when shown in Sydney in September 1942. However, I have begun with 'Art in the Soviet Union' because it will, among other things, indicate my political point of view at the time I began to write criticism.

It is virtually impossible now to recapture that deep feeling of warmth and friendship for the Soviet Union that so suddenly swept Australia during the months that followed Hitler's invasion of Russia in the northern summer of 1941. With the German army dominant over the whole of continental western Europe the early months of 1941 had brought news only of unmitigated disaster. The German invasion of Russia brought the first glimmer of hope that Hitler might be defeated. A few days after the invasion Sali Herman, an apolitical man if ever there was one, said to me, 'Hitler's made a fatal mistake. He'll never defeat the Russians'.

There was a sense in which we were all Stalinists in those days from Churchill and Curtin to the person in the street who fervently hoped that 'Uncle Joe' would defeat Hitler. The Nazis must not triumph. Against that overriding reality even the enormity of Stalin's destruction of all forms of political opposition in the USSR, as revealed in the show trials of the 1930s, paled into insignificance. There was perhaps a certain innocence in this warm-hearted support of the USSR which affected all sections of the community. But it was an innocence that supported an incontestable reality. Hitler had to be defeated.

My paper on 'Art in the Soviet Union' was not of course criticism in any sense of the word; it was a declaration of faith and hope. I had no direct knowledge of Soviet art and had put the material together from my reading. But since there are views first announced in this paper that I continue to hold—such as that concerning an élitist position in the production of art—it may be useful to spell out in some detail the situation in which the paper was prepared and given.

It was one of several papers read at the Conference on Soviet Culture held at Federation House, Phillip Street, Sydney, on 8 November 1941 and organized by the Aid Russia Committee. (Federation House continued to be an important centre of cultural activity in Sydney during the war years.) The time of the conference is significant. It took place four months after Hitler's invasion of Russia when Britain and the Commonwealth faced the might of the German armed forces alone and one month before the bombing of Pearl Harbour brought Japan and the United States into the war. The situation for the Commonwealth, with Russia as the only ally and by early November deeply invaded by the German army, seemed quite perilous.

It is not surprising therefore that the conference was a large and representative one, attended by 193 delegates from sixty-three cultural organizations. Then aged twenty-five, I must have been the youngest (and rawest) to speak. The conference was divided into sections. That devoted to medicine and science included Dr Grahame Drew, the Sydney Metropolitan Officer of Health; J. V. Duhig, Professor of Pathology at Queensland University, and Ian Clunies Ross, Professor of Veterinary Science at Sydney University. The section on education included papers by Elsie Blackshield, a Sydney schoolteacher who had visited the USSR in 1938, and John Dease, a well-known radio commentator. Russian music was discussed by Cyril Monk, a lecturer at the Sydney Conservatorium of Music, and Russian ballet by Raia Kuznetsova, trained in the USSR and a former dancer with the Bolshoi Ballet. The paper on architecture was given by Henry Pynor, who had worked in Russia as an architect during 1932–33, and the papers devoted to literature and drama were given by the writers Miles Franklin, Katharine Susannah Prichard and Frank Dalby Davison.

Despite my enthusiasm for Soviet efforts in conservation, ethnic art, and so on, it will be clear that I was less than enthusiastic about the little I had seen in reproduction of Soviet socialist realist art. But I believe the questions I raise in the paper are still relevant. Can value in art, even in modern societies, be so closely correlated with the personal freedom of the artist to do just what he or she wishes? The history of art certainly does not reveal such a close correlation. In that case has a structural change therefore taken place since, say, 1789? Does the emergence of modern society mean that value in art and personal freedom are now indivisible? The other question is this: socialist realism is so closely related to Stalinist repression that the work has been condemned on purely moral grounds. Is it possible that art of real aesthetic value has been produced under such tyrannous conditions? What, one wonders, will be the verdict a century hence? I recall how in our youth, under the influence of early modernism, we scorned what was described as the pseudo-classicism that emerged with David and the French Revolution and indeed most of Victorian painting as well. All that has changed. It would seem reasonable to assume on purely rational grounds that some Soviet socialist realist paintings are better than others. Are there masterpieces among them? Perhaps this judgement will have to be left to a time when more paintings become available to an international audience and when images of heroes of socialist labour perched on the top of buildings against the sky begin to appear less revolting to the eyes of discriminating 'western' viewers.

Although a mere tiro among Sydney art critics during the war years, I felt the need to draw attention to the fact that something unexpected was happening to modernism in Australia under the pressure of the war situation; the emergence of a style in some respects opposed to modernism, best described as social realism. The distinction between social realism and socialist realism is as important as the distinction between 'social' and 'socialist'. Socialist realism is an art of celebration, its closest affinities as a genre of painting being with history paintings of the academic type. Social realism possesses not a celebratory but a critical tone, directed for the most part at the social and moral shortcomings of capitalist society, though occasionally it can attempt a kind of stoical celebration. Consider, for example, Dobell's wartime labourers and Drysdale's cocky farmers. The other pressing need I felt during the war years was to expose the pro-fascist and anti-Semitic sentiments then widespread in Australian art circles and still given expression in the early years of the war when the victory of the Axis powers and Japan seemed a distinct possibility. During the later years of the war such sentiments were suppressed. Sir Lionel Lindsay at least was courageous enough to put his views in writing, but in doing so he spoke for a large number of his own generation.

The end of the war brought early but short-lived hopes for a better, more democratic and more community-oriented Australia in which the visual arts would play a much more significant role in Australian life. Those hopes were only partially realized. During the war years my experience of original art was limited largely to work exhibited at the annual exhibitions of the Contemporary Art Society, the Society of Artists, and other such exhibitions. The Macquarie Galleries was the one private gallery at that time that maintained a consistent standard of quality in their one-person and group exhibitions. This may have been a narrow enough base on which to begin to build a critical practice but it must be said that it was a base of original works not reproductions.

During the war years, after three camps in summer training, I was placed, with many other teachers, on army reserve. It was during the war years while teaching educationally maladjusted children at the Enmore Activity School that I gained some idea of John Anderson's philosophy mainly through four years of more or less continuous staff-room discussion with Tom Rose, one of Anderson's most able and devoted students, who was then a fellow teacher and close friend. From Rose I absorbed something of Anderson's pluralism, which greatly modified my rather overconfident Marxist approach to art without however eradicating it entirely. I came to accept Anderson's pluralism but not his apparent lack of interest in the unequal institutional powers that supported or opposed his 'plural forces' operating within society.

I have called Part II The Post-War Years and the Search for a Critical Canon, by which I mean that it seems to me in retrospect, though I could not have been aware of it at the time, that what I was then seeking to do was to develop a personal standard of critical practice by interpreting and evaluating the works of artists I admired. This was limited of course in these years to what original work was available. In 1945 I began an evening course in Arts at Sydney University. My first two years there strengthened an interest in the formal properties of art works, of the work as a self-contained artefact, and I gave less attention to social context and ideological implications. Here the work of Professor A. J. A. Waldock was influential. I read his books on *Hamlet* and *Paradise Lost and its Critics* and much admired his critical method, though I gained the uneasy feeling that the finesse and subtlety of his rhetoric tended to press the often reluctant reader, by means of rational argument about what were after all delicate nuances of meaning and sensibility, into inescapable 'Waldockian' readings of the texts under consideration. I must have been seeking a more open approach than that. But Waldock gave me an appreciation of the sense of responsibility that accompanies serious criticism. My discussions with Tom Rose had tempted me to read philosophy under Professor John Anderson. But after attending a few of his introductory lectures I decided instead to read the new course in classical archaeology then being offered for the first time by Professor A. D. Trendall. I did not take to Anderson. He seemed much too filled with his own presence—a man possessed of a Socrates complex and keen to play martyr—hero to the forces of the Establishment. It may have been a rash judgement. On the other hand I certainly gained much from attending Trendall's classes. He taught me something about formal analysis, style and the relation of both to history. Waldock and Trendall probably had a good deal of influence on what I wrote on Australian artists between 1945 and 1948. During those years only work exhibited in Sydney was available to me. So I saw little of the work of Melbourne artists such as Sidney Nolan, Arthur Boyd and John Perceval.

I have given Part III the somewhat facetious title Hotting it up during the Cold War: the 1950s. But the first few weeks after my return to Sydney in 1951 were neither amusing nor pleasant. After two years study at the Warburg Institute, University of London and travel in Germany, Italy, France, Belgium and Holland to acquaint myself with many of the great collections of Europe, I found to my dismay that the Director-General of the New South Wales Department of Education, who had taken a keen interest in my work bringing art exhibitions to country towns between 1944 and 1948, was now under pressure from the New South Wales Public Service Board and wanted to get me out of the Art Gallery of New South Wales as soon as he could. Apparently it was now deemed that my views on art were such that they might corrupt the youth of the state. It was only as the result of the direct personal intervention of Dr H. V. Evatt that I was permitted to remain. Not only the political but the whole cultural climate had altered radically during my years abroad. In 1951 it would have been impossible to publish a book like *Place, Taste and Tradition* (1945), as I found when I suggested a revised edition. The cold war had reached Australia.

Fortunately, as the result of Evatt's intervention, I was able to complete my Arts degree at Sydney. I had left it in abeyance during my studies abroad and then later, between 1954 and 1955,

I was able to find a most commodious funk-hole at the Australian National University and complete the research on eighteenth-century European perceptions of the Pacific that I had begun at the Warburg Institute. As a result of all this the 1950s were given over largely to research and teaching, particularly after I joined the staff of the Fine Arts Department of the University of Melbourne in 1956.

As the 1950s advanced I became increasingly disturbed by the growing tendency in art criticism both in Australia and abroad to proclaim the imminent end of 'representational' art. I had witnessed the emergence of this constricting element in late modernism in its early stages during my period of study in Britain and Europe between 1948 and 1950. It seemed to me that the fallacious but popular belief that it was only from art from which all representational elements had been banished that new and original work would issue was a subtle but sinister form of aesthetic censorship. If it prevailed it would destroy that dynamic pluralism that had nurtured the best work of early modernism. It was coming to Australia mostly from American sources and could only weaken the vitality of the new figurative art that had emerged in Australia during the war years and was still, in the work of Nolan, Boyd and others, being prosecuted with vigour and vitality. The dominance of abstraction could only impose a form of aesthetic censorship for which Australian art had no ready answer. This resulted in my involvement with the Antipodeans which I have discussed elsewhere. That occasion is marked here by the inclusion of two previously unpublished papers. There never was any intention of suggesting that abstract art had no part to play in the future. That would have been absurd. Rather, the Antipodean intervention sought to maintain the pluralist position that had obtained during the 1940s and not allow the severe constraints placed upon original figural art in the United States by the late modernist establishment to dominate the art scene here. In this I believe we were successful.

Part IV, Pluralism in Practice: the 1960s, covers the period beginning in July 1963 when I was offered the post of art critic to the *Age* newspaper, Melbourne, until I left for a further period of study abroad in June 1966. Writing for the general public in the *Age* was a completely different proposition from writing for quarterlies like *Meanjin*. In those days the art scene was small enough to allow me to see most shows opening each week and an attempt was made to notice most current exhibitions. This meant that even a major show could not be given more than 500 words.

Furthermore, as I had a full-time teaching post at the University of Melbourne I only allowed myself one day to see and write up all the week's exhibitions. The selected reviews of the 1960s published here were written under such conditions. Writing for the *Age* gave me an opportunity to put my pluralist position into practice. By pluralism I do not mean an even-handed attempt to be 'objective' or 'neutral'. Pluralism is not a sophisticated or fashionable way of sitting on criticism's fence. Pluralism, as I understand it, involves in practice the presentation of a personal viewpoint (at times quite strongly) but it also requires a fair treatment of artistic practices and positions that do not accord with one's personal view. If it is possible to make it clear, either implicitly or explicitly, that these practices, these positions, are not one's own, so much the better. It is in part simply a matter of decent manners; an agreement to tolerate diverse positions, not a fatuous attempt to mimic them. Of course, again in practice, the situation is never as mechanical as I have put it. In the presence of new and original art the viewpoint of the responsive critic can alter or even change significantly and perhaps permanently. For example, I have no sympathy with the metaphysical position figured forth in Roger Kemp's art but that has not precluded a warm and positive response to much of it.

Part V, Reviews, Revisions and Revisitations, covers the 1970s and 1980s. Although I have continued to engage in critical work since 1970 much of it is contained in reviews of books concerned with the art of my contemporaries, in the sense that I have used the word above, or about exhibitions of their work. This has given me the opportunity to defend my own position where I felt that to be necessary and also revise it or elaborate upon it. Fortunately the 1970s and 1980s have seen the publication of a considerable number of important books on Australian art, by Robert Hughes, Richard Haese, Humphrey McQueen, Gary Catalano, Patrick McCaughey and others. Several of their books are reviewed here. They have given me, among other things, the vicarious opportunity to revisit the work of artists I have admired in the past.

Very little pejorative criticism of the work of practising artists will be found here. Where it does occur it will be found in my early and immature writing. Personal attacks on the work of individual artists are of no permanent value. There are no invisible and inviolable Platonic standards of criticism to be maintained; it is rather one judgement against others. However, on issues such as the lingering pro-fascism of the 1940s and the abstract hegemony of the 1960s I have adopted a different line. I have tried to put my position as clearly and forcefully as I possibly could because it seemed to me that they were important issues not only for art but for the identity and continued vitality of Australian culture in general.

PART I

War, Realism and Fascism: 1941–1946

1

Art in the Soviet Union

—1941—

During the course of a lecture delivered to the Trades Guild of Learning at Birmingham in 1878, William Morris made a significant remark: 'I do not want art for a few,' he said, 'any more than education for a few or culture for a few'. Morris gave voice to the theme running through all Soviet art.

Never have we had so many conflicting views as to the nature and function of art as we have today. The western world has been beset by a dazzling display of movements and theories in art. Cubism, neo-plasticism, Cézannism, vorticism, surrealism, suprematism to mention but a few. Archaeologists have shown us the nature of art before the Flood. The formal achievements in stone of the African Negroes have been studied with an almost religious awe. But of the art of the Soviet Union we have heard little or nothing, and in the few instances where the silence has been broken criticism has usually been openly hostile. It has been said that the form of government prevailing in the Soviet Union is inimical to the growth of a vital art. It has been said that there the artist is little more than a tool of the state, that art has been narrowed to fit the procrustean bed of a rigid political doctrine. This afternoon I have no desire to prove anything, but if I can persuade you that the development of visual art in the Soviet Union is well worthy of patient and sympathetic study by everyone who has the real welfare of those arts at heart, I will be content.

Before the Revolution of 1917 the fine arts in Russia were the monopoly of the Tsarist nobility and of the Boyar and Kulak classes. This court had come under the influence of western art since the time of Catherine the Great. The art of the church,

First published in *Soviet Culture: A selection of talks at the Cultural Conference, November 1941*, Aid Russia Committee, Sydney, 1942.

on the other hand, followed the rich and ancient traditions of Byzantine art, and the greatest examples of Russian art today are the work of the early primitives of the Orthodox Church. The folk art derived its motifs from widely divergent sources, from the Scandinavian Vikings, from Byzantium and the Eastern influences from the Tartar invasions and from Iran.

The change to socialism in Russia from the point of view of the collection of these ancient art masterpieces of the church was as striking as any of those made in recent years by the great archaeological excavations. There were masterpieces hidden away in the dark recesses of the churches from which they had never been removed and hidden still more effectively by successive coats of paint. Due to the devotion and technical science of the members of the National Central Restoration workshops set up in Moscow in 1918, these works were slowly unveiled; many of them in the perfection of their original condition. Here are the words of Professor Igor Grabar, the head of the Restoration workshops:

In 1919 we had the great pleasure and privilege of taking up the task of uncovering one of the most renowned masterpieces of ancient Russian painting, 'Our Lady of Vladimir'. A masterpiece of the eleventh century, it had already been restored in the thirteenth, the background being altered and painted over, and had received similar treatment at the beginning of the sixteenth, seventeenth and nineteenth centuries. Further, there was every reason to suppose that it had been restored in the beginning of the fifteenth century by the greatest of all Russian masters, Andrei Rublév. Should one remove completely his work if beneath it there was no original but only a fragment of white ground for which he himself was responsible? Certainly not. Not only must the painting be preserved, but also every subsequent addition beneath which there is no original but only a fragment of white groundwork contemporaneous with the painting beneath. The restoration of 'Our Lady of Vladimir' was carried out in such a way that on this masterpiece there are preserved and visible the strata of all the centuries.

Hardly less important is the innovation made by the Restoration workshops in its experiments in the transference of complete layers of paint from a painting onto a fresh panel. Instead of destroying a layer of paint it has been found possible to remove it intact onto some other material. It is easy to see what extraordinary prospects are opened out for restoration work in the near future.

I have quoted at length because I think that this shows what extraordinary care was taken to preserve old masterpieces of art. Remember that this took place in 1919, when Russia was being threatened on several fronts by the armies of intervention and when the whole world was being told that the Bolshevik government had destroyed all culture and art in Russia. No really great work of art was destroyed intentionally during the Revolution. This was the considered opinion of Dr Laserson when speaking in this building several weeks ago. Dr Laserson was himself responsible for the collection of many masterpieces of fine and applied art immediately after the Revolution for the Hermitage Museum at Leningrad.

But what of Soviet art itself. The modern movement came to Russia in 1910. Moscow was kept in constant touch with Paris by means of exhibitions and periodicals. By 1914 the Muscovite collectors Shchukin and Morosov had collected over a hundred paintings by Picasso and Matisse, many of which could still be seen at the Tretyakov Gallery at Moscow in 1934,[1] for those in charge of the Soviet galleries have developed quite a passion, as I have mentioned, for taking paintings from cellars rather than for placing them in them.[2] The modern movement spread rapidly in Russia, manifesting itself in the form of rayonism, suprematism and constructivism. The names of Malevich, Rodchenko, Kandinsky and Tatlin are famous in this respect. Rebels of the art world of the Tsarist court, they came into their own following the Revolution. In 1919 Malevich and Rodchenko became professors at the Moscow Art School. They taught in art academies, designed posters, floats in decorative parades and statues to the heroes of the Revolution, and gigantic cubist façades to screen the Winter Palace during the mass celebrations.

But the workers and peasants did not like the great squares and circles covering the Winter Palace and they said so. Moreover, they had a right to say what they liked and what they did not like. A nice question in aesthetics this, and one which could only become a vital issue in a socialist society. The question was, have the people the right to determine the art which they desire or are such questions the particular province of a cultured élite? We will return to this question later. In 1919 Malevich had exhibited a white square on a white ground and called the picture, 'white on white'. This was in fact the rejection of art, and that is what Gan wrote in the art journal, *Constructivism*, at that time: 'Art is done for; there is no place for art in a society of labour. Labour, technique, organization, this is the ideology of our days'. Schism grew in the art institutes and art circles, many of the modernists went to work in industry, others left for Germany and Paris. Many, like the futurist Mayakovsky, turned to the creation of posters, newspaper drawings and placards.

From 1917 to 1921 these modernist experiments occupied the pride of place. During this period widely divergent views were expressed as to the nature of art in a socialist society. For instance, when asked by the Art Department of the People's Commissariat of Education to take part in a united exhibition without a jury, one of the prominent members of the World of Art Society said: 'Art is only for the chosen, it cannot be the property of all. It is royal, divine, and one who violates its sacredness will answer before God'.

But the leaders of Russia took a different attitude to art. Two years later Lenin was to express his view on art in this way:

Our opinion on art is not important. Nor is it important what art gives to a few hundreds or even thousands of a population as great as ours. Art belongs to the people. It must be rooted in and grow with their feelings, thoughts and desires. Can we give cake and sugar to a minority when the mass of the people lack bread? I mean this, not as you might think, only in the literal sense of the word, but also figuratively. We must keep the workers and peasants always before our eyes. We must learn to reckon and to manage for them, even in the sphere of art and culture. So that art may come to the people and the people to art, we must first of all raise the level of education and culture.

Remember Morris: 'I do not want art for a few, any more than education for a few or freedom for a few'.

From 1922 until 1932 Soviet art steadily moved from the formalist experiments of the early period to an acceptance of the general principles of socialist realism. This new art was an endeavour to create canvasses not only new as to theme, but also imbued with a new conception disclosing the life of the new man and the entire inner meaning of human relationships in the Soviet Union. Innumerable societies arose and the names of the well-known artists are legion; names like that of Aleksandr Deineka, Saryan the Armenian painter and Chaikov the sculptor are steadily building the power and influence of the socialist school of painting. I shall not deal with any of these artists individually now because of the shortness of my time, and to do justice to an artist one needs good reproductions of his work.

I have summarized the main development in Russian art since 1917, but there is another aspect which is equally important. The Soviet Union is a vast republic comprising numerous nationalities, all of which possess a definite cultural tradition and folk art. Perhaps the most famous example of the Soviet government's interest in the revival and development of traditional craftsmanship is the regrowth of art in the former icon-painting towns of

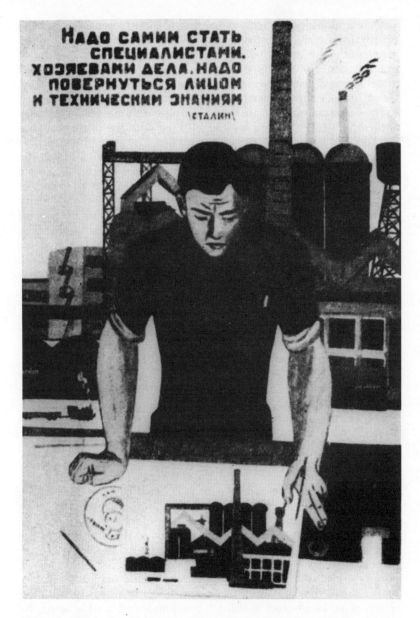

Aleksandr Aleksandrovich Deineka, *We must ourselves become specialists*, poster.

Palekh and Mnestra. Icon painting in these towns reached its zenith in the eighteenth century and began to decline in the nineteenth. Today Palekh art has overcome the craft decline of the last century and is producing exquisite lacquer work and distemper painting, the literary figures of Pushkin, Lermontov, Gorki and Cervantes being popular subjects.

The Eurasian nomads are the world's greatest masters of tapestry and carpet design, which is closely linked with the cattle breeding forming the industrial basis of nomad life. The style of the carpets under the Tsarist regime was steadily declining and technique was deteriorating. Instead of the beautiful and lasting vegetable dyes there came a flood of aniline dyes with the invasion of industrialism. After the Revolution the story changed. Many thousands of women carpet weavers in all parts of the Soviet Union were united in handicraft groups and associations. The old vegetable dyes were restored and their production recommenced by the state factories. Scientific institutions are carefully fostering the best old methods of carpet-making, developing the initiative of the women carpet weavers and transforming them from artisans into artists.

These are but two examples of the many others that could be cited to show the earnest endeavour to foster the traditional art and craft work of the varied races of the Soviet Union. In Armenia, Turkmenistan, Uzbekistan and Georgia there are flourishing schools of national arts. It is particularly interesting to note the survival of the traditional techniques within many of the new paintings from these republics.

Let us turn now to the economic position of the artist in the Soviet Union today. Planning is the basis of Soviet economics and art is included in that planning. The most important material basis is the All-Union Artists' Co-operative. This has branches all over the Soviet Union. Take the case of the co-operative in Moscow. Painters are expected to paint two pictures a year, the themes of these pictures being planned jointly by the artist and the co-operative. Artists are given commissions to proceed to new constructions, to the collective farms, to the republics of the Soviet Union, or to join geographical expeditions. In 1933 four hundred artists were sent on these commissions. The artist is given the choice of the place to which he would like to travel; one may choose the Ural building plant, another the ship-building wharves at Leningrad, a third Samarkand and Tashkent or the collective tea farms of Batum, and so on. The Soviet artist certainly cannot be said to suffer from lack of themes. And who are the patrons, the buyers of all this work? Firstly, there is the Central Buying Commission, which buys for museums; then there are also workers' clubs, palaces of culture, sanatoria and rest homes and other Soviet organizations. It is doubtful whether any country can boast of visitors numbering hundreds of thousands to the important art exhibitions in the capital cities. These, it may be added, are active visitors: they fill out questionnaires about their impressions, they excitedly discuss the positive and negative characteristics of the works. Lectures and debates are arranged at all important exhibitions. The price of oil pictures in proportion to the skill of the artist and to the size varies from 300 to 3000 roubles; some of the prices run as high as 10 000 roubles; water-colours, 150—300 roubles; engravings, 50—200 roubles; sculptures, 1500—2000 roubles and monumental sculptures between 15 000 and 30 000 roubles.

There is little doubt that the Soviet Union today has given more thought to the cultivation and improvement of the visual arts than any other country. The economic position of the artist has been assured, the art and handicraft traditions of the many national cultures preserved and developed, adult aesthetic education pursued both in the museum and the factory, and artistic ability fostered in gifted children by excellent provisions of the education system. There remains but one important question, which I have purposely left till last: the question of individual freedom and the Soviet artist. It is true that socialist themes are definitely encouraged and the earlier modernist experiments dis-couraged. Will this attitude, we may reasonably ask, encourage or stultify the growth of the new art? At present it is impossible to give the final answer to that question, for Soviet art is a living thing, and therefore the answer lies in the future. But we must be careful not to attribute an overwhelming importance to this question, for individual freedom as a measure of art values is quite useless. The artist in Egypt, Mesopotamia, Mexico, Greece and Byzantium was not free, as we have come to understand that word. The artist as a free individual agent became common only in the nineteenth century, and art since then has not attained the perfection of style of most of the preceding periods of art. We must realize also, that for the Soviet Union the question was not a mere academic discussion. Russia had to above all preserve the socialist civilization which she had brought to birth. Therefore art had to be identified with the people and their needs. Art could not be considered as above the level of the ordinary man, for along that path lay the dangers of disruption, disintegration and the death of the new society. For the apparently harmless idealist theory of art, which believes that the history of art is written in the biography of genius, has been distorted to serve the purpose of fascism. Hitler, speaking at the Nuremberg Congress of the National Socialist Party in September 1937, said: 'A true epoch-making artistic accomplishment will therefore be the work of a single, isolated, gifted man, a prophet far in advance of his contemporaries, it can never be the result of an ordinary average collective effort'.

Such is the fascist attitude to art, and socialist realism is the one principle that consistently opposes the fascist theory: it is art defending itself against its own death. Art organized, but organized for its own survival. Today the unfortunate artists of France, who built with so much ardour the little towers of the modern movement, are realizing to their sorrow that ivory is a poor material for fortification. It is true that Soviet art has created no great masterpieces, but can we justly expect masterpieces of visual art in the heroic period of a new civilization? The very slowness of growth is a source of strength to our belief, for we are not concerned with the growth of a minor development, such as the symbolist movement in poetry, or of impressionism in painting. We are dealing with something deeper and more significant, with the fundamental change that has occurred in the livelihood and belief in the future of a whole community of peoples. Today we cannot measure that growth because a culture always builds its own standards and values. But we can appreciate the possibilities of the future. It would have been difficult if we had lived in the first century of our era to realize that the strange symbols of birds and fishes painted on the dark walls of the Roman catacombs would blossom after fourteen centuries in the works of a Giotto and a Raphael or, to move farther into the past, could the celebrants of the ancient spring rites of Thrace know that one day those rites would provide the religious content of the Elgin Marbles? But today we realize that those primitive art forms possessed such great latent potentialities because they arose, not from something individual merely, but linked with the common spirit of a people.

Soviet art, too, is linked with the common spirit of men, linked with the will to survive. It is not the greatest art, but it is accumulating the experiences, the raw material, the folk law of its future, and we can say that if the fulfilment, the fruition of those experiences equals the price it is paying for them, then the art of socialism will not rank least in the achievements of men.

Notes

[1] This is literally true but from 1932, with the acceptance of socialist realism as the official style, paintings by Picasso and Matisse and many other leading artists of the modern movement were removed from the walls and kept in storage.

[2] The reference here is to the fact that the trustees of the National Art Gallery of New South Wales at that time (1941) were refusing to show modern masterpieces from the exhibition of French and British Modern Art, better known as the Herald Exhibition, brought to Australia by Sir Keith Murdoch for exhibition in Melbourne and Sydney during 1939, but held for safe-keeping during the war years by the National Art Gallery of New South Wales until 1945.

2
Some Aspects of Contemporary Art in Australia
—1943—

Last year's Contemporary Art Exhibition, held in Sydney in September, has proved one thing: there is nothing that can be called 'the modern group' in this country. What we do see among the exhibitors are a number of contemporary tendencies, differing to a greater extent among themselves than any differences which they may have in common from so-called conservative and traditional art. This results from a self-effacing selection committee, which has been more democratic than even the society's constitution, which bans representative art.

No doubt the members of this committee have been distressed at times by the vision of those heavily-bound volumes one meets in the second-hand bookshops, labelled 'Modern Art', the contents of which are now dusty Victorianism. By the abolition, in effect, of a selection committee the society hopes to establish a kind of permanent contemporaneity. While the intention is perhaps the best in the world, the effect of such a policy, as with the French Academy after 1791 and the Salon des Refusés, will probably be fatal if the society still desires to preserve its identity as a body with a defined attitude and policy. On the other hand, the society could become a valuable organizing committee that would arrange a cross-section of the painting (and the sculpture?) of the country annually. Such an organization is needed, and the Contemporary Art Society, being progressive in outlook and national in compass, is the only body that looks like fulfilling this function effectively.

The tendencies in art in this country today, as reflected in this year's Contemporary Art show, are widely divergent. It is absurd nowadays to talk about 'modern art' as a single entity; and a society exhibiting so many different and conflicting tendencies

First published in *Education*, Journal of the New South Wales Teachers' Federation, 22 February 1943.

would do well to realize that it cannot hope to speak for all its members; and its critics should realize that when they speak of 'modern art' they are using a term which no longer has any significance. The quotation from Herbert Read on the Sydney catalogue, for instance, is only a view of a section, and that not the most significant, of this year's exhibitors.[1]

Purely abstract and constructivist work is definitely losing its adherents. Eric Wilson shows that an accomplished technique and a feeling for design and colour can still build an abstract work into a very effective composition; and W. Armstrong, of Victoria, shows what can happen to abstractions without technique, feeling or design. Braque, after all, did these things much better, and it is doubtful whether any real importance can be attached to our colonial derivatives in his manner. Abstract art will not have a future in Australia; its rigid formalism has little place for the infusion of national qualities, for an art that derives nothing from its own place is as much an artistic misnomer as an art that gains nothing from its own time. In industrial subjects such as Wilson's *Hot Feed, Cold Feed, Steam*, Ebert's *Furnace Man* and *Factories—Streets—Houses* and also in Eric Thake's *Brownout*, the new content is struggling within a form evolved by the cubists from their X-ray attitude to their nineteenth-century subjects which usually look better cut to pieces anyway.

Daumier or Orozco would have been better points of departure in the search for adequate forms for these subjects.

The best painters among the modern group are not producing the most vital pictures. The paintings of S. Herman, Rah Fizelle and F. Medworth always please by their competent handling and assured technique. Medworth's experiments in various media are always a source of interest, and a constant reminder to over-ambitious amateurs that there is still a craft of painting though modernist propaganda has done much to obscure the fact.

Surrealism is not so much in evidence this year as previously. The paintings of James Gleeson are disappointing when considered in the light of the tremendous promise of last year's large picture.[2] There seems to have been a relapse to an earlier attitude without any appreciable gain. Still the actual painting of pictures is an achievement at present, and it is hoped that the reaffirmed allegiance to Dali will give way to something more personal in the future.

Painters like Elaine Haxton, Alice Danciger and Ivor Francis are charming within the limited sphere of conversational pieces—slight things in which technique and subject are in harmony. Their weakness lies in a tendency to slip back to the nasty adolescent paintings that pour from girls' high schools. Co-education might be a solution. This *Flapping Skirt* style—to coin a name from Ivor Francis' picture—has nothing particularly to do with contemporary painting and borders on the banal. Miss Haxton, with her *Street Scene, Sydney, 1942*, reproduces the Hollywood conception of the American Negro. She sees them superficially, as the eighteenth century, with its insufferable chinoiserie, saw Chinese art. A race that has consistently proved itself more artistic and rhythmically conscious when it comes to matters of plastic art could well have been spared this local comment.

Melbourne has always been the chief storm centre of Australian art, and it is from Melbourne that this year's most significant development comes. The new group is avowedly literary in its approach, and there is a strong element of propaganda in most of the paintings. Such a label is sufficient to damn them in the eyes of the more conservative, 'Moderns' and the members of the more respectable art societies. Therefore those who have the development of art in this country at heart will watch their growth with interest. The paintings of Perceval and Boyd are not nice paintings, and there is still a wide margin between the strength of conception and the painted picture, but they are at least a direct challenge to preciousness, and we have seen too much of it in the last few years in Australian art. The paintings of Bergner owe much to Daumier, but since last year his technical ability and the force of his presentation have developed. It is to be regretted that his work was not suitably hung. Arthur Boyd's paintings have a certain rawness of conception. They are ambitious works which at present levy too great a strain upon a somewhat limited technical equipment. It is precisely this strain, however, which may lead the painter to a mature style. *Progression* is a better piece of social criticism than *Blessed Are The Merciful*; it is also a better painting. The presentation of horror in painting unalleviated by any other factor, even where the realities of the subject are in every way as revulsive, usually creates in the mind of the spectator an effect opposite to that intended by the artist. Any human tendency to react sympathetically to the victims of injustice is overpowered by a physiological loathing of the disgusting. If the artists of the Melbourne group seek to arouse more than loathing, to avoid the accusation of presenting 'chambers of horror', they will have to seek to arouse a complex emotion. Robert Owen realized this when he wrote of his war poems: 'The poetry is in the pity'. This is a central problem for

Arthur Boyd, *Progression*, 1941, oil on board, 90.0 × 55.2 cm Heide Park and Art Gallery, Melbourne.

realism, and its successful solution will be fraught with significance for Australian art. Boyd's *Blessed Are The Merciful* and Nan Hortins' *Mourners* could be quoted as showing the need both to realize and to solve this problem.

The new grouping with all these deficiencies is the most vital movement in Australian art today. They are obviously painters with working-class sympathies, and painting with a proletarian bias is something new in Australian art, though its expression has been widely developed in literature. The development of painting here, as elsewhere, depends largely upon patronage. The 'squattocracy' gave the initial patronage upon which the Australian impressionism of Streeton and Heysen rode to fame and high prices. Today that particular class seems as bankrupt of ideas as of intelligent politicians, and consequently has nothing to bring to the nourishment of art. The disciples of modernism have waged wordy battles with the lingering protagonists of an art championed by an effete pastoral patriarchy, but would flirt with their descendants and gather their patrons from the owners of the large commercial houses, the young-rich, and the critics of ultra-conservative news-sheets. Such a policy invites suicide. So long as the supporters of modernism identify aesthetic sensibility with a large bank account they profess their ignorance of the real causes of the modern movement itself. The desire for this patronage is also seen in the absurd prices placed upon paintings by many amateur artists who do not depend upon painting for their livelihood. Such prices would serve a useful purpose if there were any accomplished professional painters in this country depending on the sales of their paintings for existence. The high-priced amateur painting would probably remain unsold and ensure the professional the receipt of enough money to go on painting. As there are at present no professional painters of any moment in the country, and the development of painting depends largely upon amateur and semi-professional painters, young amateurs would do well to price their pictures at a level making sales possible and in keeping with a war situation, instead of using the price as a personal estimation of what the painting might realize in Elysium. Many painters in the Contemporary Art Society have realized this and placed reasonable prices on their pictures. After all, the 'boom' periods in Australian art have passed, and their passing will not be greatly lamented.

Contemporary art has reached its adulthood and will have to begin making adult decisions, such as the cutting of apron-strings; future exhibitions, therefore, should be of great interest and importance to the development of Australian art.

Josl Bergner, *Aborigines in Fitzroy*, *c.*1943, oil on board, 62 × 49.5cm. Art Gallery of South Australia.

Notes

1 The statement from Herbert Read, published first in 1936, read:

> What we really expect in a work of art is a certain personal element—we expect the artist to have, if not a distinguished mind, at least a distinguished sensibility. We expect him to reveal something to us that is original—a unique and private vision of the world. It is this expectation which, blinding the plain man to all other considerations, leads to a confirmed misunderstanding of the nature of art. Such a man becomes so intent on the meaning or message of a picture that he forgets that sensibility is a passive function of the human frame, and that objects received in sensibility have their objective existence. The artist is mainly concerned with this objective existence.
>
> We must not be afraid of this word 'abstract'. All art is primarily abstract. For what is aesthetic experience, derived of its incidental trappings and associations, but a response of the body and mind of man to invented or isolated harmonies? Art is an escape from chaos. It is movement ordained in numbers; it is mass confined to measure: it is the indetermination of matter seeking the rhythm of life.

2 I was referring to Gleeson's 'Images of Spring Disguised in Lethal Attitudes of Duty'. It was illustrated and discussed in *Angry Penguins*, no. 2, 1941, The Adelaide University Arts Association, pp. 30–1.

3

Art and Mr Lawlor

—1943—

The article entitled Present Discontents in Australian Art in the last issue told us a great deal about the present discontents of Mr Lawlor, nothing about discontents in our art.[1] The reading of personal emotion into objective situations is the long-established principle of the myth-maker; and Mr Lawlor's article shows his undoubted ability in this direction. It is the object of the present article to examine some of these myths.

Three years ago Mr Lawlor wrote in an address to the Melbourne Contemporary Art Society: 'We must make active response to any public lecture or broadcast talk or debated opinion that has as its aim the obstruction of the movement that is known as Modern Art'. But today he writes: 'these Contemporary-Art-Society people are for the most part as far removed from any real interest in art, *per se*, as are the great majority of people'. Whence comes the present apostasy? Has he or has the Contemporary Art Society altered appreciably?

There are several points at issue. Mr Lawlor is worried by the large number of disparate experiences he received from last year's Contemporary Art Exhibition. 'Of precisely *what* genre is the experience we are undergoing before these paintings? Is it an aesthetic, a religious or a merely neural experience,' he asks. The inference here is that each picture evokes a similar experience in all of us, which is patently false. Artists are not people who spend their lives marking off the fields of various sciences, politics, aesthetics, etc. The experiences we gain from pictures are usually complex. Mr Lawlor is endeavouring to make the point that certain of these experiences are valid and that others are invalid. For Mr Lawlor the only valid experience we derive from a picture is an aesthetic experience. When he talks about the aesthetic

First published in *The Australian Quarterly*, vol. xv, no. 1, March 1943, pp. 76–81.

experience it is not possible to tell whether he means a peculiar way of regarding *anything* which certain people possess, or that it is a particular *type* of experience aroused in us by a particular type of object e.g. a work of art. By saying, 'Of precisely *what* genre is the experience we are undergoing before these paintings? Is it an aesthetic (etc.) experience', he implies the second view. But he implies the first when he says, 'the essential crux and quiddity of the aesthetic experience is that it operates in ineluctable isolation *away from the common experience*' (my italics). In short, Mr Lawlor does not know whether it is his 'aesthetic imagination' or certain qualities in the pictures seen which make possible his aesthetic experience. This confusion wrecks his argument throughout the article. Of course the important point which he does not touch at all is whether there is any such thing as an aesthetic experience. If I. A. Richards did prove one thing it was that from the standpoint of psychology there is no such thing as an aesthetic experience which is qualitatively different from any of our other experiences.[2] Yet it is just from arguments derived from psychology that Mr Lawlor endeavours to establish this badly-worn concept.

But the central point of contention was that the 'Loud majority' of the paintings were 'ideological'. According to Mr Lawlor such pictures, not being 'artistic', have no right to be shown in an art exhibition. He infers that it is not possible for a picture to possess 'ideas' and at the same time tickle his phantom elf, 'the aesthetic experience'. Presented with *The Last Supper*, Mr Lawlor would be either tickled aesthetically *or* he would be disconcerted by non-aesthetic 'ideas' which were associated with the subject. These ideas could not enter into his appreciation for if they did that would imply that an ideological painting could also have an aesthetic value, which he denies vigorously. The simple fact is that *The Last Supper* is an ideological painting in the ordinary sense of the term because it can present us with all kinds of ideas besides being judged aesthetically. Indeed if Mr Lawlor is so concerned about paintings frankly presenting 'ideas' then he should have begun his polemic three years ago when surrealist paintings were first exhibited in any quantity, because these pictures are frank endeavours to introduce a type of literary content into art. At that time, however, he was a most ardent supporter of the Contemporary Art Society and his references were then always spiced with a judicious diplomacy. In passing, I might point out that his naive belief that painters become surrealists in order to propagate the teachings of Marx and

Engels shows a complete misunderstanding of both surrealism and Marxism. Surrealism is probably the most facile of the many distortions of Marxism; its spurious political façade usually embarrasses its adherents.

If then, 'ideological' painting, as far as the modern movement is concerned, began several years ago, why has Mr Lawlor waited so long to voice his disagreement? The reason is obvious to anyone who read his article. It is not so much 'ideas' in painting to which he objects—indeed in 1939, during the course of the lecture which has already been mentioned, he said, 'I believe that you cannot paint or carve or write to any purpose unless the terms of your expression are given in the idiom, *and with immediate reference to the ideas*, that are current in the place in time in which you happen to be born'—it is rather certain *kinds* of ideas which arouse his ire, ideas which he would say are 'propaganda, inimical to questions of value'. The major portion of his article is a dissertation on dialectical materialism, which he considers a dangerous influence upon art. This is what he means when he calls paintings 'ideological' i.e. those paintings which may have derived something from their authors' acquaintance with dialectical materialism. He is not satisfied to say that such paintings from his point of view are bad art but proceeds to question the right of such artists to show their pictures in an 'art' exhibition. To this extent Mr Lawlor has joined the ranks of the red-baiters. Necessity certainly makes strange bedfellows even among art critics.

What arguments does Mr Lawlor bring forward to show that ideas have no place in a work of art? He says, 'the Truth of any human experience if judged at all must be judged in terms of value', i.e. it must be evaluated in terms of value, which is nothing but the purest tautology. Works of art are judged on the plane of value but they are not produced on that plane. Mr Lawlor fails to distinguish between the process of creating and the process of evaluating a work of art. This is a major error from one who wants to give so much advice as to how works of art should be produced. Leaving in abeyance the question whether the nature of the ideas presented by an 'ideological' work of art enters into its evaluation, let us consider whether the nature of the ideas of the artist assists in the production of the work of art. If this is beside the point for Mr Lawlor it is not beside the point for artists who do not talk about pictures but paint them. Dante did not write the *Inferno* to Mr Lawlor's pale goddess of 'creative responsibility', or to satiate our 'aesthetic experiences,' rather he was driven to it through a whole labyrinth of ideas among which were his idealized love for Beatrice, Thomastic scholasticism, the political intrigues of his time, and so on. All these things were aspects of the ideological tensions of his age and he reacted to them in his various capacities of poet, philosopher, Christian and lover, and the generation of actual verse forms, e.g. the sonnet and *terza rima* developed directly as the most adequate formal vehicle for the aesthetic expression of those complex ideological tensions. Without the sustaining power of his religious and political beliefs Milton's longer works would never have been written, simply because there would have been no *need* to write them. Imagine some emasculated Herrick lacking his charm, if you are a devotee of intellectual pastimes, and you have a Milton without his 'non-aesthetic' beliefs.

The poetry of Gerard Hopkins was not written because he found an interesting little device (Mr Lawlor would call it a 'gadget') known as 'sprung' rhythm, but because that rhythm literally sprang from the complex non-aesthetic beliefs of the poet. Ideological beliefs have always entered into the production of works of art, and they remain in them crystallized in their aesthetic forms. Indeed Mr Lawlor himself, with his own brand new aesthetic 'absolute' (or is it just a poor re-hash of Croce and Bergson to the logical detriment of both) Creative Responsibility, finds it necessary to smuggle in 'content' or 'ideology' in disguise to make his system work. He says, 'Creative art is the formulation of profound aesthetic *symbols*, which serve, when historically determined, to reinforce the spiritual authority and logical continuity of the tradition in which it is generated' (my italic). Aesthetic symbols, we might ask, of what? If the symbol is considered as being inseparable from the aesthetic imagination then it is a symbol of itself, i.e. it is not a symbol at all. If it is a true symbol it is a symbol of something 'non-aesthetic'. In this way Mr Lawlor introduces 'ideology' to make his system work. Again he says, 'the artist continually arrives at annihilating conclusions', but we are also informed that 'the aesthetic experience operates in ineluctable isolation away from the common experience'. If so then what annihilating conclusions are arrived at? The only answer is that acting in isolation the aesthetic experience begins to annihilate itself.

And this is precisely what happens. For the belief that the artist can only derive inspiration from participation 'within the tradition' is a particularly dangerous type of aesthetic incest, which has itself become an ideology, perhaps the only ideology which could really be said to be inimical to existence of any given art style. It is the type of ideology which manifests itself historically at the ends of 'styles' and is common to Egyptian, classic and Byzantine art in their last stages, and it is present of course in much of the art of our own age.

I say that this belief in the 'non-participation' of the artist in his social milieu, is itself an ideology. Since ideologies have a history it will be interesting to trace the modern development of that to which Mr Lawlor subscribes. Croce, the Italian philosopher, gave it definition when he wrote, 'the aesthetic fact, therefore, is form, and nothing but form'.[3] Croce maintained that art was 'intuition', and although opposed to fascism his theory, which posed art as a peculiarly non-material activity, influenced the fascist attitude to art. Gentile, his student, became one of the best known of the fascist philosophers. 'Art,' says Gentile:

is the self-realization of the spirit as subject. Man becomes enfolded in his subjectivity, and hears but the voice of love or other inward summons. Living without communication with the world, he refrains from affirming and denying what exists and what does not exist. He simply spreads out over his own interior world and dreams.[4]

Compare Mr Lawlor: 'it [i.e. art] is non-revolutionary in its operations, because its magnetic field or psychic potential is entirely beyond the scope of political and societal judgment'. Mr Lawlor's views are also closely allied to those of a house painter of some moment, who once said, 'A true epoch-making artistic accomplishment will therefore be the work of a single, isolated, gifted man, a prophet far in advance of his contemporaries'.[5] Mr Lawlor says 'the title of artist is only applicable to the man who recognises art as the ultimate criterion of his being, toward which all his mental and spiritual faculties are in a state of continual polarisation or magnetic inspiration'.

Now I am not inferring that Mr Lawlor is a fascist or that Hitler does not know a great deal about the nature of art. But I do say that there is no appreciable difference between Mr Lawlor's ideas about the nature of art and the fascist theory of the nature of art. What we have to remember is that it is just with this idealistic façade about art being the peculiar province of a few gifted individuals that the fascists have been able to cut ruthlessly and lethally at the very roots of European culture. Nor has the 'idealistic façade' and its association been confined to European countries. In 1933 Michael Gold, of the United States, evidenced Archibald MacLeish's poem, 'Frescoes for Mr Rockfeller's Centre', as an example of the 'Fascist Unconscious'.[6] If any further evidence is needed to demonstrate the interdependence of the idealist façade in art and a potentially fascist outlook, Mr Lawlor will again furnish us with an example. In *Comment*, January 1942, Mr Lawlor has an article in which he intimates that Alister Kershaw is the poetic genius we have all been waiting for. Mr Kershaw has in the same issue what he might call a prose poem. Here is a typical extract:

The mediocraties, the less-than-men are marshalled for attack. They, the Many, gods of the golf club and the dance floor, they are at our throats. We, the poets, the natural aristocrats are menaced by the rabble. En garde, En garde: but let us not close ranks, *let us become a group. Let us move swiftly, alone, to crush the infamy*. But it is not so easy as one would think to obliterate these sans-culottes. Consider the latest cackling conceit in the latest cackling novel! Consider the Marxists—those swinish disciples of equality and fraternity—consider the tennis court and the bridge parties! Listen to the insane toccata of talk in the ballrooms and the studios! They are everywhere, these sub-human cretins. Let us get the smell out of our nostrils; they stink, massed pullulatingly together, how they stink! [my italics]

This from Mr Lawlor's genius! If Mr Lawlor knows anything about ideologies he will have known for exactly a year now that the above is a perfect expression of the fascist ideology in Australian literature.

Is this how art becomes the ultimate criterion of your being, Mr Lawlor?

Notes

[1] *The Australian Quarterly*, vol. xiv, no. 4, December 1942, pp. 33–43.

[2] I. A. Richards, *Principles of Literary Criticism*, Kegan Paul, London, 1934, ch. 2, The Phantom Aesthetic State.

[3] Benedetto Croce, *Aesthetic*, tr. Douglas Ainslie, Macmillan, London, 1909, p. 16.

[4] Giovanni Gentile, *The Reform of Education*, tr. D. Bigongiari, Harcourt, Brace & Co., New York, 1922, quoted in Melvin Rader, *No Compromise*, Gollancz, London, 1939, p. 266.

[5] Adolf Hitler, 'Lecture on Art and Culture, Nürnberg Party Conference, September 7, 1937', quoted in Rader, p. 267.

[6] Michael Gold, 'The Fascist Unconscious', *New Republic*, July 1933.

4
The New Realism in Australian Art
—1944—

The generation of Cézanne is not our generation. It is just when a civilization or an art movement seeks to canalize the stream of art to its own rules and canons that its influence wanes and the stream breaks over the banks into the forbidden meadows. Yet all societies, for they are social institutions, gather sets of ideas, conventions and finally dogmas. This is as true for modernism as any other art movement. Peter Pan was never more than a beautiful myth. How then can art societies expect to remain always young, eternally contemporary? Most of the idols of the modern movement—Picasso, Braque, Matisse—today are old men. They have painted their pictures, the critics have praised them or abused them, some have made their fortunes, and others have died hungry. The period of their propaganda is over. We have to study and collect what they have contributed of value to art, throw out the rubbish, and not allow the limitations of the aesthetic which bound them to bind us.

Of recent years there has been a definite change of attitude among those who profess modernism in art, and the term includes the varied group of ideas and practices flowing from the Cézanne watershed. In the early years of this century, the modernists' appeal was to archaeology, history and science. Today the emphasis is placed on aesthetic passion and the sanctity of genius. This was to be expected, for the earlier appeal brought with it a crop of bad mistakes. T. E. Hulme, for instance, prophesied that from the modern movement would grow an art, 'hard, cold and linear'. It was to be a geometric art quite different from the organic arts of Europe. Clive Bell prophesied similarly. It was to be an art that would catch the 'spirit' of machinery in its abstract and geometric forms, a modern post-Byzantinism.

First published in *Meanjin Papers*, vol. 3, no. 1, Autumn 1944, pp. 20–5.

But the latest development of contemporary painting has been, on the contrary, a trend towards a realism in which the previous insistence on abstract values has given way to a new representational art quite unlike the illusionist academic painting from which modernism reacted so successfully and violently during its period of growth.

Epstein never allowed himself to be carried away by the excesses of modernism. It was his opinion that 'to think of abstraction as an end in itself is undoubtedly letting oneself be led into a cul-de-sac, and can only lead to exhaustion and impotence'. Whether it is *Genesis, Adam, Consummatum Est*, or any other of his greater works, the power of the idea has guided the artist's creation. Yet the pure modernist always views the presentation of 'ideas' in art with suspicion. The late Eric Gill, one of England's finest engravers and carvers, was always sceptical about the claims of the 'aesthetic' higher criticism. Henry Moore, leading exponent of abstraction in English sculpture, has under the pressure of war conditions, returned in his pen drawings to the realism of air-raid shelter themes. The Mexican muralists Rivera and Orozco, after passing through a transitional stage of abstractionism and subjective painting, during which they developed their technical equipment enormously, reached realism and maturity in an art based on the life and history of the Mexican people.

In Germany, before the crushing of all creative art under Hitler, modern art was already on the long and hard road back to reality. It may be observed as a reaction from the mysticism of Kandinsky and Klee. Otto Dix and George Grosz among painters, Gropius the architect, Ernst Barlach the sculptor, came under the influence of modernism; all of them later rejected the subjectivism of its aesthetic.

Today in our own country there is a similar restlessness. The paintings of Yosl Bergner, Noel Counihan, V. G. O'Connor and Arthur Boyd among Victorian painters, and in New South Wales the work of Russell Drysdale, William Dobell, Herbert McLintock, Douglas Watson and Geoffrey Collings, all point in the direction of a new realism stemming from the contemporary movement. Even the work of such a highly personal painter as James Gleeson shows a movement from purely subjective themes that characterized an earlier phase of his work. The Museum of Modern Art in the United States, that very respectable Mecca of American modernism, has recently paid lip-service to the growing realist trend by its exhibition of Realism and Magic Realism.

The development of this realist tendency from the ranks of the moderns should be distinguished from the rise of modernism itself. Like Hellenistic art and Saïte Egyptian, modernist art exhibits all the qualities of a true decadence but in a greater complexity than any of the earlier prototypes. The cul-de-sac of neo-impressionist form provided the technical *casus belli*. But the movement which is affecting art today and bringing new paintings to the walls of recent exhibitions arises from quite a different source, although the most vigorous roots are undoubtedly embedded in the positive achievements of the modernists. Nevertheless, they differ from the conservative modernists. Many artists today want to paint 'about' rather than just paint. This is heresy to the older modernism, for content and subject are still anathema to them, still part of their aesthetic taboos. The new realism in Australian painting adopts rather the humanist attitudes to be found in Brueghel, Van Gogh, Goya, Daumier, and the Australian, S. T. Gill. It is much less suited than modernism to decorate the homes of millionaires with advanced views. Four years ago in this country it would have been a hope or a prophecy; today it is a fact.

Why has this realist tendency developed in the art of almost every country in the world, particularly where previously an abstract modernist phase had gained widest recognition?

It has appeared because you cannot bind artists forever by a theory which does not face up to the facts. For the intellectual tragedy, the tragedy of art, both in this country, in the United States, and in the countries of Western Europe, has been the continued refusal of the bulk of artists of those countries to admit what they had seen enacted under their eyes. They had been witnesses of the political expression of those forces which, once in power, began a conscious and calculated attack on the traditions and the living representatives of Western European culture. They saw the exiles coming out of Europe, the scientists, the writers, the philosophers, the musicians of our generation. But they said it was not their business. These things were not within the ambit of art; these things were not the responsibility of the artist. The forces causing all the disturbance, the intolerance, the murders of Jews and the beatings in the concentration camps—these things were political and social; they were the concern of the politician or of the economist or the propagandist; they could never be the concern of the artist. They comforted themselves with the thought that these things should be left to those whom they concern. The artist should cultivate his significant experiences; his concern was with form, with empathy, with subjective truth. It was their

John Perceval, *Survival*, 1942, oil on board, 122 × 93.5 cm National Gallery of Victoria.

business to see the world from a whale's transparent belly, but Nineveh was not their responsibility.

It was in the face of this aesthetic isolationism that the writers and artists of the world saw a country with a tradition in art, in literature, and in thought, which had given us Dürer, Goethe and Beethoven, trample its past under the heels of its storm-troopers. And they said it was not their business. They saw the expressionist art which had flourished under the Weimar Republic hung up in an exhibition of Degenerates, and they still said it was not their business. The Bauhaus of Walter Gropius became a Nazi drill hall. The writings of Thomas Mann were officially burnt. Twenty years before, in his *Memoirs of an Unpolitical Man*, Thomas Mann had written, opposing in the name of freedom and culture, the artist's participation in political activity. After he escaped from Germany he wrote: 'I see now that the German bourgeoisie erred in thinking that a man could remain unpolitical...for the political and social are parts of the human: they belong to the totality of human problems and must be drawn into the whole'. The Spanish war brought from Picasso the cry: 'I am on the side of the people', and it produced his *Guernica*. It brought the greatest Catholic thinker, Jacques Maritain, to a condemnation of fascism in Spain. But Garcia Lorca is dead; Rolland recently died in a Nazi concentration camp; Stephan Zweig committed suicide; Einstein is in America; Freud in an English grave. We have witnessed a 'Decline of the West' that was not a prophecy but a political programme. These things are more than matters of military strategy or political opinion.

Today, in this country, it is important for us to know the conditions which made the destruction of Western European cultural tradition a possibility. What aesthetic policies were used *before* the political coup d'état, *before* the wholesale persecutions of artists and writers, the exodus of the scientists, and the *autos-da-fé* of National Socialism?

For their own purposes the fascists built up a spurious façade of 'culture', a metaphysical creed, a *Weltanschauung*, and a medieval mysticism which stressed the 'spiritual' and spurned the material. The material conditions of life and production, environmental factors, economic conditions, the advances of technology—all these were secondary and unimportant manifestations of the spiritual qualities manifested in religion, war, patriotism, nationality, and art. When the fascist talks about art he is a mystic and an idealist. Their 'idealism' is manifested very plainly in the various aesthetic theories which they have embraced to further their purposes. The official fascist attitude to art derives largely from the theories of Croce and his follower Gentile. Croce maintains that art is intuition; the artist's feelings and expression are in fact his art; the art-work is only a practical activity, a method of publicity.

It may seem strange that a regime as callous as fascism should adopt an idealist attitude to art. But this attitude has served its political purpose for them. It derives from Hegelian thought in Germany, and in France from the theories of Bergson. The approach is anti-intellectual; emotional values are all-important. Art is a personal emanation, always a thing of the individual passion. It was this attitude that Julien Benda criticized in 1929, when he pointed out that these attitudes would eventually undermine the complete fabric of French culture. He was a reliable prophet.

Others, too, saw the danger of such a theoretical approach to art. They reasserted a vigorous humanism, and something of the anger of Morris and Ruskin, Tolstoy, and Cherneshevski. Such an attitude is at the base of the art of Grosz and Gropper, Barlach and Dix. It is in the writings of Ralph Fox, John Cornford and Christopher Caudwell. They saw that isolationism in art led to disastrous implications. Behind these theories, enunciated by all kinds of respectable people, was the fascist who drew his revolver on hearing the word culture, and behind him the dancing witch-doctor with his bones and spells; and in the final analysis, the idealist theory of art, the fascist and the witch-doctor, have always been inimical to the growth of art, as they have been to the growth of science, and those factors which constitute human progress.

Today it is necessary to choose between these two attitudes to art as a social activity. Too many artists have been murdered, too many books have been burned along the primrose path that leads the intellectual towards the passive acceptance of fascism, wherein blood and race become the source of all artistic intuition. Today the artist cannot honestly serve the forces of social decay, he cannot embrace those theories which can be so easily turned to the destruction of art itself. He cannot be passive in the face of these things, for it is not a school of art that is threatened but the survival of art as we have known it as an aspect of human sensibility and human freedom.

And so to accept realism is not to retreat. It is simply to be prepared to do what Swift, what Milton and Voltaire would have done under similar circumstances. Once Milton could write in anger 'On the Massacre of the Piedmontese'. Today a whole race in Europe is in danger of being exterminated. And this is not all. Today art that is honest will be still capable of anger, though it has been diluted for years by a thin asceticism.

Yet among artists we have mostly witnessed a strange indifference not unalloyed with a strange fear. Those who refused to do anything to resist this threat to their existence as artists could only stare in hypnotic satisfaction at the forces threatening to engulf them. They were prepared to analyse their fears and to write about the mysterious universality of the death instinct. The only thing they were not prepared to do was to meet force with the force of their own beliefs, to defend the cultural tradition, to use their brushes and pens as weapons.

George Grosz, brilliant German artist and satirist, before he fled Germany, flung a charge at his brother artists: 'Your brushes and pens which should have been weapons are but empty straws'.

Today there is a Nazi flag flying from the top of the ivory tower, and the Hamsuns, Pounds, Kershaws and Lindsays who still keep apartments there, pay, in effect, their rent to Dr Goebbels. Today calls for a Milton or a Goya. It was in a somewhat similar situation that Milton once wrote: 'I cannot praise a fugitive and cloistered virtue, unexercised and unbreathed, that never sallies forth and seeks her adversary, but slinks out of the race where that immortal garland is to be run for, not without dust and heat'.

It is because there are artists and writers in the various countries of the world who are prepared to accept the dust and the heat, and risk the sadism of the concentration camp that we have this new development in writing and painting, this tendency towards a new realism. For art can do many things, but it cannot exist for long upon the patronage of a lie.

5
The Studio of Realist Art
—1945—

In the art chronicle of the last issue of *Meanjin* Herbert McClintock, with some aptness, pointed out that in New South Wales the stale argument between the modern and the academic painter had become of less importance than the basic opposition of two schools of contemporary painting, the romantic revivalists and the contemporary realists. To state the position as simply as it may be stated, the centre of gravity of art controversy has shifted from representation versus formalism and abstraction, to aestheticism versus realism.

Unfortunately a great many modernists have adopted a wave-theory aesthetic and have decided with a sublime disregard of the facts that we live in an 'architectural' age, and that plastic art must therefore be abstract or 'architectural' to be modern. The academization of the abstract is almost within view. I shall not be surprised if it is from the ranks of the post-impressionist moderns of the 1920s that the chief heresy hunters of the vital artists of the 1940s and 1950s will arise. And the apparent impersonality of abstract art should make of it as safe an occupation as any academician would desire.

Paintings that treated social themes and portrayed aspects of contemporary life in Australia with no small measure of passion and significance were to be found in the odd corners of exhibitions of the Contemporary Art Society as early as 1939. But their accent was not always the best Parisian, and they were soon suspected of certain ecumenical divergencies from the central dogmas of non-representation.

This difference of opinion and practice resulted, as opinions usually do, in the creation of a new group. The Studio of Realist

First published under the title 'Art Chronicle' in *Meanjin Papers*, vol. 2, Winter 1945, pp. 107–8.

Art was formed in Sydney in March this year to promote an art which has been at the best of times regarded as a sort of heresy by the majority of post-impressionist moderns.

The studio has been a success since its inception. Regular art classes in advanced and elementary drawing and in painting are well attended. A series of fortnightly lectures has been most successful. With its well-stocked art library and the regular monthly bulletin *Sora* it is fast becoming the most vigorous art centre in Sydney. The studio was founded by James Cant, who studied in Sydney, London and Paris, and worked as a painter in Spain in 1934, Hal Missingham, who is at present awaiting appointment as director of the National Art Gallery of New South Wales, Roy Dalgarno, widely known as the first artist to be commissioned by trade unions in this country to paint industrial life and activity, Dora Chapman, formerly of the Adelaide School of Arts and Crafts, and Roderick Shaw, painter, designer and book illustrator.

What is most impressive about the studio is the vigour of its activity and production, and the tolerance of its principles. These qualities are the marks of its contemporaneity. There have been many attempts to produce a national art but it is likely that the contemporary realists will be the first to produce it. If they do it will come as a by-product of their realism; not by a preoccupation with *plein-air* landscape, nor by archaistic myth-making, but by a passionate portrayal of the Australian people of their own time, as they live, think, work and play, by an understanding of their problems and ideals, and, above all by a firm belief that their own people are at least worthy to be the subject of art.

6

The Fascist Mentality in Australian Art and Criticism

—1946—

Both aestheticism and the sentiment of nationalism in art comment in Australia took on, between 1910 and 1940, the characteristics of a pre-fascist mentality. These characteristics arose partly from the existing social conditions in Australia and partly from the influence of overseas developments. Melvin Rader, of the Department of Philosophy, Washington University, whose *No Compromise* is one of the best analyses of its ideological features, cites the social origin of fascism in these terms:

Financed by rich capitalists, it attacked chiefly trade unions and workers' organisations. Its development accordingly, cannot be understood apart from the crisis of capitalism. The post-war chaos and world depression meant a rising tide of popular resentment and radicalism. Fascism has been promoted as a counter-movement to crush the insurgency of the masses. It had been growing within the womb of the old order for more than a century, but the world crisis nourished its growth and brought it quickly to maturity.

The features mentioned by Rader—support of rich industrialists, post-war chaos, world depression, rising resentment and radicalism, capitalist crisis—were present in Australia as in other countries. They provided the social basis for an indigenous fascist development in Australia. But, in addition to these local factors, there were overseas influences—the writings of Nietzsche, Spengler and others—who gave a measure of theoretical credence, and the sanction of 'authorities' to the local developments, particularly in the realm of art comment.

It will be possible to deal only with those attributes of pre-fascist mentality that are in some way connected with art comment

First published in the *Communist Review*, June 1946, pp. 182–4 (pt 1), and July 1946, pp. 215–17 (pt 2).

and criticism. What are these attributes? Rader has analysed a large number with great care. Some of those which are relevant to our purpose here include: the doctrine of racial supremacy, the belief in society as an organism, a hatred of democracy, the fascist praise of rural life, the identification of modern art with Bolshevism and Jewish exploitation. Have these attributes revealed themselves in the 'culture climate' of Australia?

Nationalism in its heightened forms is usually identified with the dominant 'race' of the nation. In this way, nationalism tends to transform itself into racism. We may note symptoms of this transposition in the phrases of J. S. MacDonald: 'the racial expression of others will not be ours', the supremacy of 'British-blooded stock', and similar statements. The same writer gives evidence of his belief in the possible development of an Australian racial élite when, in dealing with the art of Arthur Streeton, he writes: 'If we so choose, we can yet be the elect of the world, the last of the pastoralists, the thoroughbred Aryans in all their nobility'. Such a statement combines the fascist love of rural life, emphasizes the Aryan myth of racial supremacy, and champions racial purity.

The Caesar-worship and pessimism of fascism owes a great deal to the writings of Oswald Spengler who maintained that 'cultures' were organisms and, as such, had predetermined life-spans. This view has been embraced by P. R. Stephenson, who relates it to Australian conditions when he writes:

The only Spenglerian point worth considering is whether Australia is going to decline with Europe or whether there is some force in us which enables Australians to enter into the 'Spring' phase of an entirely new Pacifico-centric culture. Alas the overwhelming majority of Australians appear to be mentally Europo-centric, not Pacifico-centric. More, they are Euro-decadents. They prefer, for example, to fall with Britain in the Atlantic than to rise with Japan in the Pacific. 'Save Great Bunyip, save Thy little ones!'

This is no more than a poor attempt to turn the argument of *The Decline of the West* to Australia's benefit. But the argument has weathered very poorly in the light of recent history. The exclamation at the end, 'Great Bunyip, save Thy little ones!' is to be considered, presumably, as an invocation to a new Australian paganism to become a racial religion in a pro-fascist Australian state. This may seem a far cry from the Bunyip worship of the Australian Aboriginal. But here we have another instance of that archaism which has affected many social institutions in recent

years although they were considered previously quite immune
from such illogical developments. Rather than be sceptical of
such a possibility, it would be well to read Professor Toynbee's
warning, written after a detailed analysis of the development of
archaism in contemporary society, in connection with Hauer's
paganism in Nazi Germany: 'Hauerism is evidence that Western
souls were no longer proof against being captivated by a religious
archaism even when this offered itself in an elaborate fancy dress'.

But many years before either J. S. MacDonald or P. R. Stephenson
wrote these statements advocating racial supremacy, the poet
William Baylebridge had written his *National Notes*, which were
printed and circulated privately, 'largely to members of Parliament'. That an obscure Australian poet writing before the 1914–18
war was able to advocate a 'philosophy' that was almost completely identical with the philosophy of Hitler and Mussolini, is
further evidence that fascism is a phenomenon growing out of
specific social conditions; that the nationalism which it brandishes
is, in fact, a symptom of international capitalism in decay.

In his *National Notes* Baylebridge states that: 'When the mind
of a nation is set free and a direction of research given to it, all
the explanatory and hunting instincts are awakened'. The 'hunting
instincts' of the nation so aroused, it will then be possible to
embark upon an imperial domination of the earth. 'Man's principle
in creation we must now posit in himself. Our present goal (to be
supplanted when reaped by one of larger touch) shall be the
overrunning of earth by Australians, strong-necked, natural men.'
These supermen, Baylebridge maintains, can only be bred from
Australian women who must help to populate the country with
great rapidity, and must eschew any activities that will militate
against their sole mission of motherhood. 'When we shall have
bred this higher human activity, it is not possible that it will
allow itself to be chained up in any particular stall—it will devour
the earth.' It may be objected that the idea of a race of supermen
Australians 'devouring the earth' is so ridiculous as not to be
worth serious consideration. But the stupidity of such 'philosophy'
is not in question. We are concerned here solely with the existence
of these ideas and their relation to the Australian milieu. It may,
of course, be objected that this obscure poet has little relation to
Australian thought in general. And this is undoubtedly true. Yet
we must not underestimate the spread of 'irrationalism' in the
intellectual circles of Australia, as of elsewhere. T. Inglis Moore—
who was awarded a prize in the Australian celebrations of its
150th anniversary, and whose book *Six Australian Poets* was published by the Australian Literary Fund, and, therefore can be

Victor O'Connor, *The Refugees*, c. 1942, oil on board, 55.9 × 50.8 cm, The Joseph Brown Collection.

taken as fairly representative of Australian critical thought—selects Baylebridge as one of his six best Australian poets. We are not concerned here with the aesthetic merits or otherwise of Baylebridge's work, but the selection by Moore at least indicates that Baylebridge is not merely an unknown rhymester, but a man with a following and influence. Speaking, not of Baylebridge's poetic ability, but of his thought, Moore insists that, in his poem 'The New Life', 'the poet stands out as a thinker in advance of his time, whose ideas, formulated twenty years ago, are only now winning acceptance'. It may be remarked at this stage that at the time when Moore's book was published in 1942, the 'ideas' of Baylebridge were not finding acceptance, though, in their cause, Europe was being turned into a concentration camp, as 'blood and soil' rode on its triumphant way. The 'ideas' were finding a grave. For *The New Life* of Baylebridge is an amazing anticipation of the ideas presented in the 'dawn ceremony' of the Nazi storm troopers, entitled Men, Fighters and Soldiers. Rader described the ceremony: 'The participants are a band of music, a male speaking choir and three principal speakers, namely the 'Believer', the 'Doubter', and the 'Caller'. The Doubter records the defeats in German history; he is eventually silenced with the dates of victories'. This should be compared with the titles of the early poems in *The New Life*, which include 'Our Task', 'The Mean', 'The Executors', 'The Call', 'The Rejected'.

It must be stressed here that T. Inglis Moore states explicitly in his essay on Baylebridge, after noting the fascist nature of his ideas: 'His creed is not mine, for I hold that the State was made for man, not man for the State'. And this is borne out in Moore's own war poems, particularly his fine 'Festival of Freedom'. But when a critic writes of the illogical *mélange* of quack-theorizing that makes up the great body of Baylebridge's 'thinking'—'It is not only the statement of a metaphysic; it is also the hymning of a faith held with religious passion, or rather, perhaps, of a vision attained through the mystic mood'—then he certainly prejudices his claim to critical integrity. A collection of ideas about birth, love, death, race, war, and so on, may make a 'metaphysic', but before we talk about a poet's thought, it should also make sense.

One of the minor attributes of fascist thought is the idealization of rural life as compared with the life of the city. Rader remarks: 'Fascist literature is full of panegyrics to the spiritual character of rural life. The metropolis, in contrast, is represented as the den of materialism'. This tendency, which might be considered a reversion to the heyday of Australian squattocracy, is evident in the belief held by J. S. MacDonald that Arthur Streeton's paintings:

point the way in which life should be lived in Australia, with the maximum of flocks and the minimum of factories. But we have to be like the rest of the world, feeling out of it if we cannot blow as many get-to-work whistles, punch as many bundy-clocks, and show as much smoke and squalor as places that cannot escape such curses... Let others if they are bent upon it, mass-produce themselves into robotry, thinking and looking like mechanical monkeys chained to organs whose tunes are furnished by rivetting machines.

The conception of the state as an organism or a group-mind is one of the central features of fascist literature. It is to be found in its mature form in Baylebridge's *National Notes*: 'The God that we, as a nation, shall have made ourselves, is perhaps the only one to which man has yet never offered serious worship and sacrifice'. The Nazi ideal of complete and final national regimentation is paralleled when he says: 'Every man then, thinking in a truly national character, will consider himself but as a means and instrument of national service'.

One of the commonest confusions among pro-fascist writers is the identification of the development of modern art with the growth of communism on the one hand, and Jewish exploitation on the other. Writing on Culture and Commerce, in 1939, Norman Lindsay says:

To be sure the uprush of communistic principles among all peoples has had one extremely disastrous result, for to their claim to a share of the world's culture the lower orders have taken to practising art themselves; hence the peculiar uproar of disintegrated values labelled Modernism. Later and more discerning generations will undoubtedly define this movement under the heading The Wharf Lumper in Art.

Wharf labourers have been blamed for many things, but only a Norman Lindsay would blame them for the art forms of, for example, Salvador Dali. Hitler of course felt very much as did Lindsay in the matter of modern art. He passed laws against it, called it Jewish, international, foreign, degenerate. He forced modern artists such as Klee, Kandinsky, Beckmann out of their art schools, and drove them from the country. Their works were removed from museum walls and hidden or sold abroad.

But Lindsay's statement is not an isolated case; anyone who takes the trouble to go through the material in art publications in Australia in the period between the wars will find ample evidence of the widespread nature of the 'Bolshevik–Modernist' confusion. Before leaving the matter it is perhaps worth quoting E. Wake Cooke's contribution: 'There is a curious parallelism between Bolshevism and the Modernity movements; Lenin promised Russia a heaven and gave it a hell! The Modernists are actuated by the same spirit'. If Mr Wake Cooke had been in a position to examine the facts he would have found the modernist painters, at the time that he wrote his criticism, were far too absorbed in the investigation of their own private heavens and hells to worry about presenting sidereal gifts to the Soviets.

Perhaps the most obvious, because the most terrible and ir-rational of its tenets, has been the fascist persecution of the Jews. This trait developed much later in Australia than the other Fascist traits that we have noted. But the 1940 Exhibition of the Contem-porary Art Society brought a virulent attack upon the Jewish contributors to that exhibition in the form of a letter from Sir Lionel Lindsay to the *Sydney Morning Herald*. Lindsay's book *Addled Art* confirms the anti-Semitic nature of his art-criticism. But as several million Jews have been done to death on the altar of anti-Semitism since Lindsay wrote his notorious letter, he has considered it advisable to include a qualification, by which he hopes to attack 'Jewish' painting and at the same time absolve himself from the charge of anti-Semitism. Lindsay patronizingly admits that there are some 'good' Jews: Heine, Disraeli, Einstein, Monash and Phillips Fox. This is not a new qualification.

Sigmund Freud is numbered among the 'bad' Jews, and this is accounted for largely because—quite literally—Lindsay does not like the look of his face. 'Glance at Freud's face. The look of concentration in the eyes is confounded by a general expression of sulky disquietude and their sadness tempered by a vague hostility. It is the face of a man soured and ill at ease with himself or the world.' The sourness, according to Lindsay, following his predilection for racial arguments, is due to one extreme of the Jewish character. If Lionel Lindsay had been a Jew living through the 1930s in Vienna, he may have been able to find other reasons for the 'sadness tempered with hostility'. It is very doubtful whether an intelligent man could feel anything but sad and hostile at Goebbels' 'description' of the Jew to the Nuremberg Party Conference, in September 1937: 'This is the world enemy, the destroyer of civilisation, the parasite among nations, the son of chaos, the incarnation of evil, the germ of decomposition, the plastic demon of the decay of humanity'.

The general tenor of *Addled Art* is strongly anti-democratic. Lindsay has the same hatred of democracy as the leading fascist theorists Gobineau and Chamberlain, and the fascist writer Alfred Rosenberg. He speaks of the 'mob's invasion of art' and that art can only survive this invasion if bad art is discouraged. To Lindsay a democracy cannot produce great art. He objects to art being included in the school curriculum because art cannot be taught. By including art in the curriculum, 'the democracies level and lower all cultures'.

The pre-fascist mentality of *Addled Art*, however, is not limited to its anti-Semitism and a hatred of democracy. There is the same emphasis upon a natural élite that provides the leaders, to be found throughout fascist writing: 'Natural man, guided by a profound instinct, destroys the weak and malformed at birth. Mistakes of nature, he knows that if they were allowed to propagate they would menace the vitality and continuity of the tribe. The weak chicken is pecked to death.' Like Hitler and Mussolini Lionel Lindsay is also a red-baiter: 'The tactics of the international Communists would serve: (the "bolshevik—modernist" confusion) corrupt, undermine, flatter the groundlings; put the boot in. The thing was to kick the stuffing out of the aristocrat Drawing'.

Anti-Semitism has not been isolated to one or two critics in Australia. In a statement by Alcedo Gigas in *The Publicist*, we read: 'We Kookaburras think that the Australian community cannot be possibly saved or advanced by Jews: we think the Jews' advocacy of a so-called internationalism and their antagonism to nationalism constitutes a menace to Australians'. Ghettos, Ku Klux Klan Kookaburras, Bunyip gods and Jindyworobaks are some of the archaic fossils left by the ebbing of objectivity in Australian thought and criticism that has proceeded steadily since the 1890s.

The final answer to the increasingly reactionary nature of the 'criticism' proceeding from the pens of Lionel and Norman Lindsay has been written by Jack Lindsay, son of the latter, nephew of the former: 'Wherever we probe this "German culture" we find a regressive entanglement of dark magic thinking and flat scholasticism, which if left to itself, would revert to a barbarous Medievalism. So rapidly can the mass-roots of culture be cut'.

This article has endeavoured to show that there is a direct line of theoretical descent from the aestheticism which grew out of the Melbourne Bohemian circles of the 1890s, and the increasing mysticism associated with the practice and criticism of landscape painting, to the development of an arrogant nationalism, and finally to an arrogant mysticism which takes on all the attributes of the fascist mentality. There is to be observed during the 1920s and 1930s the gradual growth of the anti-human tendencies of fascism in Australian cultural development as in certain aspects of its political development. Nor must we delude ourselves that those same tendencies have been finally and completely defeated. Their reappearance in whatever form must give us cause to be vigilant. For the final common denominator of these 'cultural' tendencies is to be found in the concentration camps of Dachau and Belsen.

PART II

The Post-war Years and the Search for a Critical Canon: 1945–1948

7
Noel Counihan
—1945—

In *The Happy Prince* Oscar Wilde has the prince say to his messenger the bird, 'you tell me of marvellous things, but more marvellous than anything is the suffering of men and of women'. On hearing this remark the bird, had he been an Australian art critic, would have accused the prince of spreading left-wing political propaganda.

For though suffering has been one of the great themes and problems of art throughout history there have always been those who would place it beyond the pale of painting. It is well known that suffering is easier to bear in art when it is softened by time or gathered into a universal symbol. Owning no plantations in Dixie we can feel for Uncle Tom; knowing the gods could not possibly want to single out our own little lives for their exquisite agonies we readily share the burden of Oedipus Rex. But there are artists for whom the salve of time and the cushion of myth will not do, for whom suffering begins, like charity, at home.

Such artists are realists, the stormy petrels of art; among them are Brueghel, Caravaggio, Goya, Daumier, Barlach, Grosz. Noel Counihan belongs spiritually to this company.

The artist who dedicates himself to the portrayal of suffering comes to grips with one of the great problems of art. He must transform by his technique and expression that which is often squalid and repulsive in real life into something aesthetically valid. Individual and social conflict are drawn upon for artistic conceptions that must become beautiful yet remain true, attain the values of art without rejecting the values of life.

Counihan began his career as a caricaturist in Melbourne at the age of nineteen. When he was twenty he lived for a year on the

An extended version of the article in *Present Day Art in Australia*, Sydney Ure Smith, Sydney, 1945, pp. 28–30.

Noel Counihan, *At the Corner of Nightingale Street*, 1944, oil on board, 58.5 × 50.5 cm. Private collection.

dole and depicted the life of the unemployed during the depth of the Depression in an exhibition of drawings held in 1934. Not until 1941 did he begin to paint in oils. Since that time he has exhibited with the Contemporary Art Society, the Studio of Realist Art, the Victorian Artists Society, and held seventeen one-man shows.

Counihan's art has grown directly from his own experience and political faith. He knows the people he paints and identifies himself with their lives: the mothers prematurely aged by poverty and domestic squalor, the dole queues, the old men and women waiting through the day at the out-patients departments of public hospitals, the miner with dusted lungs. His world is, for the most part, a sombre world but real enough. His paintings ask us what we are even as we ask them what they are, testing our charity as we judge their value. When we have exhausted all the fashionable clichés—that it is propaganda, that it is representational, that it has been done before and done better—we must still face the art itself. Is it worth saying, worth painting, well said, well painted? And we come to the fact, disturbing to those who cultivate their sensibility at the expense of their natural feeling, that Counihan is prepared to see steadily what most of us are only too ready to turn away from. Propaganda or no propaganda, illustration or no illustration, the conscience of the nation is held in trust by artists and people like Counihan who have the strength and desire to turn over the stones of our smugness and reveal what lies beneath.

Few Australian artists have been inspired for long by politics or suffering; their achievements have been won in other fields. The poets and the novelists have spoken for the common man. But it is of the greatest importance for the maturity and diversity of our art that we can number one unflinching critic of society among our best painters.

8
Justin O'Brien
—1947—

Justin O'Brien's painting has flowered suddenly in the years since the end of the Second World War. A teacher of art in Sydney before the war, the experiments of a younger generation of Australian artists meant little to him until the war years changed the tenor of his life. The spiritual turbulence that must result when a sensitive nature is suddenly uprooted from its customary surroundings, propelled violently through military campaigns, and deposited for a number of years as a military prisoner in a strange country, left its mark on him. His earlier and more conventional art gave way before new creative vitality. As an Australian prisoner of war in a German prison camp—an Austrian fort on the Vistula—he had time to think about his art, and to discuss his problems with some fellow prisoners who were also artists. And because of the existence of the International Red Cross, which provided brushes and pigments, he was able to paint as well. Material to paint on was, I understand, a difficulty, but in this regard the prison guards were not by any means uncooperative. It was in such a situation fraught with material difficulties but rich in spiritual possibilities that O'Brien's art began to emerge.

When he came back to Australia after his release at the conclusion of the war he held an exhibition at the Macquarie Galleries, Sydney, together with Jesse Martin, a fellow prisoner. The work was immature, derivative, tightly designed, and yet had in it the urgency of sincerity. It was obvious that O'Brien had been deeply attracted by the spiritual intensity of Byzantine painting. The weight of the contours, the burning depths of the colour, and the hieratical splendour of the gestures of Byzantine art had awakened

---

This article was written for the Department of Information, Commonwealth of Australia, in May 1947, in response by them to a request for an article on O'Brien received from a British agency.

processes in O'Brien's personality that had not found expression before.

As its origins may suggest, there is a considerable element of religious expression running through O'Brien's work. He is not in any way attracted by the showy humanism of the religious art of the High Renaissance. Furthermore his religious themes are more quietly presented, are kindlier in feeling, than the Byzantine iconography from which they derive so much. The *Triptych* in the Hall—Best Collection, Sydney, hints at the elegant delicacy of Siennese quattrocento; particularly the frail loveliness of Sassetta. Such Pre-Raphaelite references bring to mind the paintings of Stanley Spencer. But O'Brien's traditionalism seems much more a matter of mood than of intellection; its humour is less consciously quaint, less firmly knit, than Spencer's.

If the spiritual intensity of Byzantine art has helped to give O'Brien's painting integrity and a sense of direction, the opulent patterning of Persian art has softened it and given it charm. Brilliant colour is applied in two-dimensional fashion, with little modelling, the faintest hint of perspective, between strong flowing lines. A fine facility for the handling of reds in splendid profusion is emerging, a quality that gives O'Brien's paintings a feeling of delicious abandon, that is, in fact, a most conscious art based upon nice judgements as to the shape, tone, and intensity of his colours. By preserving his contours he is able to invest his painting with strong linear rhythms that add considerably to their vitality. Then again there is a certain incongruity in the subjects and situations which his paintings present to us, a quality to be found most fully in folk-art. It is O'Brien's combination of brilliant colour patterning, his spirituality, and suggestion of folk humour, that constitute, to my mind, the peculiar charms of his art. Perhaps its true emotional equivalent is to be found neither in Byzantine nor Persian paintings but in the late Celtic art of the Lindisfarne Gospel.

The work of many contemporary painters has obviously helped to develop his methods and mould O'Brien's vision. Frequently we catch a glimpse of the sombre passion of Rouault. His sense of spatial arrangement and rhythmical freedom obviously owe much to Matisse, and his treatment of the figure owes perhaps a little too much to the early Picasso. Perhaps the most conspicuous weakness of his art is the limited range of its thematic material, and it is possible that his art will become mannered before it matures unless he can refresh it with a greater diversity of personal experiences.

A recent painting of Sydney Harbour revealed how well he

Justin O' Brien, *Greek Burial*, 1947, oil on board, 88.8 × 65.0 cm. Private collection.

could interpret the world of his immediate experience in terms of the vision which his interest in Byzantine and Persian art has developed. The colourful quality of Sydney Harbour has intrigued painters since the time of Conrad Martens, but few have sought to portray the colour other than naturalistically. The attempt, provided in O'Brien's painting, to present a subjective interpretation based upon colour harmonies felt rather than seen is therefore greatly to be welcomed. Incidentally, this painting was entered in the Wynne Art Prize for the best Australian landscape painted in 1946. Because so many paintings had been forwarded in recent years to this competition the trustees of the National Art Gallery of New South Wales decided to show only what they considered to be the best two hundred landscapes entered. O'Brien's painting, full of splendid colour, and sparkling with freshness and vitality, was probably the most original, certainly the most vivacious painting entered. It was rejected as being not good enough to be shown.

Lately O'Brien has been seeking to widen the scope of his art by realizing the plastic reality of his volumes without sacrificing the translucent brilliance of colour which is his outstanding technical achievement. It will be interesting to see just how successfully he can solve this problem, for it is a central one for the development of his art.

9

The English Portraits of William Dobell
—1947—

There are few better indications of the originality of an artist's work than the internal consistency of his style at the various levels of its development. We become impressed by what we feel as the inevitability of a process of unfolding. New influences are assimilated; new personal observations, ideas, and sentiments are met with; new techniques are tried, and are either discarded or absorbed. But at each level of achievement we feel that the artist's own personality is the master of his creative machinery. It is this sense of his continual presence that separates the true artist from the eclectic, who garnishes his nest with bright ornaments, or the charlatan, who merely struts and sings other people's songs badly. This feeling of an inevitable and yet natural process of unfolding is to be found in William Dobell's paintings, and several aspects of the process can be traced through a study of his portraits.

The portrait *Consuelita*, in the Heywood Collection (South Australia), painted in 1933, three years after he had arrived in London, presents us with the characteristics of Dobell's first style. Here he begins to investigate the plastic and structural problems associated with portraiture as an art-form. The contours are as sheer as archaic statues of Greek athletes; the perfect symmetry of the body being broken only by the effective placing of the clasped hands which, to harmonize with the conception of the painting, are rendered without detail, massively. The head has been reduced to as simple a geometric shape as is consistent with the requirements of portraiture; the precise central parting of the hair, the regular curve of the brows, the firm mouth, the long, evenly-modelled neck, and the expressionless face of the sitter, indicate the artist's careful avoidance of naturalism. The contours and

First published in *Arna*, Journal of the Faculty of Arts, University of Sydney, October 1947.

volumes of the figure are simply established; the massive arms, firm neck, and heavy breast arouse no feeling. They are parts of an architectonic structure. The tonal construction has also been simplified. The light yellow sweater that clothes the flask-like shape of the body, the warm browns of flesh and table, and the silky blacks of the hair could hardly be stated more simply. The colour scheme is characteristic of much of his early work, with its harmonies of fleeting greens, rich browns and yellows, heightened with touches of red and strengthened by the judicious use of black. *Consuelita* marks the extreme development in Dobell's early work towards the achievement of solidly realized construction.

It was in the same year that *Consuelita* was painted that a number of young English painters, sculptors and architects formed themselves into a group and adopted the title of Unit One. This group demanded that English art must reassert its structural qualities, that it must beware the ever-present romanticism and colloquialism that recurs in English painting. They were artistic rebels and extremists in their own way, and Dobell had little in common with their theorizing and, so far as I know, little contact with them. There is nothing in Dobell's art that may be compared with the steel-like precision of Paul Nash's seascapes, or the metallic portraits of Wyndham Lewis. Yet such is the penetration of aesthetic attitudes that their concern with coherent design and structural logic is to be seen clearly enough in *Consuelita*.

That there was another side to Dobell's art is seen in the tiny *Woman in Café*, in the Murdoch Collection (Melbourne), painted in the same year as *Consuelita*. It is one of his finest genre paintings (it can hardly be called a portrait) and reveals the emergence of new qualities in his art that are to grow in importance in later works. *Consuelita* leaves us with the feeling of the studio-posed portrait; this painting, we are equally sure, is the product of a casual sketch in a London restaurant. As an effective placement of a single figure upon canvas it will bear considerable study. The exquisite relation between face and cup has been repeated in reverse tones in the background. The handling is broad and preserves the immediacy of a sketch. This painting, in particular, bears an affinity with the paintings of Richard Sickert.

Woman in Café may well be compared with *Woman in Restaurant*, in the Schureck Collection (Sydney), painted one year later. In the latter are the first signs of that social comment for which Dobell has since become so well known. In the earlier painting he has captured with fine sympathy the reticent, contemplative mien of a woman in a little London coffee house. Her sister of *Woman in Restaurant* belongs to a different social world; she is overdressed and pretentiously vulgar. Dobell's approach to his subject is different in each case; the quiet humanism of the first painting is replaced by the gentle but obvious satire of the second. Again, in the second, the tonality has become stronger; heavy blacks are thrown against assertive whites in which the beginnings of an impasto technique are appearing. The swelling curves of the woman are repeated in the curves of the backs of the chairs, the whole design creating a rococo effect recalling Hogarth. Here for the first time, too, appear those ample curves of fat women, which Dobell has used so often, both for their expressive quality and their usefulness in design, in his later paintings, as Rubens and Renoir and so many others had done before him.

These two paintings lead directly to the manner in which Dobell painted between 1936 and 1938. The paintings of this time show a greater freedom of conception and more assurance of handling. He became interested in people, not merely as pegs upon which to hang works of art, but as people. In the portraits and genre paintings which he produced at this time he was able to express in convincing works of art the social scene of London in the mid-1930s the way he felt about the affectations and peculiarities of its people and its contrasts of pretension and poverty.

The portraits and social studies painted during this period fall, I believe, into three main classes. First, there are the little sketches or notes of people that Dobell observed and stated directly. They include such paintings as *The Little Milliner*, *Woman Watching a Funeral*, *Film Crowd Workers*, and *Tired Nippy*. Secondly, there are the satirical sketches, in which Dobell observes and then makes a personal comment. The group includes *Mrs South Kensington*, *Miss Tatty*, *Drunken Bridesmaids*, *My Lady Waits*, and *The Duchess Disrobes*. In the third group are some of Dobells' finest paintings. Here the purely satirical spirit has been modified and assimilated into a mood that is more complex and more difficult to define. The contemplative spirit to be observed in Dobell's early landscapes reappears. His observation remains sharp, and his humour is still penetrating, but he is able to see his subjects 'in the round' both visually and psychologically. This group includes *The Sleeping Greek*, *The Charlady*, and *The Irish Youth*.

The Little Milliner, with its shorthand notation of form, is a good example of the first group. No more than a sketch, it shows Dobell's ability to state an observation with a fine economy of

William Dobell, *The Irish Youth*, 1938, oil on canvas, 52.0 × 43.5 cm. Private collection.

means. What a contrast to the conscious organization and precision of *Consuelita*. During these years a distinct expressionist quality emerges in his work wherein forms are distorted to carry the burden of his expression. He portrays the tiredness of the *Nippy* by a distortion of form. There are two types of distortion in painting: there is distortion to achieve a sense of formal unity, as we find in the paintings of Cézanne; and there is distortion to achieve a sense of emotional unity, as we find in the paintings of El Greco and the great painter satirists. It is this latter type of distortion that we find in Dobell's art. The distortion of the legs in *Cockney Mother* contributes little to the effectiveness of the design of the painting, but it is of considerable importance in conveying the emotional impact of the artist's expression.

Miss Tatty, in the Packer Collection (Sydney), painted in 1936, may be taken as a typical example of Dobell's satirical method. It is social comment that is partly grotesque, partly sardonic, but always good-humoured. The image, which consists of a rapidly roughed-in impression in light pigment on a dark ground, has been stated swiftly and with an air of abandon. Dobell has seized on the floral decoration of the hat, the pom-pom hair-do, the gloves, the necklace, the fur, and the walking stick, to portray habits of dress that are an index to habits of mind. At the other end of the scale we have Dobell portraying a different morality in the very charming little *Drunken Bridesmaids*, in the Blaxland Collection (Sydney), with its delightful colour scheme of soft blues, vivid yellows and audacious streaks of red. We can imagine what Miss Tatty would have to say to the unladylike conduct!

It is upon such paintings as *The Sleeping Greek*, *The Charlady* and *The Irish Youth* that Dobell's position as an original and creative artist depends in no small degree. In these paintings we find a true aesthetic fusion of the contemplative element to be found in his early landscapes and those powers of observation which he developed during the lean years of the Depression. *The Sleeping Greek* possesses the palpable yet impersonal sensuousness of some Greek sculpture; it is Praxitelean in its moody composure. Notice the fine placing of the head in the picture-space, and the sympathetic modelling of the features. The attraction of the painting is hard to define in words, but the cause of it is due without doubt to the welding of a plastic and psychological interpretation of the subject.

This synthesis of the plastic and the emotional will be found in the striking *The Irish Youth*, a painting which, in my opinion, marks the height of Dobell's achievement as an artist in England. He appears, this Irish youth, suddenly before us, gaunt and grinning like a defiant scarecrow. But Dobell has endowed the scarecrow with life and feeling; the more it menaces the more inimitable is its appeal. Here Dobell has succeeded in rendering more than externals. The satirical comments, on the other hand, are external comments. We are not asked to sympathize with or understand the thoughts or sentiments of *Mrs South Kensington*. They are made for her, we feel certain, by her family, her social circle, and her favourite newspapers. But in *The Irish Youth* we can feel the full impact of a living human being upon the artist. In the angularity of the forms, the emaciated face, and the startled owl-like eyes there is pulsating life. The presentation is as simply conceived as any of Dobell's portraits. The hands are hung limply by the sides, and the head lunges from the shadows. Yet a conscious artistry governs the construction. The V-shaped head is repeated in the lapels of the coat; the inverted V of the hair in the collarflaps. The long nose and the tie accentuate the leanness of the figure while they state the different planes of the head and the body. The consciousness of this art may be seen by comparing the painting with the sketch for it in the Packer Collection, wherein Dobell had not yet reduced the forms to a simple coherent statement.

Yet it is not *The Irish Youth*, but *The Red Lady*, in the Collection of Colin Anderson (London), painted about a year before, which gives us an idea of the way Dobell's art was tending in the years immediately before his return to Australia. When we recall *Mrs South Kensington* or *The Sleeping Greek*, the first thing which is noticeable in *The Red Lady* is the artist's return to a consciously elaborated linear rhythm which becomes the organizing element of the painting. I do not mean that the paintings preceding *The Red Lady* ignore the importance of line in their composition, but that its use is generally subsidiary to the conception. The idea, in other words, was not conceived at the outset in terms of line. But in *The Red Lady* we have a return, in a new way, to the method of pictorial organization that we first met with in *Consuelita*, here replaced by a series of interconnected spheres. But whereas the use of line is, in a sense, a return to his earlier method, Dobell's use of colour is an important innovation that we see continued in such paintings as *The Strapper*, *The Student*, *Brian Penton* and *Joshua Smith*. No doubt the picture owes much to the colour and verve of the expressionist painter Chaim Soutine, yet it is a highly original work which, while returning to an early manner of construction, retains and indeed indicates a growth of Dobell's observational powers and mordant wit. He has given his Red Lady gargantuan dimensions. She could be one of Rowlandson's sailor wenches after she had married a duke and grown plump and prosperous and sour.

Between 1936 and 1938 Dobell's art reached maturity. The influences to which he had been subject during his Australian student days were foreign to his true nature. There was nothing in the modified version of naturalism taught at the Julian Ashton School to which he could respond naturally, beyond its penchant for hard drawing. The early influence upon his portraiture in London is from Italy—from Francesca and Pollaiuolo. But Dobell's primary affinities were with the North; it was to Rembrandt and Van Gogh, and such artists as Daumier and Goya, whose paintings were highly charged with emotional content, that he went for his inspirations.

When Dobell shook off the self-conscious attitude of the studio and ceased to be overawed by the personalities of the past, a personal art began to emerge based upon the people and life of London during the 1930s. His art becomes intelligible when seen as one more contribution to that mode of creation in which the expression of feeling produces emotional unities rather than the intuitive ordering of lines, spaces, and tones into formal unities of purely aesthetic appeal. The early traces of eclecticism; a touch of Corot in the early landscapes, of Vermeer and Francesca in the early portraits and genre studies, departs from his art of the mid-1930s. The influences have been assimilated and he bends them to his own requirements. Far in the background is the deep humanism of Rembrandt with his magical control of paint and his sympathy for all men. Rembrandt has been a kind of sheet-anchor for Dobell's art, preserving it from facile cleverness and deliberate stunting. In *My Lady Waits* and *Duchess Disrobes* we catch a reference to Daumier; in *The Dead Landlord* we hear faintly the tragic laughter of the Goya of *Los Caprichos*; but by the time these pictures are painted we are in the presence of an artist who has something original to say and the means to say it.

10

Eric Wilson

—1947—

Painting in Australia today is, I believe, richer in its variety and more mature in its values than it has ever been. A great deal of the variety and quality is due to that colony of Australian art students and artists who made London their headquarters during the 1930s. Among this group were to be found William Dobell, Arthur Murch, Russell Drysdale, Jean Bellette, Donald Friend, David Strachan, New Zealanders such as George Duncan and James Cook, and many others. Some were there for only a few years, but others, such as Dobell, for most of the decade. In the contribution of this group to Australian art the work of Eric Wilson, who died at the early age of thirty-five, occupies a distinctive and important place.

Born at Liverpool, New South Wales, in 1911, he studied at the Julian Ashton School, Sydney, and won a travelling art scholarship in 1937. He began his London studies at the Royal Academy schools under Sir Walter Russell, and worked later under Mark Gertler and Bernard Meninsky at the Westminster School. This led to his joining the Académie Ozenfant. The Westminster School was attracting at this time quite a number of Australian art students who had kicked the dust and gum-leaves of a local landscape tradition behind them. Its influence and its approach to painting would certainly form a section of any serious study of twentieth-century painting in Australia.

In such early works as *Fog and Sun*, in the possession of the Armidale Teachers' College, painted by Wilson before he left Australia for London, we have what has been a characteristic beginning for so many of the Australian artists of his generation: a landscape pleasant and lyrical, drenched in the soft sunlight of

---

This essay, here slightly revised, was first published in *Meanjin*, vol. vi, Summer 1947, pp. 245–8, shortly after the artist's death.

an uncertain and hesitant impressionism—to contemporary tastes a little too sweet. Yet even in this painting the habit of disciplining his art, which was to become such a feature of his later work, is apparent. The subject is reduced to its essentials, the handling is even and meticulous.

London and the Continent provided Wilson with a deepening of experience and contact with international values. He worked chiefly in landscape, using a palette of greens, blues, greys, and suppressed yellows, in subdued but rich variety. *Mill at Rotterdam* (in the collection of J. M. Garland), which he painted in 1939, has the soft purple-greys and delicate handling of early English topographical water-colours. In later works the tones deepened, running down into masterful blues that darkened into heavy shadow in his last years. With that change in colour went similar changes in his methods of construction and handling of pigment. *Doorways in Venice* (in the possession of Lloyd Rees) is an austere two-dimensional pattern with severe verticals and a sharp angularity of rhythm. Compare this with the rich colloquialism of *Bridge over the Liffey* (in the possession of Mrs S. Goodman) which, with its vibrant swirling movement, is one of Wilson's finest paintings, the closest that his restrained art ever came to a personal expressionism. A study of Wilson's European landscapes of this period and those painted contemporaneously by William Dobell— for a time they were closely associated—is well worth while. There is a marked similarity in their use of colour. There are technical similarities such as hatched brushwork and a common interest in the realizing of textures. Yet how different are the personalities! In Dobell it is emotion, in Wilson it is intuition for space and volume that predominates. The conflict in Dobell's work is the conflict of the humanist seeking to discipline the emotional impact of his subject-matter by his conscious awareness of the importance of structure. The conflict in Wilson's work is the conflict of an artist seeking to surprise emotional feeling by an intense exploration of the harmonies and proportions of his subject-matter. Yet strangely enough there is a greater measure of personal expression in Wilson's landscapes than in his abstracts or portraits, whereas Dobell's landscapes are invariably painted with a reticence unknown to his portraits and genre paintings.

Wilson's approach to painting was that of a classical artist; he sought for forms purged of individuality and romance. A study of his sketches in relation to his completed paintings makes this clear enough. In his *Mill at Delft* he seizes upon the massive bulk of his subject, dwarfing as it does the whole neighbourhood. He subordinates everything to the assertion of the substantiality, the mastering physical presence of the mill. His pictures of fishermen by the Seine present them as forms that are as immobile as the stones of the Embankment. Everything is impersonal, shaped and placed for an architectural purpose. All this was the natural consequence of his never-ending search for the basic structure and quiddity of his subject-matter.

I do not mean that Wilson's work lacked sensuous qualities. There is sensuousness enough in the way he presents, with a touch that almost caresses, the texture of stone in old streets. There is the real warmth of poetic feeling in *Roland Street, Belfast*, and in the delicate pinks that play softly over the greys in *Rue Charonesse*. The sensuousness is there right enough, but it escapes vicariously, as though the artist mistrusted the spontaneous flow of personal feeling. Everywhere we find evidence of how he has restrained the sensuous to impersonalize his art, so that his sense of the intuitive relations of things, which remained with him the central consideration always, might assert itself. If this asceticism at times inhibited his personal expression it did provide problems the pursuit of which made his art a thing of ordered growth.

Portraiture presented problems that he was never able to master satisfactorily. He sought to bring a monumental quality to the presence of his sitters, but the demands of naturalism were usually too insistent. The result was not a welding of the ideal and the real, the synthesis that he sought but, all too frequently, a gawkiness of pose and a sense of strain. Sometimes his very persistence for the essence of a characteristic shape or volume resulted in heavy and laboured handling and surfaces with an unpleasant oleographic sheen. But he did produce two memorable works in portraiture. *Girl in a Striped Dress* is conceived and stated with simplicity and finality. The girl's physical presence has been realized within severe conventions without a trace of hesitancy in the artistry. It has the sparkle and freshness—if not the abandon—of the freest of his landscapes, being painted in those London years when life must have been full of zest and richness for him. *The Inmates*, the other painting, in the Art Gallery New South Wales collection, is entirely different in conception and mood. The drawings made for the heads in this painting are exceptionally good. We catch a glimpse of personal distress externalized in the faces of these old men with their vacant eyes, and the unknown sufferings of their broken lives. This does not appear often in Wilson's work. Usually he disciplines his emotions so severely that they only appear as ghosts transmuted into colours, shapes and volumes.

It is not surprising that an artist with Wilson's interest in form and construction should turn to exploring the problems of abstract art. The abstract paintings derive from the tradition of Braque, through Ozenfant. Yet they reveal the personality of the artist as certainly as any handwriting. Here, as in the landscapes, there is a movement from pastellate delicacy of tone, as in his *Hospital Theme*, to the weight and sombre harmonies of *Abstract No. 9* (Memorial Exhibition catalogue), to my mind the finest abstract yet painted in this country. It is in his abstracts that his considerable craftsmanship is seen at its best. In them it is always subordinated to its architectonic purpose; the skill of sheer handling reminding one of the austere art of Eric Gill, an artist whom he resembled in more ways than one. The best of the abstracts are the clearest expression of his artistic rationalism. But it is in his landscapes painted abroad, such as *Scott Street, Glasgow*, in the National Gallery of Victoria, or *Rue de la Bonne, Montmartre, Paris, 1939*, in the Art Gallery of New South Wales, that provide us with the finest expressions of his own personality: a personality that was contemplative, intelligent, and somewhat ascetic; seeking for the essence, rather than the overtones; for the substance of things, rather than the emotions evoked by them. Perhaps he sought for the impossible: perhaps impersonal harmonies in art, the goal of so many of the finest artists—among them Francesca and Vermeer—lead, when set up as ideals, too often to aesthetic frustration. But one thing is certain. The attitudes which Wilson stood for provided an important contribution to Australian painting which he advanced both in his practice and his teaching. No one has pursued the problems of abstraction in painting in this country with a sensibility more carefully cultivated and disciplined to the requirements of abstract art, or with finer impersonality; and without impersonality and a sense of discipline abstract art develops into the cult of the accidental.

By its very nature it was inevitable that Wilson's art should be restricted in its appeal. He possessed a Sibelius touch—presenting glasses of cold water to critics who sought sentiment and emotion. Yet his work breathes a respect for the traditions of his craft. One feels instinctively that he approached great paintings with fine humility. Only in his last works do we note the appearance of a feeling of frustration; the tones are deeper, the colours less pure, and inspiration gives way to technical bravura. But in these last paintings we find him still struggling as tenaciously as ever with

Eric Wilson, *Hospital Theme, The Sterilizer*, 1942, oil on board, 81.2 × 47.0 cm. Art Gallery of New South Wales.

new problems. It is greatly to be regretted that he did not live to continue his work in the presentation of contemporary Australian landscape which he began so shortly before his death, for he was equipped as few contemporary artists in Australia are equipped, to present us with something of real significance in a field which still awaits a new interpretation.

Integrity, discipline, sensibility and intelligence; these are the virtues of Wilson's art. They are virtues that weather well. The reputation of a living artist is measured against the achievements of his contemporaries and such fortuitous factors as his social and family connections, the 'bedside manner' he can cultivate for the benefit of his patrons and his ability to amuse people at cocktail parties; at his death he begins to measured by the achievements of the dead. Wilson possessed enough wisdom and humility to remember those disturbing facts. His *œuvre*, though small, will find a secure place in Australian art.

11
Comments on Style Change and Criticism in Sydney
—1947—

Those who have examined the paintings of the younger generation of Sydney artists over the past few years, with regard not to the character of individual achievements but to the general nature of all the work produced, cannot fail to have remarked the considerable stylistic change occurring at the present time. We are witnessing nothing less than a complete revolution—or a revulsion—from those qualities which the avant-garde of the Sydney painters of the late 1920s and early 1930s sought after with so much enthusiasm and singleness of purpose. In those days firm contours and linear rhythm were prominent in the advanced art of Sydney. Painters aimed at an objective and at times cubistic simplicity of form. Colour tended to be flat, bright, and gave the appearance of dryness. There was little emphasis upon lustrous or animated textures. Brushwork, though frequently obvious, was rarely used to achieve impasto surfaces. Art, at this time, became a kind of visual mathematics. There was a general desire to escape from the Edwardian rococo of Norman Lindsay and the thin atmospheric lyricisms of Hilder by searching for an art without associations either moral or literary, but concerned with the fundamentals of structure and design. A Byzantine formalism was sought after and admired by those with advanced tastes. To some artists the discipline reduced itself to a kind of pattern-making, but others were able to realize form in three dimensions with a true feeling for plasticity. Among those artists whose work reflected something of the stylistic spirit of those times were Douglas Dundas, Rah Fizelle, John D. Moore, Roy de Maistre, Margaret Preston, Grace Cossington Smith, Grace

First published in the *Society of Artists Yearbook, 1946–47*, Sydney Ure Smith, Sydney, 1947, pp. 47–54.

Crowley, Roland Wakelin, Thea Proctor, Rayner Hoff and several others.

This style was not, of course, native to Sydney painting. A reaction from the *démodé* academic impressionism of the local schools, it was the Sydney version of an international movement in art which gave us the architecture of Le Corbusier and Frank Lloyd Wright, the sculpture of Meštrović and Archipenko, the typography of Eric Gill, the paintings of Duncan Grant. In literature it found its counterpart in the critical theories of T. E. Hulme, in the poetry of the T. S. Eliot of 'Prufrock'. It was summed up for the visual arts by Roger Fry, when he wrote, 'It cuts out all the romantic overtones of life which are the usual bait by which men are induced to accept a work of art. It appeals only to the aesthetic sensibility; and that in most men is comparatively weak.'* It was an art, in short, of fundamentals; an art of subtraction, not of addition.

In the second half of the 1940s however, we find ourselves viewing on all sides a return to an art of addition. 'The romantic overtones of life' are once again sounding in the art around us. Current exhibitions reveal the extent of the stylistic reversal. Clarity of contour, clear colour directly applied, the sharp articulation of planes in the structural organization of a painting, the grace of linear rhythms are all being sacrificed with increasing frequency in the effort to obtain a heavy romantic tonality, in which planes, contours, and tones are being used not so much as elements of organization, but to evoke literary sentiments such as 'mystery', 'poetry', and 'melancholy'. It is in the work of younger artists and students that the change is to be seen most clearly, but it is, nevertheless, general and widespread.

What, we ask, has caused this change? It could, of course, be attributed to the spirit of the time, which is about as helpful as attributing the change to Beelzebub. The spirit of the time is a kind of orphanage where critics with a spiritual turn of mind are in the habit of leaving their more troublesome mental children. Or we might, with an equal obscurity, attribute it to one of those organic theories of art in which it is argued that such style changes proceed from the natural and internal processes of art itself. We could then say that what we are witnessing is a movement from the 'architectural' to the 'painterly' phase of the movement in art which originated with Paul Cézanne and the post-impressionists. In my own view the reason is to be found in a series of isolated but analysable elements. An interest in surrealism brought back an interest in literary elements in painting via the dream; the satirical and psychological overtones of Dobell's painting and the tactile quality of his modelling brought back an interest in characterization and a greater attention to the construction of volumes. To these may be added the social emphasis of some painters of contemporary genre, on the one hand, and the interest of several Sydney painters in a romantic version of seventeenth-century classicism, on the other. It is interesting to note that in Melbourne, where not all these factors have operated, the change of style has not proceeded to the same extent.

Now it is one thing to say that the art of Sydney today is stylistically different from the art of the early 1930s, quite another to say that the standard of art has improved or declined since that time. Is Sydney art today better than the art produced by the most adventurous of our artists in the early 1930s? Can we say that the return to tonality, to literary association, to romanticism, has improved the general standard of Sydney painting? There is no a priori reason why tone should be of greater significance in art than line, flat colour of more value than modulated colour, that plasticity should be of more importance than flat decoration. Complexity in art is not necessarily better than simplicity. The sophisticated is not necessarily better than the primitive.

Now the danger for the free development of painting in Sydney lies in the fact that much current Sydney art criticism is making just these assumptions. Those qualities of the current style which emphasize romantic values have been praised for their evocation of such vague literary sentiments as 'reticence', 'melancholy', 'nostalgia', 'mystery', and 'spiritual values'. Such qualities have been by implication identified with artistic goodness, though they could with equal fitness have been associated with artistic badness. The danger which has arisen is that paintings appealing to a different set of critical values may be unduly discounted. Painters who use brilliant colour, flat patterning, and firm contours, or who paint in the classical or abstract manner derived from the post-impressionists, may be condemned as mechanical, insensitive, or even incapable, when, in fact, they are only expressing themselves according to another mode of creation which appeals to a different kind of sensibility.

Critics should beware of a unilateral criticism that sets up personal reactions and preferences as absolute standards. Criticism, of course, must preserve the myth of the absolute standard before it can operate; it is, according to Samuel Alexander, 'a conspiracy among the informed'. Objective criticism, as distinct from personal taste, is not possible without reference to the artist's purpose and his normal mode of expression. Whether or not we agree with Herbert Read's equation of realism, surrealism, expressionism and constructivism as the four modes of artistic expression, with Jung's four psychological types—of thinking, feeling, sensation, and intuition—the theory could very well have a beneficial influence upon practical art criticism in Sydney. A critic who holds such a theory is forced to admit that a man can be an artist and not feel in the same way about experience as the critic does. A pluralistic theory of artistic creation should engender critical tolerance. Unfortunately, current criticism here does not distinguish between differing modes of expression and differing standards of value. Upon values there must be no compromise; a critic must maintain standards. But an unwillingness to recognize differing modes of expression produces criticism which is unilateral and intolerant. We cannot explain the excellences of the painting of Rembrandt by using the critical terms of reference peculiarly suited to explain the excellences of Paul Cézanne. The critic must always guard against his values becoming submerged in the current style of painting. Lessing's adulation of the *Laocoon*, Ruskin's hatred of Whistler's paintings serve to remind us that even the most practised critics frequently express nothing more than the prejudices of their times.

This brings me to my final point. Painting in Sydney is becoming increasingly romantic, and the tendency is being aided by 'romantic' criticism. Whether or not this movement towards romanticism will produce finer paintings we do not yet know. But it is certain that in the present situation some other valid forms of artistic conception, such as the impressionist, the abstract, the realist and the classical, are likely to be discredited because of the power of fashion.

Note

* Roger Fry, *Vision and Design*, Chatto & Windus, London, 1920, p. 10.

12
Sali Herman
—1948—

The word 'taste', which is so useful for the art historian, is both tempting and dangerous for the critic. Its subjective associations, its close connection with what is fashionable in such uses as 'in good taste' and 'the prevailing taste' render it treacherous. There is a sense, however, in which it may be of value for criticism. A work of art is a union of material, form, and theme. Between these elements of his art the artist establishes those relations from which we derive the satisfactions peculiar to art. Now the fine adjustment of these several elements constitutes, it seems to me, what may be called taste; a sense of aesthetic discrimination operating to control each element of the artistic process for the benefit of the whole. This sense of harmony, discrimination, taste—no word quite brings out the meaning—was, of course, one of the great qualities of Greek art. Apollo, we may recall, became their god of the arts—a charioteer, a driver of half-tamed horses. And that is what the artist is: a charioteer, holding the reins of many fractious steeds, who succeeds when, by giving them rein and curbing them to his own will, he is able to drive them to his destination. Taste, in other words, is a kind of equilibrium established by an artist between the several elements operating in his artistry. We cannot judge art solely by this criterion of taste, since we must consider not only the nature of the equilibrium an artist establishes between these elements, but the nature of the elements themselves. 'The tigers of wrath are wiser than the horses of instruction', wrote William Blake; and it is right that we should rank artists who are brought to destruction—as Blake was in his later poetry—seeking to drive the tigers of their wrath, higher than we should rank artists who develop an exquisite style while driving teams of white mice.

First published in *Meanjin*, vol. vii, Spring 1948, pp. 172–6.

Some of the greatest artists have had no taste. Their art possessed them like a demon and drove them on. Such artists, unable to maintain the equilibrium of a personal taste, occasionally wreak havoc upon those years of harmony and balance which arise in the arts of civilizations from time to time. The bull-like demon of Michelangelo, for instance, wrecked the exquisite china shop of the High Renaissance and left the artists who came after him to assemble the baroque from the broken pieces. It is sometimes more important that a taste, particularly when it has become a bad habit, should be broken, than that it should be cultivated. Yet art, whether in its personal or social manifestations, always seeks its unities. All artists drive better if they have learnt the use of their reins, whatever may be the quality of their steeds.

I am concerned here with the nature of taste because, just as it is essential to understand how Drysdale's art is based on the realization of symbols if we are to appreciate it fully, so it is necessary to realize that the art of Sali Herman is controlled at its source by an intuitive sense of discrimination which controls each aspect of his artistry. I find it difficult to call to mind any contemporary Australian artist who paints in better taste. For he controls the several elements of his art better; he holds the reins better.

In the first place Herman's paintings are well built; they are, we might say, sound in wind and limb. He begins with good structure, but—and this is where his taste is in evidence—it is not demonstrated too mechanically. He does not thrust his architectonics under our noses to prove that he has learnt the grammar of art. Though the bones of his art are well-knit they are worn decorously beneath the skin, not in the manner of those crustaceans among our painters, to whom design is a claw and a carapace to protect the cold flesh within. Compare the direct presentation of the structure of *The Black House* with its dramatic associations, and the structural reticence of that exquisite urban landscape *Park at the Cross*. The structure in both cases grows from the theme: the first demands bold treatment; the second, an underlying patterning of the forms that charms by its quiet presence.

We find a sensitive discrimination, too, in the other elements of his artistry. Knowing how to use colour to achieve emotional effects such as the heat haze surrounding an army camp, or the sombre drabness of an old tenement, he will not allow his emotions to take charge completely. He is aware that colour also has its architecture. So each of his paintings has its relations of

Sali Herman, *The Black House*, 1941, oil on canvas, 53.2 × 72.6 cm. Private collection.

warm to cool colour, of dark to light tones, of flat to modulated surfaces, of rough to smooth textures. Colours by their presence will call up their complementaries; straight lines with their precision will call up curved lines with their elegance; and the hardness of walls is usually broken by the fragility of trees. He loves to soften the strong rhythms of buildings with the delicate tracery of branches, the curved arc of the moon, the soft arabesques of foliage, or the jaunty notes of some chimney pots. The prodigal impressions of nature become the ordered symbols of his art.

And to the impersonality of his art he brings the delightful contrasts of human interests; a boy sitting at a doorstep, a canary in a cage, women gossiping from windows or leaning from verandahs, a fisherman or 'bottle-oh' on his rounds, washing lines, rubbish bins, and dogs—hundreds of dogs. Whistler used to sign his pictures with a butterfly, and Herman really signs his pictures—or most of them—with a dog. It should be noted, of course, that in Herman's paintings the human interest is always subordinated to the whole plan. Nothing is placed haphazardly. The gossipping women gossip to relieve the impersonal tensions of the painting, yet they are, nevertheless, a part of those very tensions, a part of the planning. In this way he preserves his art from the literary emphasis of illustration, while realizing how well a fund of humour and the precise observation of people and their peculiarities can embellish a picture and make it more human and more lovable. Here, particularly, he holds the reins between formal and human values with great skill.

What emerges is an art in which each element is given its due prominence. Structure does not dominate colour, nor colour structure. He does not affect tones, impastos, or colour schemes that become, of themselves, 'signature tunes'. Only in the weaving of the whole tapestry does the personality of the artist emerge. And it is, I believe, because he has considerable mastery of his instruments that his art reacts so fully to the different emotional possibilities of different themes, so that there is little conscious mannerism in his work. The stylist in art will produce his own manner with the slightest thematic provocation; he will be clever, or gay, or sombre, or mysterious, or difficult, according to his chosen manner on every occasion; all will be cut to the procrustean bed of his style. The stylist would solve the problem of driving the fiery horses of creation by taming one or two after unyoking and disowning the rest. The artist who has learnt to control the several elements of his art is able to respond more naturally than the stylist to the particular expressive possibilities of his theme.

One other aspect of Herman's art calls for comment. Just as Drysdale has given us a new vision of Australian rural landscape, so Herman has portrayed the urban scene of Sydney with greater sensitivity than any artist of his generation. Many painters, such as Conrad Martens and Arthur Streeton, have been attracted by the physical beauties of Sydney. Usually it has been left at that. Only a few paintings with a real feeling for the truly urban qualities of the city come to mind. We have Streeton's *Redfern Station*, Conder's *Departure of the S.S. Orient* and Nerli's *A Wet Evening*, and—if we include Melbourne in the consideration—Tom Roberts' fine *Bourke Street*. The 1890s gave us these little masterpieces and we then had nothing that could come near them in either feeling or observation until Herman began to produce such paintings as *The Black House* and *Park at the Cross*.

It may seem strange that the majority of Australian painters have lived either in Sydney or Melbourne, yet have not drawn extensively upon their local surroundings for the material of their art. They have gone to the country—or at least to the suburbs—to paint the eucalypt, to north Italy to paint the hill towns, even to the Pacific Islands or Africa to paint the 'noble savage'. Most of the art of Australia is still an uneasy compromise between the gum-tree and the 'grand tour'. We are either arrogantly nationalistic or arrogantly cosmopolitan in matters of art; and our paintings become the expressions of our attitudes rather than the sensitive realization of our feelings. How often a rapid Cook's tour of the European galleries has left our artists suffering for the rest of their lives from a chronic aesthetic dyspepsia because they fear the charge of provincialism. How like those pilgrims who once gathered the waters of the river Jordan in little bottles to christen their offspring, hoping that its virtue would remain even when brought to their own unholy homes. Indeed a great deal of the belief that artists can be helped to produce great works of art by coming into physical contact with other great works of art is merely another form of that belief in sympathethic magic so prevalent among us. Time and again it has been left to the migrant to this country to look at the local scene in a new way: the Swiss Louis Buvelot, the young Englishman Tom Roberts and, in our own time, Sali Herman, have reacted with sensitivity to what they have seen about them in a new country.

Herman has rummaged about the congested areas that girdle the commercial heart of Sydney: Woolloomooloo, Surry Hills, Glebe, Pyrmont, Balmain, continuously making sketches of buildings and people. He has painted the parks, the ferries, the old buildings, and the wharves of Sydney. It is not that he has deliberately chosen such material, rather he paints the city because he lives in it, drawing freely on what comes to eye and mind. No doubt it is because he paints prolifically and with a characteristic *joie de vivre* that he does not always avoid the dangers that beset the artist of taste. When he does not guard against it his art, like that of Rupert Bunny, an artist whom he resembles in more than one respect, can cloy by its sweetness. Drysdale at his worst runs to melodrama, Dobell to a stilted academic constraint, and Herman to a soft and sugary romanticism. The romantic vein in his work, whether expressed in the terms of the tropical luxury of the Solomon Islands paintings, or the primitive qualities of some of his genre studies, does not always ring soundly. His lyricism, indeed, is frequently faulty in its upper registers; his is cello music, he is not to be trusted on the violin. When he tries the violin an impish quality frequently asserts itself that we may enjoy as good fun but not always as good art.

Herman was a student of George Bell, and learnt much from him. But the fine discrimination which is such a feature of his art belongs rather to a long association with the art of Europe and, particularly, to a close connection with the work and aims of the French impressionist and post-impressionist painters. In his work the French synthesis of intelligence and taste has been wedded to a sensitive observation of the local scene of this country. Conder, before he assumed the afternoon-tea Satanism of the English Decadence, and Roberts and Streeton, before they became famous Australian artists, during one or two wonderful moments in their art of the early 1890s achieved that union of intelligence and taste. They had just experienced personally the new vision of impressionism and brought their experience wonderfully to bear upon the colourful world they found about them. Herman works rather in the idiom of the post-impressionists, yet there is a great affinity of feeling and purpose between his art and their art of that time. Certainly his sensibility has more in common with theirs than with those artists who still trade in the currency—now devalued—which the Heidelberg impressionists first began to strike.

13
Henry Moore
—1948—

In Australia we usually realize what is happening in the world of art later than everyone else. Original works by Bonnard, Matisse, Cézanne, Gauguin, Duncan Grant and other moderns were first displayed here in 1939, long after their reputations had been established abroad. So it is not surprising that local criticism is often a system of echoes repeating what has already been said abroad, but more fitfully if not more faintly. Even the 1939 Melbourne Herald Show of French and British Modern Art could only present, because of its nature, a few examples, at most, of any one man's output—certainly not enough to make possible an independent judgement as to the range and quality of an artist's work. What we saw was obviously very good when judged by local standards. And there we had to leave it, for the simple reason that the conditions of criticism did not exist fully. For it is not possible to make an honest judgement upon the significance of an artist's achievement until we have seen all, or at least a considerable portion, of his work. In Australia therefore criticism must confine itself to the work of local artists, and make tentative appraisals only of the smattering of work by artists with considerable overseas reputations which reaches this country from time to time. Then there is still another difficulty. Before we saw those works by Bonnard, Gauguin, Matisse, Grant, and others, in 1939, their reputations had already been well established; many, indeed, arrived surrounded with the aura of old masters. Their influence upon contemporary taste, both here and abroad, had gone like heralding angels triumphantly before them. Theirs were not paintings only but icons; the icons of the Church Militant of

First published in *Hermes*, Magazine of the University of Sydney, 1948, as a review article based on the British Council's exhibition of Moore's work which toured Australia in that year.

Modern Art, and the emotions which they aroused were as often religious as they were aesthetic.

The works of Henry Moore arrived here too, it must be admitted, with all the mystical potency of religious symbols adhering to them. We will not, unless we are careful, approach them with a pure heart. For are they not accepted abroad by the judgement of the most discerning as evidence of British resurgence, nay more, leadership, in the plastic arts?

Indeed the fear of coming to grips critically with the work and ideas of Henry Moore characterizes much of the writing about him. We meet with much interpretative explanation but little criticism. The problem of presenting the sculptor to the public has largely occupied his critics. They have endeavoured to bring his audience into sympathetic relation with his work. For we must know what a man is trying to do before we can decide whether he is likely to achieve his purpose and whether it is worth achieving. Yet a sympathetic feeling for an artist's aims may result in bad judgements as frequently as good ones. What a master John Ruskin was at preparing an audience, by a kind of critical softening-up process, to react enthusiastically to mediocre paintings! An understanding of aims is essential to appreciation, but it is not yet criticism. And when an artist's aims do not measure up at all points to what he has achieved such an approach may be misleading. Something of this sort, it seems to me, has occurred in the case of Henry Moore.

In the first place we must be fully aware that Moore's work exists in its own right, in its own stone, or wood, or lead; not in anything that Henry Moore, or anyone else, including myself, should say, in words, about it. My problem is concerned rather with the fair brokerage of honest criticism. Words have grown about the works of Henry Moore, in a few years, like the tropical rainforest which once grew about the Mexican sculptures he admires. No doubt there is good reason for this growth of words about his work. But we must hack our way through all of it back to the stone, wood, and lead of his sculpture before we can look at it with our own eyes.

In 'The Sculptor's Aims', published in *Unit One* (1934),* Moore makes four salient points: first, the need for the sculptor to be true to his material; second, the need for full three-dimensional realization; third, the need for a continuous study of natural objects; and fourth, the need for vision, vitality, and expression in sculpture. I shall not concern myself with the last two points; no one will question the fourth point, and as for the third, even the mystic will probably be a better mystic if he observes well. The first two points, however, truth to material and full three-dimensional realization, raise some interesting questions. Some contemporary critics of sculpture appear to accept them as primary canons, the infringement of which inevitably produces bad sculpture. For this reason, and because they enter so frequently into the practical criticism of sculpture, it is most desirable to examine their meaning and their validity as aesthetic canons.

What exactly is meant by 'truth to material'? 'Stone', writes Henry Moore, 'is hard and concentrated and should not be falsified to look like soft flesh—it should not be forced beyond its constructive build to a point of weakness. It should keep its hard tense stoniness'. It is claimed that a sculptor must understand the nature of his material so that his finished work will, among other things, express the true nature of the material. Now the sculptor does not change the physical nature of his material. His wood remains wood, his stone remains stone when he has finished with it. He changes not the substance but rather the shapes of solids, and changes shape in accordance with his aesthetic purpose. But the shapes that any solid substance may possibly assume are determined by the physical nature of the substance. Sandstone, for instance, will not assume the capillarity of glass. So that the sculptor in glass will have a different variety of shapes to work with than a sculptor in sandstone. But truth to material means more than this. For the sculptor each solid has a great but not an unlimited number of shapes which a quantity of it may assume. Some of these possible shapes, says the contemporary sculptor, are not true to the material. That is, considered aesthetically, every solid will have a variety of shapes which are 'true' to its nature and a variety of shapes which are not true to it. What exactly does this mean? It is suggested that one of the ways in which a shape is not true to its substance is when the shape suggests to its audience not its own substance but some other substance; when stone is modelled, to repeat Moore's example, in a shape that suggests the palpable qualities of flesh. It is then that we feel stone as flesh; and this, it is maintained, is a quality of bad sculpture. For 'stone must preserve its stoniness'.

The weakness of this argument, it seems to me, arises from the nature of sculpture itself. It cannot be denied that as soon as a sculptor begins to carve or model in his material he begins to invest that material with values it did not posses before. He gives his stone values and meanings other than the values and meanings of natural stone. The stone, however abstract the carving may be, becomes a symbol fraught with human significance. The sculptor, by imputing other values to the stone, is being true to his intuitions rather than true to his material. Even when he sets out with no other purpose than to be true to his material he can only carve or model it according to his knowledge of its physical structure and its possibilities and limitations under his sculptural processes. And since he can never know all there is to know about the physical nature of his material and is limited by the tools with which he works, he can only be true to his knowledge of the material. In other words, the artist can only give us the truth about himself in this regard, for he is always turning his material from what it is to what he wants it to be. Indeed the sceptic may suggest, at this point, that the best way to allow a piece of stone to be true to its material is to leave it alone. But the contemporary sculptor will probably reply that he can help a material to realize its true nature. Like the good teacher he will seek to draw from his pupil, the stone, the inherent possibilities of its nature.

It is true, of course, that the sculptor who works during a long period with a certain material learns a great deal about its physical nature and may project his own personality into it by that aesthetic process of feeling which has been called 'empathy'. He senses his material as something living, and seeks to give that life an ordered growth. This form of 'truth to material' is another variety of the pathetic fallacy so common to all the arts. Behind such a process there seems to be the contemporary sculptor's intuitive and mystical desire to work upon his material in a fashion similar to that of the forces of nature, to adopt the sculptural methods of the wind and sea, and work in harmony with them. Though such an attitude may be, in a sense, the negation of human purposiveness in sculpture, yet it may mean an extension of our sensibility to the beautiful forms that are wrought by nature's agents. And if the basis of our aesthetic pleasure derives from the apprehension in works of art of a formal order which springs ultimately from the order of the natural world, then a knowledge of the methods of nature's sculpture may be a key to the practice of good art. Nevertheless, 'truth to material' can never be more than a useful practical maxim which expresses the compromise the artist establishes between his sculptural activity and the passivity of his material. Was it not Whistler who pointed out that he mixed himself with his materials; and the slogan, truth to material, is not unlike a recipe for making jam; so much sugar to the kind of fruit, so much artist according to the nature of the material. The recipe differs according to the artist, the material, and the age. The Hellenistic world had a sweeter tooth than archaic Greece and, sickened by the saccharine sentimentalities our grandmothers relished, we prefer our sculpture to be tart and even bitter to the taste. So our sculptors keep their woods wooden, their leads leaden, in vision as well as in substance.

Perhaps we may accept 'truth to material' as a maxim that throws light upon a new and experimental approach to sculpture, yet not elevate it to the position of a sculptural canon. If we insist that the nature of the material must completely direct the formal construction in order to vanquish the tyrant of representation, we may find that we have aroused the even more intractable tyrant of abstraction. For the creative artist is always master of his material and this means that he will fashion it according to his own nature, which can never be completely subordinated to the nature of his material.

Moore's second contention, that sculpture fully in the round has no points of view exactly alike, is even more debatable than the slogan 'truth to material'. It is well known that students of sculpture are taught to think of their creations as solid masses in space and that the sculptor in the round should be realizing his work from all points of view simultaneously. But it is one thing to create working simultaneously from many points of view and quite another to make each point of view, each plane and contour, different from every other. The sculptor's conception may require that several points of view be identical in contour or, at least, nearly identical. This, indeed, seems to be what has occurred in Moore's own *Madonna and Child*, in the Northampton church. An increase in the number of points of view may add to the variety at the expense of the unity of the conception, and lead to a diversity which is aesthetically unpleasant. This, to me, is what has occurred to Moore's *Figure* in Armenian marble (1932), in the collection of Eric Gregory. It is rather the relation of the contours, planes and volumes of the sculpture to the meaning or the function of the sculpture, not the multiplication of the faces for their own sakes, which makes a piece of sculpture satisfactory. The processes and torsions of a piece of bone have a beauty which arises from the exquisite adaptation of form to function. Variety of face, plane and contour does not make an object sculpturally pleasant merely because of the variety. An oak tree, for instance, is less symmetrical, presents points of view infinitely varied, yet as a sculptural shape it is not as satisfactory as any of its own acorns, which are far more symmetrical and have less facial variety.

To disagree with Moore's theories is not, of course, to disagree with the work of the practising artist who does his real thinking in and with his materials. An examination of his work even in the small exhibition brought to Australia in 1948 by the British Council does, I believe, indicate a movement towards the canons of sculpture of the constructivist and abstract sculptors, but it also indicates quite clearly his modification of those canons, and even a movement away from them in recent years. Moore has grown in stature as an artist not because he has fully realized his theories but because in practice he has modified them.

The earliest of his pieces in the exhibition arranged by the British Council is the *Mother and Child* in Hornton stone, from the Manchester City Gallery, which was carved in 1925. It is rendered in large, simply-stated masses. The planes are sharply articulated, only the form of the free breast serves to herald the fully rounded forms of his later work. What gives the carving its sinewy vigour is the finely conceived movement of the broken spiral which proceeds from the right arm of the mother around the block to the head of the child. An exquisite relation has been established between the mass of the mother and the mass of the child. Yet it is an immature work in which the Egyptian and African references are not fully subordinated to the expression of the theme. The compact quality and blockiness seem to be a characteristic feature of his early work. There is much more opening out of the forms and more rounding of the volumes in *Reclining Woman* (1930) in green Hornton stone. The dominant rhythmical motive now traverse the upper surfaces of the stone instead of running spirally round the core, as in the earlier piece. In the protuberances isolated from the body of the stone, breast is opposed to breast, hand to hand, and knee to knee. Yet the opposition in each case is not a symmetrical one. Then the hemispherical forms of the breasts are opposed to the sharp articulation of the hands, the contrast of this being broken in the formal compromise of the knees, which hesitate between rotundity and blockiness.

In *Mother and Child* and *Reclining Figure* the relation of the whole to the parts is fixed in a static unity. But in the *Composition* in Cumberland alabaster (1931) the whole conception has been based upon a gyratory movement. Lines, planes, volumes, turn continuously upon themselves. Asymmetry predominates. The structure and pattern of the alabaster have helped to assert the

Henry Moore, *Reclining Woman*, 1930, green Hornton stone, 59.7 × 92.7 × 41.3 cm. National Gallery of Canada, Ottawa.

nature of the rhythmical structure, and the perforation of the block has helped to emphasize the movement of the form.

These three pieces indicate a distinct movement in Moore's work from the representational to the abstract, from the sharply articulated form to the ovoid swelling form, from a specific symbolic reference to a more general symbolic reference. In the alabaster composition the representation of eyes, hands, and arms exist only as naturalistic 'vestiges' when compared with the representation given them in *Reclining Woman*. The volumes of the neck, shoulders, arms and breasts are still suggested, but now they grow unobtrusively from the rhythmical implications of the alabaster. The nature of the material rather than the nature of the mental symbol has become the first source of reference for the sculptor. It may be well to ask ourselves from where such a piece draws its particular appeal.

There is, in the first place, the sensuous appeal of the material; the instinctive feeling for the mass, weight, and texture of the material as stone. We could, of course, enjoy the same sensations in a piece of uncarved stone, a pebble, for instance, or a bone. It is not an appeal which the sculptor gives to the material but which he can preserve in it by not endowing it vicariously with the sensuous appeal of another material, such as flesh.

Closely related to our appreciation of the sculpture as material is our appreciation of the formal arrangement of the contours, planes and volumes, and their unity and interrelation. Appreciation of form is closely related to appreciation of material. The crisp, brittle hardness of marble suggests a different set of formal relations from those assumed naturally by a pliable substance such as lead. Even an examination of the photographs of Moore's work will reveal how he has succeeded in evolving one system of formal relations based on the human figure from Hornton stone, another from wood, and another from lead.

We may separate from the appreciation of the material, which is sensuous, and the appreciation of form, which is intuitive, the referential or symbolical significance of the sculptured shape. As the representational element in Moore's work becomes less obvious, the symbolic reference becomes more generalized. Just as the word 'freedom' possesses considerably more emotive power than the word 'telephone' because its reference is to something less objective, so the forms of Moore's sculpture frequently achieve intensity by the substitution of the more general for the more specific symbol. Whether these symbolic values possess meanings for us because they call to mind certain archetypal images which are part of our mental nature, or whether they arise from a direct association of ideas does not, it seems to me, matter very much, for the added emotional intensity which such meanings evoke is there, no matter from what mental level it arises. The *Composition* (1932) in African wonderstone, for example, captivates immediately by the sheer perfection of the treatment of the material, but it gains in emotional intensity from the symbolical references which we glimpse playing in the shapes, and lose again, just as we might glimpse a dolphin leaping in the sea and then lose it from sight. At times, indeed, the meanings will not rise fully to our consciousness. We apprehend them only as grey shapes turning in subliminal depths, being vaguely aware that we have known these shapes before and that they belong to a part of our mental nature, though we cannot fish them out to examine in the dry light of our thought.

Let us turn for a moment to the wood carvings in the exhibition. The *Figure* in ebony (1930) from the Ventris Collection is expressionist in conception, and this seems to be true of a great deal of the work which Moore produced in this year. Witness, for instance, *Head* (1930) and *Reclining Figure*, both in ironstone; the angular gothic vitality of the *Seated Figure* in lead; or the *Reclining Figure* in Corsehill stone. All these pieces have contours, surfaces, and volumes agitated with emotion. Not until a decade later, and then in the medium of drawing, does his work again attain to these strange human and sub-human gestures—in the shelter drawings. The immediate future after 1930 was with the exploration of shapes, surfaces and materials for their intrinsic possibilities. So that *Figure* in beech wood (1931), with its quiet medieval reminiscence, leads from the gestures of the ebony *Figure* to the abstract *Composition* in walnut wood of 1932. Here we meet again the internal gyratory movement that he had given to the Cumberland alabaster composition of a year before, which has already been mentioned. In the walnut-wood composition an ellipse turns in and out upon itself, buds, blossoms, and folds up within its own contours. Referential meanings have been suppressed. We are confronted only with the fashioning of a material and the movement of a form.

From 1932 to 1936 Moore's work became increasingly abstract. In the two square forms of 1936 in Hornton stone in the exhibition, the planes, contours, incisions all take the simplest form. His works become, at times, almost a plastic equivalent of the paintings of Mondrian. 'My sculpture is becoming less representational', wrote Moore in 1937. For years he had sought the abstract, the monumental, the final relation between form and material. The war years witnessed a change in the direction of his art. What occurred was not a recantation of aims, but a bending of old principles and old knowledge to a new purpose. His art—there is no reason why we should shy at the conclusion as some of his critics seems to—became more representational than it had been. His art leapt suddenly to the challenge of a human situation that had never before found expression in art, and his work achieved greatness where before it had only achieved perfection. A flood of human passion surged through the channels of formal analysis which he had built so assiduously through the 1930s. And because he had built well the channels held; his structure was equal to his passion. It is in the shelter drawings that his art, which had rotated in a system of enclosed perfection, suddenly became eloquent. The symbolism became more powerful, more precise, and more contemporary, while at the same time it became more universal—revealing how men and women suffer and yet endure. As Herbert Read admirably puts it, they 'constitute the most authentic expression of the special tragedy of this war'. It would have been difficult to prophesy that Moore's art, which had perfected itself by a denial of social relevance, should have achieved its most complete expression in another medium with an art which combines formal perfection with direct social relevance.

It seems that Moore's work will not remain an expression of his theories, particularly those concerned with asymmetry, three-dimensional realization, and abstraction. In his work of the 1940s Moore returned, in several respects, to a form of art which he had discarded earlier in his career. But he returned in a new way and as a creative artist. He continued to respond to the challenge of life rather than to work too closely in accord with his precepts of 1934. And is it not true that these precepts were rather slogans in the struggle against academic and representational sculpture that was waged in the 1930s and 1920s? 'You may drive out nature with a pitchfork but she will keep coming back', wrote Horace. His comment may be applied to Moore's development as an artist. Moore has been too wise an artist to throw out all nature from his art. Yet it is not without interest to contemplate that it was just those elements of it which he discarded through the 1930s that re-emerged a decade later in the shelter drawings, and in the *Madonna and Child* in the Northampton church.

Note

* Herbert Read (ed.), *Unit One: The Modern Movement in English Architecture, Painting and Sculpture*, Cassell, London, 1934. The book derived its name from the group of eleven artists who held an exhibition in 1933 claiming to express 'a truly contemporary spirit'. The group included Henry Moore, Paul Nash, Ben Nicholson and others.

14
Australian Portraiture
—1948—

The trustees of the National Art Gallery of New South Wales awarded William Dargie the 1947 Archibald Prize, for the fifth time, for his portrait of Sir Marcus Clarke, a trustee of the National Art Gallery of New South Wales. The portrait is completely lacking in distinction. The general quality of the exhibits was below that of recent years. There were, however, several portraits both in craftmanship and vitality far superior to the winning portrait. There was more vitality, for instance, and more soundness of construction in Joseph Wolinski's portrait of Howard Ashton, however lacking it may have been, like Dargie's portrait, in arrangement. There is quite a Dobellian veracity in the painting of Ashton's head. There is some sound painting, too, in the head of Professor Harvey Sutton by Joshua Smith, although the effect of the whole picture is unpleasant. But Joshua Smith's painting of Dr Hugh Poate reveals his decline as a painter, perhaps under the pressure of commissions since his fine dual portrait of his mother and father.

Carrington Smith is one of the few painters in Australia today who can think pictorially and paint good portraits at the same time. Although there is considerable distinction in the portrait of Professor A. L. McAuley it cannot compare with his portrait of Hester Clarke, which should have won the Archibald Prize of 1944. Other portraits which rose considerably above the general level include the portrait of Harold Beck by L. S. Pendelbury, a sympathetic and consistent treatment, and the portrait of Miss A. M. E. Bale by I. G. Hill.

Why is it that Australian portraiture is at such a low general standard? The answer is to be found, I believe, in the fact that

---

Part of an article first published in *Meanjin*, vol. vii, no. 1, Autumn 1948, pp. 28–9.

our art grew to adulthood under the aegis of impressionism; and impressionism, whatever its achievements, did not, could not by its nature, create great portraiture. At most it evolved slick and juicy portraiture in the manner of Sargent, or our own W. B. McInnes. For the impressionist, by the nature of his art, has to be impartial; and the good portraitist is never impartial. The impressionist can only paint the surface of things; the good portrait must penetrate below the surface, must be psychological as well as visual. For men are not turnips; to paint them well you have to adopt some sort of attitude towards them. That is why Vermeer and Cézanne were not great portrait painters. They were impartial. They made great pictures out of heads but not great portraits. The great portraitist either glorifies or debunks, he ennobles or satirizes; he accepts a man's assumptions concerning his own importance, and writes—or rather paints—him up, or else he penetrates those assumptions, and paints him down. Look how Reynolds, believing in the grandeur of office and the power of the state, will paint an admiral, and think how W. B. McInnes, Meldrum, Dargie, or Joshua Smith would paint one. I am not comparing as to achievement, but as to conception and attack. Reynolds will paint a spirit and a tradition; our painters chase after lapel shadows, wrinkles, the shine upon buttons. A good portraitist, in short, will bring out the hero a man would like to be, or the villain he is.

15
Russell Drysdale
—1948—

I do not suppose there is any painter in Australia today whose work enjoys more general recognition among collectors, critics, and his fellow-artists than Russell Drysdale. His art lies at the cross-roads where many views and opinions meet. His paintings are widely discussed, much sought after, and reasonably well known abroad. The high respect in which his art is held in art circles is not so apparent among the general public. Objections are made that his people are not real, that he gives a false impression of rural life in Australia, that he is too stark, and so on. Even so, his art has already met with a wide measure of public acceptance.

Born in 1912, Drysdale did not decide to adopt painting as a career until he went abroad in the early 1930s and saw examples of contemporary British and French art. They made a considerable impression upon him and on his return to Australia he entered the art studio of George Bell in Melbourne. No individual teacher of painting in this country during the past two decades has exercised a greater or more beneficent influence than Bell. He has been able to get the personalities of his students working actively in their art better than anyone else. Artists as varied in their talents and approach as Sali Herman, Donald Friend, Alan Sumner, and Drysdale himself, testify to Bell's ability to develop the artistic potentialities of his students without cramping their style. Drysdale has acknowledged the great value to his development as artist of those years with George Bell. His early works, painted under Bell's direct influence, are capable studies in the formal organization of colour and design.

Drysdale visited England and Paris again shortly before the

Not previously published.

beginning of the Second World War and became particularly interested in the work of the younger generation of English artists who were seeking to liberate English painting from the school of Paris. It was not, however, until the one-man show held at the Macquarie Galleries, Sydney, in March 1942 that his work became known for its highly individual qualities. A visit to his home town of Albury after his trip abroad impressed him with the fact that in the contemporary Australian rural scene was a wealth of material which, if used with knowledge and sensibility, could form the basis of a completely new approach to Australian painting.

Drysdale is a natural genre painter; and good genre painters are hard to come by. Many an artist will attempt a figure group on occasion, but most have neither the time, skill nor patience required to create good genre. The age, it seems, in many respects, is against it. So far as Australian art is concerned, the art of figure composition, to misquote Kenneth Slessor, 'is an art practised by the ancients'. Artists have got out of the habit of composing frequently with the human figure. And then, quite apart from composition, the good genre painter has to seize upon that which is most characteristic of his figures and the situations in which he presents them. In such paintings the special problems of landscape, still-life, and portraiture tend to merge. Among Australian painters, three have been outstanding; Samuel T. Gill, Tom Roberts and Russell Drysdale. There have been others, of course, such as Fred McCubbin and George Lambert, who have produced memorable works in the same field, but they do not reach, to my mind, the same stature. Gill, Roberts and Drysdale have each expressed an important phase of the Australian life of their time through the medium of their own personalities. They have combined personal with social truth. Gill gave expression to the Australian gold-fields with their boisterous vitality, their egalitarianism and their humour. Roberts painted the stories and activities of a pastoral Australia in such paintings as *Shearing the Rams*, *The Breakaway*, *The Straggler* and *Bailed Up*. Drysdale's art marks the first distinct break with the landscape and genre tradition in Australian art which Roberts did so much to establish. True, artists such as Gruner have given us significant variants of the impressionist tradition, but they have not departed completely from the aesthetic assumptions of the Heidelberg school as Drysdale has done.

Looking at any of Drysdale's paintings it is clear enough that his colour is distinguished, his sense of design strong and vital, and that he has achieved a highly personal style. But what is the outstanding quality of his work? It resides, I believe, in his ability to seek out the beauty and significance existing in contemporary situations and things, and to bring them within the ambit of art. It is an ability similar to the image-making process of poetry. Drysdale, in a word, creates his own metaphors. He is not satisfied with the aesthetic clichés of a past generation. It is illuminating to compare his method with that of some contemporary Australian poets. The poetry of T. Inglis Moore shows a continual search for new images drawn from the local scene to express his poetic ideas. In 'Emu Parade' he writes:

> *Rust in the world's stained wheat, fly in the*
> *rotting fruit!*
> *White ants of greed in our faith's hollowed fences:*
> *Where the long drought of disbelief had dried*
> *each root*
> *Stripped udders of the age gave no responses.*

In such poetry the imagery greets us a little self-consciously but the poet is at the central business of poetry, writing out his ideas and feelings in the terms of his personal experience. Or there is Slessor's remarkable couplet from his 'Country Towns':

> *At the School of Arts, a broadsheet lies*
> *Sprayed with the sarcasm of flies*

These poets are attempting to think poetically in terms of the images they have derived from contemporary Australian life and landscape. They are not content to repeat images sanctioned by tradition and usage. In so doing they contribute in their own way to the living body of English verse. Now Drysdale works at his art in a similar fashion, transforming his experiences into aesthetic images that are particularly relevant to our time.

From this it follows that the central fact to grasp in the appreciation of Drysdale's art is the emphasis he places upon what is central to the presentation of his idea. He is always seeking the characteristic symbol. Having found his symbols he labours to present them with all the dramatic force that his technical resources will allow. Take, for example, the long road that runs through *The Home Town*. One will meet such a road anywhere in Australia. Yet in Drysdale's presentation there is something about it of the nightmare roads of Chirico and Dali. So much has been done to emphasize the road that it dominates the whole conception and we see it not only in its natural geographical setting but with a

Russell Drysdale, *Hometown*, 1943, oil on canvas, 50 × 60 cm. The Robert Holmes
à Court Collection.

deeper psychological resonance. Or take again the Australian pub
with its characteristic wrought-iron columns and balustrades.
There is not a town in Australia without its 'Moody's Pub'. For
the pub has been the dominating social centre—for the males of
the district, at least—in most Australian towns since their beginnings. In the same way Drysdale will make use of water tanks
upon trestles, spindly trees, sheets of galvanized iron, and rust-
ing wheels for their evocative quality. He sees them not merely
as objects in a landscape but in their social context as cultural
objects, in the true sense of that debased word. By his intelligent
use of symbolism Drysdale has been able to give artistic expression for the first time in our history to the one-horse town of
Australia: the small community which is something more than a
camp and something less than a village. And in revealing the
nature of these towns he has laid the basis for a new point of

view in our art. His art has risen from the challenge of his subject-matter and again and again he has gone back to these towns seeking what is most characteristic in them as social phenomena. His other virtues as an artist will be found to rest upon this intuitive ability to pick out the symbols of a culture in the most commonplace of things.

If Drysdale's art is a realization of symbols rather than a realization of impressions it will follow that the technical methods which he adopts in his artistry will differ from those of the impressionist painters of the generation before him and their latter-day followers. Ideally, impressionism seeks to present, as well as it can, the visual truth of the subject during a moment of its existence. This means that the statement should be as instantaneous as possible, the brushwork direct and visible, the values succinctly realized and affirmed, the colour a record of well-observed visual fact. Drysdale's method differs completely from this for the simple reason that he is not concerned with stating colour facts under certain conditions of light and atmosphere. His trees, his roads, his women, cannot be presented by impressionist methods since they are symbols existing outside of purely visual experience. Drysdale uses visual fact only as a means to an expressionist end. Instead of attacking his subject-matter directly, in the manner of an impressionist, he prefers to ambush his symbols by a prolonged series of feints and deployments, the process being something like this. First, a series of sketches and then the conception of a symbol from the sketches. This will be followed by a slow realization of the idea, by means of the several symbols of which it is composed, using a process of indirect painting which will include considerable underpainting, scumbling, the continuous modulation of colour, and finally glazing. Selection, reduction, modification will be active through all these processes. In this way he rids himself of the tyranny of appearances. The symbolic reference is built up as the painting nears completion. So the meaning grows organically with the structure, colour and texture of the painting.

An art such as Drysdale's, which seeks, like the sculpture of Henry Moore, to 'penetrate reality', will freely distort the forms of nature. Drysdale, in seeking a symbolic presentation of men and women eking out a miserable existence upon a drought-stricken countryside, elongates his figures to increase the impact of his idea. His people are the organic manifestations of their environment, as are his trees. Both are conceived as integral parts of the poetic expression of the painting. They do not exist in their own right, but exist both in expression and shape only as parts of the totality of the presentation.

He uses colour in the same way as he uses line and tone, as an agent in the realization of symbols. Frequently he will use an observed natural colour—a red dust-covered sky, for example. But the business of establishing the symbolism may mean that the colour will be heightened in hue, modulated, suppressed in tone, and so forth, in the painting process. Furthermore, like many expressionist painters who depend upon the dramatic brilliance of their colour for their emotional effects, Drysdale is not adventurous in the use of colour itself. A palette of warm colours ranging from browns through the reds and oranges to the yellows—with a judicious admixture of greens and blues—is constantly called into service. This colour scheme has become part of his personality as a painter. But opposed to this comparative conservatism in the choice of colours is the care which he lavishes upon drawing out the full luminosity of his colours. A great deal of the conscious process of his artistry is concerned with this search for full luminous colour. Certainly few Australian painters, living or dead, have been able to achieve the resonance of hue that Drysdale attains in such a painting as *Sofala*.

Contrast *Sofala* with a typical landscape by Sir Arthur Streeton, such as *Cremorne Festival*. Using colour in a high tonal key throughout, achieved by the liberal use of white pigment, Streeton attains to a visual truth in its own way profound. The danger of this method is that the search for 'true' values frequently means a loss of colour richness. Today many of Streeton's pictures possess an unsatisfactory washed-out appearance. Now there is another method of presenting the sensations of colour and heat that we associate with Australian landscape. Colour produces its tactile as well as its visual sensations, otherwise we could not call some colours hot and others cold. By the building up of reds, browns, oranges, and so on, in their full colour intensity it is possible to evoke sensations of heat and dryness in a way quite distinct from the purely visual methods of impressionism. This is Drysdale's method; a subjective expressionist method rather than an objective impressionist one.

Just as with Streeton's, so Drysdale's method has its own peculiar pitfall. Streeton's colour, when at its worst, suffers from pernicious anaemia. Drysdale, when he oversteps the limitations imposed by form and idea, allows his presentation to become melodramatic. An element of sensationalism appears in the riot of colour richness, and one seeks in vain for a quiet note, a passage of grey, or just a suggestion of green among all the heat. It is in the later paintings of the 'erosion' series in which this weakness is to be found most plainly.

At its best, however, Drysdale's colour grows naturally from the formal structure of the picture, yet it never remains a passive agent in the formal conception. He uses colour as the sensuous embodiment of the poetry of the idea. Therefore it is never purely harmonic in its relations but is, rather, eloquent in the assertion of the theme, belonging in spirit to the tradition of Rembrandt, Daumier and Rouault.

Despite the weakness already noted it is the 'erosion' series of paintings which mark the highest level of Drysdale's achievement to the present. In these pictures he depicts the struggle of trees for life in a dry wilderness. Man is not present in person but he is there for all that, presiding over the desolate wastes like an evil genius, a creator of wildernesses, a being capable of disrupting the natural rhythms established through ages of time between climate and vegetation, capable of reducing, by his voracity and stupidity, a verdant plain to a desert. There is no humour in these paintings. Trees writhe like bodies convulsed with torture; nor can we be sure that they are not bodies like trees. It is in such paintings that Drysdale reveals that he possesses a sense of tragedy.

Let me repeat what I said at the beginning: Drysdale creates his own metaphors. He is original at that point of the artistic process where a creative artist must be original, at the point of conception. He has seen *new* beauty, and has cut it from the very chaos and drabness of his own time. Like Piers the Plowman he ploughs a good furrow; and indeed his example looks as though it will yet turn several local pilgrims, who have wandered disconsolately about the earth in search of a saviour, to the salvation to be found on their own doorstep for the price of a good day's labour with their own eyes and hearts.

PART III

Hotting it up during the Cold War: the 1950s

16
Fifty Years of Painting in Australia
—1951—

Before I can hope to talk about Australian art during the past fifty years I must try, like St George, to kill a dragon. The dragon is that oft-repeated assertion that the history of our art is the story of how an English way of looking at things here was replaced by an Australian way of looking at things here. Only when we put that dragon out of mind can we begin to appreciate the real course of art in this country.

What happened was quite different. During the 1880s and 1890s picturesque and romantic attitudes of vision, mainly of English origin, were rapidly replaced by *plein air* and impressionist techniques of painting, largely of French origin. Where, we might ask, in the year 1900 were the three men who had done most to bring this change about? Conder was in Paris, Streeton in London, and Roberts, together with Longstaff and Phillips Fox, was planning his second trip abroad. As William Moore put it, after the Genesis came the Exodus. And the turn of the century was a period of exodus for Australian art.

For in 1900 Australia was not much concerned about art or artists. Somebody complained in a Sydney newspaper: 'Among the thousand and one methods suggested for the accomplishment of Federation one sees, so far, nothing that would lead the visitor to suppose this country had any appreciation of art'. To make up for this official neglect the Society of Artists held a Commonwealth Exhibition of Australian art in January 1901.

Let us glance at one or two of the exhibits in passing. Here are some fresh water-colours by Julian Ashton—at the age of fifty the

First published in *Meanjin*, vol. x, no. 4, Summer 1951, pp. 354–8 by courtesy of the Australian Broadcasting Commission, being originally given as a talk entitled 'Painting and Sculpture' in the Fifty Years of Federation series, and broadcast on the interstate programme at 2 p.m., Sunday, 29 April 1951.

most influential man in the art world of Australia. For the next fifty years Australian art will be almost a story written by his pupils. And here is a dawn landscape with a satyr piping to sheep among fantastic art nouveau vegetation, by Sid Long, the young president of the society and one of Ashton's pupils. Soon the poets O'Dowd and McCrae will be painting verbal pictures not unlike these landscapes.

And here another Ashton pupil, George Lambert, shows his big picture *Across the Black Soil Plains*. Such work-a-day subject matter in the Roberts' manner will soon be out of fashion. Official commissions are now coming to those who ten years before had challenged official taste. Roberts spent the first years of the new century painting his big picture of the *Opening of the First Common-wealth Parliament*. Conder, writing to him from Paris, obviously had some misgivings: 'I hope the big machine will be a success, but it must be an awful job to do,' he wrote. 'I should think Parliamentary coves are usually so beastly ugly.' Shortly afterwards we find Longstaff painting the portraits of King Edward VII and his Queen for the Sydney Gallery. Lord Beauchamp, Governor of New South Wales, was inviting artists to his garden parties. In Melbourne Sir Baldwin Spencer was developing the first important private collection of Australian pictures. Madame Melba was buying too. Gradually, very gradually, Edwardian Australia began to support some of its painters. Conventional portrait painters had the most to gain. The year 1900 was the year that Archibald commissioned Longstaff to paint Henry Lawson's portrait and in that commission, I'm sure, lay the germ of the future Archibald Prize. In Melbourne, Bernard Hall, as director and teacher at the National Gallery, was talking much about Velasquez, Raeburn, and the importance of values. He had just trained two young Scotsmen. Hugh Ramsay, the more talented of the two, died young. Max Meldrum, the other, returned to Melbourne in 1912 to expound for years a theory in which tonal accuracy became the chief end of painting. In short the emphasis on portraiture was bringing impressionism from the open air back into the studio.

The young men of the day were reading Whistler's *Gentle Art of Making Enemies*, though they learnt, as they grew older, that the success of their exhibitions depended in no small manner upon the even gentler art of making friends in the right places. The older generation still enjoyed the pre-Raphaelites and the moral exhortations of John Ruskin. In March 1906 Holman Hunt's painting *The Light of the World* burst upon the country with the force of a religious revival. Fifteen thousand people fought their way to see it in three hours at the Melbourne Gallery. Sermons were based on it; ministers of religion explained its mystic symbolism up and down the country. Then next year, Norman Lindsay, grandson of a missionary, began to exhibit with the Society of Artists. From his pen and brush there poured tumultuous mobs of hairy satyrs, Spanish dwarfs, lusting gods, and an inexhaustible flood of naked and buxom ladies, enjoying themselves among peacocks on arcadian lawns. The crowds that had adored the *Light of the World* as high art were horrified and denounced the new paganism. 'Art', said Norman Lindsay, 'was creative energy', as he rode to battle against the wowsers of the whole world. It must have been very exciting. And in the same year J. J. Hilder first exhibited those delicate water-colours that recall the lyrical verse of John Shaw Neilson.

What then is the scene before the First World War? Norman Lindsay is tilting vigorously at Victorian conventions and the local complacency to art; Lionel, his brother, with Syd Ure Smith, is fostering an interest in etching and the graphic arts. Elioth Gruner is rising early to paint the frosty dawns, and Hans Heysen in South Australia is turning the gum-tree into the dominant symbol of the Australian landscape. The war itself produced little Australian art of outstanding merit, as the War Museum at Canberra testifies. Only David Low with his *Billy Book* and Will Dyson with his lithographs of the Western Front produced things truly memorable.

After the war the Australian portrait painters and landscape painters who had made their reputations in the first decades of the century, their wander years over, settled more or less permanently in the country. These were the years that George Washington Lambert, now an Associate of the Royal Academy painter, sculptor, and horse-lover, came and saw and conquered. They called him Australia's first master, and people would nudge one another when he came into the theatre. After the years of Genesis and the years of Exodus had come the years of the Leviticus, when the older men began to lay down the law for the guidance of the young.

Let us keep Australian art healthy and sane they said and not allow the madness now going on in Paris and London to creep in here. For over twenty years two men, James S. McDonald and Lionel Lindsay, moulded critical opinion in the country. Lindsay was the better critic, writing with real penetration and knowledge of the things he enjoyed and with a kind of Ruskinesque fury about the things he did not enjoy. And one of the things he disliked was post-impressionist painting and the experimental schools that flowed from it. For such reasons Australia was cut off from the liberating vitality of the modern movement for longer than most other civilized countries. Paul Gauguin had passed through Melbourne and Sydney in 1891 and noting their civic architecture had called them 'burlesques of the grandiose'. The Spanish painter Casas influenced the work of Tom Roberts, as later he influenced the art of Pablo Picasso; but Edwardian Australia knew nothing really of post-impressionism. True, Rupert Bunny talked of their work when he came out in 1911; and Francis Hodgkins, exhibiting a year later in Sydney, revealed some references to Gauguin's work. But the first painters in Australia to react to the work of Paul Cézanne and Van Gogh were Grace Cossington Smith, Roland Wakelin and Roy de Maistre, in 1914.

From being at first a heightening of decorative colour and simplification of design in the art of Arnold Shore, William Frater, and John Moore, the modern movement proceeded to even more formal treatments of figures and landscape in the paintings of Rah Fizelle and Grace Crowley, achieved a spirit of joy in Sali Herman's rich colour, a touch of mystery in Desiderius Orban's romantic formalism, and a superb classical abstraction in Eric Wilson's artistry. It invaded the field of commercial and industrial design through the activities of Annand, Morrison, Missingham, and R. Haughton James. As early as 1924 it had begun to open our eyes to the primitive splendour of Aboriginal art, first in the writing, and then in the vigorous experimental art of Margaret Preston. And as we came to the later 1930s with war looming ahead, ideas from the fields of psychology and politics became more usual at contemporary art exhibitions: in the surrealism of James Gleeson, the powerful if somewhat hysterical premonitions of Albert Tucker, and the sombre realism of Noel Counihan. Yet the modern movement, for all its experiments and emphasis upon originality, did not lose touch with tradition. Jean Bellette has drawn strength from Massaccio and the Venetians; Donald Friend and Arthur Boyd have at times made delightful and significant play with the later Flemings; Persian art and the trecento have helped Justin O'Brien to find his Irish religious self. Finally, expressionism triumphed in the two citadels of conventional painting in this country, in the portraits of William Dobell, and the landscapes of Russell Drysdale, who in the view of many are the two finest artists the country has produced.

If in this Jubilee year we were asked to pronounce a provisional judgement on the art of the first half of the century, I think it would be along these lines: the great promise that gleamed for a moment in the late 1880s and early 1890s was not realized; within a decade the painters of the Australian school were mainly concerned in gaining recognition at the Royal Academy and the Paris Salon, more than in producing original art. Their desire for sales and success hardened the arteries of their sensibility and their imagination. The modern movement certainly has had its fashionable painters and nine-day wonders, too, but its finest achievements are also the finest achievements of Australian art.

17
Art in the Dog Days
—1953—

The Archibald Prize is awarded in the heat of Sydney's mid-summer. Perhaps this is why the exhibition is closely followed by exhibitions of bad temper. Each year someone solemnly pronounces that the standard of the portraits displayed is worse than ever before. Each year someone suggests that the prize should not have been awarded at all. And each year the newspaper critics take a day off from criticism to pour abuse upon the heads of the trustees of the Sydney Gallery. Everyone—and that of course includes the winner—loses his head and, rushing into print, vociferates loudly upon the nature of portraiture and the nature of art. The 1952 award was no exception.

William Dargie won the prize for the seventh time with his portrait of Mr Essington Lewis. It is a good photographic likeness but it is dull, abominably dull. I cannot believe that Mr Lewis is as dull as this picture has made him—for posterity. Not even McInness with his sleek, oily efficiency was ever quite so boring. Certainly no one can expect William Dargie to paint portraits like Oskar Kokoschka, but one can expect from a representational painter some spark of imaginative insight that will make a personality more than a treacle of pigment. But Mr Dargie seems to go in horror of the imaginative life. In this regard it may be recalled that he was a pupil of A. D. Colquhoun, the pupil of Max Meldrum. In William Dargie's work then, we have Meldrum at two removes. And whereas there remains a certain astringency of vision and a sturdiness in the portraits of the old maestro himself so that he was never entirely seduced by the blandishments of the camera, Dargie's portrait of Lewis attains the smooth finish of a fashionable photographer's studio portrait after the retouching. It has

First published in *Meanjin*, vol. xii, no. 1, Autumn 1953, pp. 55–8.

taken, seemingly, two generations of Meldrum's teaching to stifle the spark of invention. For William Dargie's portraiture is nothing less than Meldrumism purged of its eccentricities, Meldrum modified, Meldrum without tears.

Williams Dobell's portrait of Hedley R. Marston is disappointing. Dobell, I cannot help thinking, is resting on his Wangi Wangi oars. The manner in which Dobell has presented the pose and mien of the figure has many antecedents in his earlier work, and there is not the same coherence in the articulation of the design that we have become used to in the past. Who, we might ask, really owns those quizzical eyebrows—Marston or James Cook or some simian original roaming about in Dobell's private archetypal zoo? And whether that belly truly belongs to Hedley Marston or to Walter Magnus may well be a point not beyond all conjecture, but its final attribution must await some future historian. Nevertheless Dobell's return to a broader handling is to be welcomed. There was an unpleasant fussiness about his 1951 entries and the present portrait is certainly better than those. But he has not recaptured the insight and the unity of conception that went to making *The Cypriot* and *Joshua Smith*.

Carington Smith's *Lucien Dechainaux*, though not quite so happy as some of his other portraits that linger in the memory, reveals again his pictorial intelligence, his attention to pose and gesture as aids to the presentation of character while ensuring, with a fine judgement, that the design controls all. In this regard he has a better sense of values than Ivor Hele whose *Brigadier Wills* is so anxious to claim our attention that it thrusts its oversized head well out of the picture-plane like a baroque saint. Here again the problem of Hele's art is apparent. His conventional technique (despite the vigour of the handling) cannot cope with his expressive desires. He is a kind of Dobell caught in the matchbox of his art training. And Arthur Murch's portrait of Dr Charlton affects me in a similar way. Is it really possible to make a such a modified pointillist technique (Seurat's great masterpieces are so classical, so serene) serve strong expressive intentions? For this is what Murch seems to be attempting. It would seem that Dobell's 1944 vintage is still new enough to crack the stylistic bottles distributed in our art schools during the 1920s and 1930s

Critics who declare mournfully that the standard of the portraiture displayed is declining year by year pay scant regard to individual cases. Jerrold Nathan's *Henry Edgecombe* is one of the finest portraits I have seen from this artist. It is restrained and well handled and there is a touch of vitality about it. William

Pidgeon's *Hon. Mr. Justice Kirby* is stated with economy and conviction and avoids that feverish handling of paint devoid of real conviction which have marred his entries in previous years. Both these paintings are at least personal triumphs even though they passed unnoticed amid the general hullabaloo.

Charles Bush was awarded the Wynne Prize with his *Summer at Kanmantoo*. Here we have not Meldrum but Drysdale without tears. It was Drysdale who opened the eyes of Australian painters to the pictorial possibilities of our society's artefacts when strewn over a primeval landscape. As recently as 1943 it took a touch of genius to make pictures from such things, but today, ten years later, bedsteads among the boulders are all à la mode. And then again the self-confident assertion of Bush's impressionism does not reveal the poignant sunlit mystery of his theme. His shortcomings as a colourist are manifest when we compare *Kanmantoo* with Herman's *La Perouse*, which radiates a gentle happiness so subtly conceived that the painting's quality is easily missed among its more strident neighbours. Here at least is a mature style which has freed itself from intellectualism. Here it is the experience lived through then recollected and refined that matters. The boy under the pale moon who pushes his boat through the turquoise water might have been no more than a romantic cliché; it is the adequate realization of the colour poised between assertion and suggestion, between the moods of joy and melancholy, which saves him and stamps the painting with the authenticity of a work of art. Elaine Haxton's two paintings reveal a happiness more assertive, more strident and decorative than Herman's. They are perhaps a little too self-confident, particularly in their structure, to be fully satisfying yet they are certainly among the best things in the competition. Herman and Haxton are the incorrigible humanists of Sydney's art world. They seem to possess a natural distaste for wallowing openly in the now fashionable little puddles of Despond considered so necessary to an artist's philosophical health. Yet the images of an uneasy world are often caught most admirably in the retina of Haxton's bright eye.

Lance Solomon is one of the few Australian painters who can still squeeze some originality from the old blue and gold tubes of the landscaping 1890s. And although he seems to be saying much the same thing each year and saying it in much the same way, it is well said and worth saying. But his stylism is so deliberate that it allows him little scope. Our other painters who still paint 'blue and golds' lean more heavily than Solomon upon our erstwhile great. Charles Meere and Herbert Gallop would resuscitate Gruner,

Rhys Williams in his *Hills at Attunga* would resuscitate Streeton, and R. E. Campbell in *Glanmire Near Bathurst* would drown Hans Heysen.

Mary Brady's landscape is well constructed and not without a touch of poetry. Her portrait in the Archibald has its own distinction. She deserves to be better known. Arthur Evan Read takes the joy out of his paintings by being too methodical. His sense of design is still cramping his apprehension of colour. Kenneth Jack's painting of Captain Blair's House is a well-composed and thoroughly spooky stage-set. But the Gothic machinery creaks too much to be effective.

The Sir John Sulman Prize for a subject or genre painting was awarded to Charles Doutney. It is an immature piece; the massing of the groups and the ordering of the spaces is unconvincing. Yet the attempt has been made to solve compositional problems in a painterly and architectural way. No doubt he will continue to study Francesca and Seurat. Elaine Haxton's *The Kite Flyers* is a better painting. She has a keen eye for the pictorial possibilities of the unexpected. Her manner of painting has American affiliations (as has often been noted) but these are a welcome change after the more usual French, Italian and English tie-ups to be observed in contemporary Sydney painting. And her delightful themes—unless I am much mistaken—are transmuted observations. Herman's *Shearingtime* is ambitious but it cannot be numbered among his successes. The same may be said of Gleeson's *Tristan* with its lurid unpleasant colour and its fussy redundant symbolism. Hinder's *Subway Escalator* is well-conceived and admirably controlled, and the technical mastery leaves little to be desired. But it is all so derivative of early Italian futurism; and it does not benefit from the inevitable comparison with Umberto Boccioni. Hinder's *Flight into Egypt* with which he won—and won deservedly—the 1952 Blake Prize was a much finer painting. One of the most charming paintings in the whole show is Sam Fullbrook's little *La Perouse*. Fullbrook has an instinctive feeling for colour and an unusual sense of design which are both compelling without being assertive. He is one of the most interesting of the younger painters working in Sydney today.

18
The French Art Exhibition in Sydney
—1953—

The exhibition of paintings and tapestries by living artists of the School of Paris at present touring the Commonwealth is the finest exhibition we have seen in Australia since the Exhibition of French and British Modern Art brought out here by the late Sir Keith Murdoch in 1939. It brings us once again after fourteen years into touch with the most influential school of contemporary art.

The general effect of the exhibition is one of full, rich and brilliant colour. French painters, like most Europeans, have passed through anxious times since the war ended but they are careful how they express their anxiety. There is no self-pity in this exhibition.

The abstract paintings provide one of the most notable features. They vary greatly in range and quality. Very few of them are pure abstractions, that is painting in which internal relations of line and colour are the only things that matter: abstract in the manner of the paintings of Piet Mondrian and Ben Nicholson. The man who comes closest to them is Hans Hartung who has perfected his own way of painting. He turns his tools of trade into precision instruments and reduces painting to the purity of its initial acts. His loaded brush is drawn across dry canvas or moist colour and we can trace, if we wish, the history of its movement. Hartung makes great use of black, for by its transparency he can suggest quite subtly a sensation of space, and his calligraphic method makes it possible for him to suggest rather free and transient perspectives. His paintings have the lithe sinewy grace of Chinese writing and their perfection is irresistible to those who are quite pure in their aesthetic. But the perfection is gained at enormous expense, for the paintings are like signs in a language never to be

First published in *Meanjin*, vol. xii, no. 2, Winter 1953, pp. 165—74.

deciphered. A phrase coined by Arnold Toynbee, 'the idolization of an ephemeral technique' fits them well. Here, more than anywhere else in the exhibition, the means has become the end.

Hartung is, however, an artist to his fingertips. De Stael, in the two paintings shown, is merely clumsy and insensitive; it is hard to understand why they were included. Abstract painting is a trap baited for the unskilled and the cocksure. Note, for instance, the paintings by Denise Chesnay and Suzanne Roger, both weak in construction, both dull.

Fortunately most of the abstracts are much better than these. The two canvases by Manessier, for instance, are among the delights of the exhibition. *Late October*, a long panel of rich and sombre beauty, is a distillation of colour from autumn's transient shapes—warm, poetic, harmonious. *The Sleeping Harbour* is even better. There is something intensely evocative in its varied and weighty line, and in the massing of the blacks against their ochrous background. The painting is in a strange way a wedding of the art of Rouault and Mondrian. The catalogue quotes the artist as saying, 'My canvases are to be witness of something felt by the heart, and not an imitation of something seen by the eye'. Yet it is clear that in these paintings, for all their abstracting from reality, the image of the thing seen still lingers like the memory of a treasured experience.

Léger's three paintings reveal him as a master of decorative colour. But his art has lost the mystery and excitement of discovery which it once held. One feels before these paintings that colour is now Léger's profession and that he can demonstrate it like a perfect juggler. He has become the great decorator of the School of Paris and that doubtless explains his popularity, for beyond a sensitive apprehension of colour his art makes few demands; to my mind it has become too self-assured, somewhat rubicund and flabby. There is more vitality in the work of Soulages who uses abstract constructions for an expressive purpose. He is not interested, as Manessier is, in extracting the formal essence from a momentary experience, but is content with a personal display of force. Yet his colour is good and the emotional impact of his painting is contained admirably within the formal composition. Lanskoy is more intimate, sweeter in colour, seeking rather to ingratiate himself with the spectator than to command. Whether such themes as 'the scent of water' and 'prolonged desire' lend themselves to abstract pictorial treatment must be an open question. Certainly colours have been shown to be related to emotional states of mind; but whether anything more than a purely

Hans Hartung, *T- 1954-20*, 1954, oil on canvas, 145.8 × 95.5 cm. Australian National Gallery, Canberra.

arbitrary relation can be established between a complex notion such as 'prolonged desire' and a complex pattern of non-
representational colour is something I am inclined to doubt. Yet
Lanskoy's paintings have a pleasant charm of their own, to which
the titles are an enticement.

The little oval Braque is unassertive but repays the closest
examination. It reveals what a fine engineer Braque is of pictorial
form. He is always conscious of the stress, strains and tensions
which can be set up in a work of art to provide it with a sense of
space ordered and perfected into classical beauty. Braque opposes
the curved to the angular, the textured surface to the plain surface,
monochromatic colour to pure colour, representational motifs to
abstract motifs always with a restrained, masterly judgement.
Metzinger lacks the austere classical finality of Braque but his
cubism is still full of the joy of material things and the colours
and patterns which can be made from them. His geometry, we
might say, is only skin deep. Nor is this joyousness confined to
the early cubists. There is a splendid realization, for example, of
abstract and yet sunlit colour in Maurice Estève's *Vivarium* and
in Raymond Legueult's *Feathered Hat*—so sensitive, free and
vivacious. In such paintings—and Jean Aujame's *Nude with
Chrysanthemums* and Roger Bezombes' *Portrait of Maria Casares*
may be numbered among them—we can observe how much the
French know about the technique of painting without pretension.

The art of painting naturally brings us immediately to Matisse;
not that we can appreciate the full stature of his art from this
exhibition. His *Quay St. Michel*, however, reveals the admirable
directness of his approach and his fine sense of colour. Painted in
1900, this little landscape has the pure colour, the assertion of
personality and the enjoyment of sensation for its own sake
which the fauves inherited from the impressionists. *Quay St.
Michel* might be said to depict one of the themes of this exhibition,
the humanist theme, here expressed as a frank enjoyment of
colour and sensational experience. The theme runs through painting after painting in this exhibition despite the diversities of
style to triumph in the pagan glow of the Gromaire tapestry and
linger in a ripple of late medieval laughter in Dufy's *Le Bel Eté*. It
is this recurring note of humanism which provides what the
broadcasters call the 'continuity' for the exhibition. How close to
Matisse, for instance, is Yves Alix's *Taking in the Nets* in feeling,
colour and the enjoyment of experience, though it was painted at
a time when sensational pleasure has become almost pictorially
indiscreet. Again, Villon's art is here seen to be quite close in

essential feeling to the art of Matisse and Alix though he is more analytic in his manner of expression. The investigation of colour and shape that produced his *Orange Trees* still evokes a memory of red soil, fruits, vines, and the clear air of mountains. It is important to realize that *The Flageolet Player* is descended not only from Cézanne's Mont St Victoire landscapes but also from Manet's *Bar at the Folies Bergère*.

One of the outstanding paintings of the exhibition is Lagrange's *The Guests of Arcueil*. Like Villon, Lagrange manages to combine brilliant impressionist effects with an architect's interest in the definition of form and space. Like Villon, too, he makes great play with triangular constructions. Line is used to indicate changes of plane but not to contain colour. The edge of the free colour is thus left to suggest a quite different kind of line—an 'impressionist' line. And this line sets up a kind of contrapuntal rhythm with the more heavy structural line. It should be observed, however, that even the heavy lines only suggest the presence of planes, they do not define them. By such means Lagrange seeks to solve the problem that has occupied the attention of so many modern artists and, as we have seen, many of the artists represented in this exhibition: the pictorial fusion of permanent structure and transient impression. The vigour with which Lagrange has tackled this problem, and the interesting solutions he suggests for it, is evidence, surely, that there is still a good deal of vitality in the art of the French painters of the younger generation.

The exhibition is, however, extremely uneven in quality. Indeed so many second-rate paintings have been included that the general standard attained is well below the standard of the Murdoch exhibition of 1939. In some respects the lower standard may be inevitable since the terms of reference were more restricted than those of the earlier exhibition, and the selectors, it would seem had to depend to a large extent upon pictures that happened to be in the stacks of the Paris commercial galleries at the time of selection. Even so it is difficult to understand why some of these paintings were chosen to represent the artistic achievements of contemporary French art. Eugene Kermadec's *Light and the Nude*, for example, is no more than a clever piece of commercial doodling; Leon Gischia's *Three Vases* is insipid in feeling, superficial in construction and pertly unpleasant in colour; Masson's large *Day Diagram* would be more at home in an enlightened retail store. There is, of course, a place for superficial painting if it is enjoyable and charming at the same time, and does not attempt to pass off inanity as profundity. No one would want to exclude Victor

Brauner's superbly nonsensical, Egyptianizing, *Oppression of the Object* from the exhibition, though we might all weep upon reading in the catalogue that the third dimension appeared in his exhibition at the Galerie de France last October. Neither are we likely to mind Vera Pagava's equally archaistic interpretation (she clings quite closely to the form and colour of typical proto-Corinthian vase painting) of the *Battle of Marathon* by means of a style of Greek painting which had already disappeared over a hundred years before the battle began. After all, digging up the past is one of the chief excitements of what the public used to call 'futuristic' painting. It would be interesting to know, however, just what induced the selectors to include Joan Miró's *Forty-Eight*. If the exhibition had been arranged on historical lines there might have been some reason to include this genuine example of the Dadaist movement, though a piece of Dada *objet d'art* such as a broken lavatory seat, would serve better to illustrate the aesthetic philosophy of the movement. But in an exhibition for which works were selected, presumably, for their quality as works of art, *Forty-Eight* is somewhat out of place. Perhaps the most charitable way of explaining the inclusion of the painting is to assume that the selectors put it in as a publicity decoy-duck.

Although most of the paintings have been conceived in a spirit of joy, which accepts even when it transforms the natural beauty of material things, the darker side of contemporary life has not been neglected. There is a group of surrealist paintings which the selectors have chosen to keep small. The most compelling painting of this group is Yves Tanguy's *The Dark Garden* wherein the painter has been able to say something—and to say it successfully in contemporary idiom without recourse to religious iconography —about the mysterious nature of the origin of evil. Coutaud's *Memories* too has something significant to say with its many images of time, growth and dissolution, its seeds, clocks and anthropomorphic rocks. But the symbols are too much like the captions inserted in a comic strip to help the visual narrative. They have not been thought out in terms of the structure of the painting. Prassinos' monochromatic *Herd* is an interesting example of a semi-abstract technique being used to evoke a feeling of vague disquiet. Here at least the symbolism emerges from the total pictorial conception whereas Coutaud's symbols are literary appendages. The least interesting of the surrealist paintings is Max Ernst's *The Year 1955* which, painted in 1925, is taking a prophetic pot-shot at the date of the last war or the next one. It is better for artists to leave such things to the astrologers and David

Low. The finest paintings in the exhibition which convey to us something of the quality of our own uneasy times is to be found not among the professional pessimisms of the surrealists but in the paintings by Picasso and Marchand.

Picasso is not as adequately represented as he was in the 1939 exhibition but here we find a Picasso who was not available to us then. Painted in April 1940, *The Orange Bodice* does provide us with some measure of the violence of Picasso's personal reaction to the invasion of France. The motive behind Picasso's distortion of the features in this painting differs considerably from the motive behind his distortion of the figures in, say, *Les Demoiselles d'Avignon* wherein the distortion is partly expressive but largely constructive and analytic in its intention. In this painting the distortion is completely personal and expressive in intention. By opening up the breasts like a pair of winged seeds Picasso had created a motif which governs the design of the painting. The result is startling, grotesque, and brutal. It bears comparison with those maps, equally terrifying, which we studied thirteen years ago as the Nazis swept across Northern France. Compared with this painting *The Lady with the Green Bodice* is far more austere in colour, more solid, martial and compact. If the orange lady has been demented the green lady has been brutalized. What a contrast the two paintings make! How different the exaggerated 'military' shoulders, the firm squat neck, the flattened breasts, the tight beak-like mouth, and the small bulging eyes of the green lady from the lacerated forms of the orange lady. If in the divided forms of the one we have a spiritual symbol of France divided against herself then in the closed and compacted forms of the other, painted three years later, we have a symbol of the French Resistance. There is no better key to a sympathetic understanding of these paintings than the war poetry of such writers as Paul Eluard and Louis Aragon. Eluard's *La Halte des Heures*, for instance, provides a fairly close literary equivalent, it seems to me, for the feelings expressed by *The Lady with the Green Bodice*. Much of the power of Picasso's art lies in just this ability to find potent symbols for his private feelings, and symbols which, for all their potency, can be stated with utter simplicity in a completely pictorial language.

André Marchand's *Spring* is the one painting in the exhibition which comes close to being a masterpiece—certainly it is quite unforgettable. Among paintings in which colour predominates, the daring brilliance of Marchand's colour is like a trumpet call sounded beyond them all. It is an ambitious painting and it does go out of its way to claim our attention, but it is a mistake to be put off by its insistence. Marchand has been courageous enough to take the oldest—and the most hackneyed—theme of the arts for his subject. The debt to Picasso is obvious but the quality of pure lustrous colour in broad masses, the sonorous black and the firm calligraphy which give the painting a strong graphic quality brings to mind fine examples of medieval Islamic pottery. Despite its apparent simplicity the painting is full of subtlety; the judicious use of the 'white' line, the modulation of the blacks, and the control of complementaries all bespeak a master of colour construction. The painting has gained, too, because Marchand has chosen a traditional subject to provide harness and rein to his roving imagination. The colour, so satisfactory for its own sake, gains in significance by reason of its symbolic references just as the figures do. As for the subject itself it is clear that there is no romance or sentiment in Marchand's interpretation of spring. It is not seen here as the season of wonder that it was for Botticelli or the season of playful eroticism that it was for Boucher. Bringing the world to birth once every twelve months is here seen as an extremely onerous and utterly feminine mystery not altogether without its compensations. Marchand's spring is a very old, primitive and pagan spring, a 'cruel April' that requires no masculine gods to prompt it into existence.

The group of primitive paintings are, for the most part, disappointing. The clean, dancing colour of Bombois' *Washerwomen* and the prim clarity of Lefranc's *Saumer Castle* (so like a page torn from a book of hours) are the most successful paintings of the group. Bauchant's *Butcher's Shop* has some pertinent observations of people but the handling of the paint is tired and the size of the painting makes it doubly boring. Madeleine Luka's *Cadet from Saint-Cyr* has a sweet, vulgar simplicity which directs its appeal to simple and jaded tastes. One little painting by Henri Rousseau would have been worth them all. But he alas is dead and ineligible for inclusion in the exhibition. If any demonstration were necessary it is clear from this group that primitive painters can often be as dull as academic painters.

Those who are inclined to dismiss the exhibition because of the unfamiliar nature of many of the works, notably the abstract paintings, should pay attention to the large numbers of pictures which adhere closely to the world of familiar appearance. Apart from the natural and understandable enjoyment to be gained from the Utrillos and the confident certainty of Vlaminck's two still-life paintings there is quite a large group by younger men, among them Brianchon, Despierre, Chapelain-Midy, and Planson whose work has an academic competence. At times this competence is combined with keen sensitivity, as in Planson's delicate *Springtime at La Ferté*, or with a true imaginative feeling as in Chapelain-Midy's *Still Life with Owl*. In fact naturalistic painting is more strongly represented in this exhibition than our first impressions might lead us to suspect. A study of the paintings with the aid of the catalogue does reveal something of a 'return to realism' among the youngest painters showing work. Jean-Pierre Capron, for instance, who was born in 1921, paints a somewhat mysterious *Fishing Port near Venice* full of cool, sombre colour. The drawing is well thought out but quite conventional; it is the colour that Capron relies upon to arouse an emotional appeal. And far better than Capron's painting is Minaux's massive *Country Still Life* which is splendidly painted and organized with great pictorial skill. Born in 1923, Minaux has a healthy respect for craftsmanship and combines breadth of handling with an unusual and classical feeling for the disposition of mass. Bernard Buffet (b. 1928) is another young painter who prefers a representational though highly stylized manner of expression which makes much use of greys bounded by strong rigid lines, and a lighter 'incised' line to modulate his colour areas. *The Painter* may be limited in its appeal yet it is a sensitive, workmanlike and thoroughly sincere composition. Vera Pagava, whose work I have already mentioned, also prefers representational forms though her work lacks Capron's touch of mystery, Minaux's plastic achievement and Buffet's sensitivity.

I think it would be a mistake to come to any conclusions about the nature of contemporary art in France from the evidence supplied by this exhibition. But the work of the young painters I have just mentioned is an indication that French painting is not heading, as contemporary American painting seems to be, sternly towards the northern latitudes of non-representational painting. Of the painters represented Soulages is the only painter under thirty-five producing abstract paintings of a high quality, Prassinos and Lagrange are the only painters under forty in which the non-representational element is as strong as the naturalistic element. Lapoujade's piece of grandiose map-making, of course, is neither a good painting nor an abstract one.

It was with a sense of real loss that we heard of the death of Raoul Dufy while the exhibition was showing in Sydney. No painter of the School of Paris painted so naturally or with less pretension. *The Yellow Sideboard* is simplicity itself yet how well it reveals Dufy's unerring skill for knowing just what will make a picture! Immediacy was his great virtue as it has been many a painter's vice; and immediacy remained a virtue with Dufy because he seems always to have been able to recapture that sense of wonder which makes precious the moment in which a work of art is conceived. And Dufy's simplicity is never sullied by the imp of the perverse which so often mars the art of Joan Miró and Paul Klee.

The exhibition includes four paintings by Georges Rouault. Rouault is a man with an enormous popular following and much of this is due to the fact that he paints religious pictures. It is difficult, however, on the evidence of the paintings shown, to agree that he should be paid the customary obeisance. The trouble with Rouault, it seems to me, does not derive so much from the archaistic quality of his art, though it is true that the colour, the distortions and even the textures of his paintings depend largely upon different types of medieval art, but from their complete lack of any feeling of spontaneity. Everything is so carefully calculated, so deliberately planned to achieve a required effect upon the spectator: the mountainous impasto, the 'hocus-pocus' leading, and the rather monotonous palette of emotionally 'intense' colours. These pictures have the eloquence of skilled oratory but lack an inner personality of their own. Nevertheless the traditional elements in Rouault's art make it possible for him to fashion images which are, to say the least, most compelling. *Exodus* has a simple and sombre beauty of theme, and its overtones of meaning give it a force of its own. *Tiberiade* is to my mind the finest of the Rouaults and much better than his *Passion* whose masochistic, lamb-faced Christ I find, like the mixture of religion and eroticism in *The Little Sorceress*, quite nauseating. It would be unfair, however, to take these four paintings as typical of Rouault's best work. Yet it must be said that, considering his reputation as a colourist, it is a pity that four paintings were included that from the standpoint of colour are so indubitably dull.

For rich, singing, resonant colour with much of the quality of Chartres glass, one has to turn from Rouault's icons to Marc Chagall's *Trough with Two Pigs. The Black Glove*, too, has much of the essential Chagall, his colour, his fantasy, and his exquisite touch of sentiment. Of all the well-known men whose work is included in this exhibition Chagall is certainly the most fortunate in the pictures selected to represent his achievement.

There are quite a number of extremely interesting paintings, notably those by Vulliamy, Picabia, Morand, Goerg, and Gromaire, that I cannot attempt to discuss. The exhibition, despite its imperfections, is a magnificent one and the tapestries, themselves artistic triumphs of no mean order, give the display a resplendent atmosphere. It should do much to stimulate a greater interest in art in Australia; no doubt we shall meet its influence in Australian painting for some time to come. Everyone who has helped to bring the exhibition here deserves our heartfelt thanks. One can only hope that other governments will seek to emulate the gracious generosity of the French government. In the visual arts far more than in any of the other arts, Australia suffers from its continued isolation from the art centres of the world. Obviously the Australian government and the Australian galleries should do all they can to make such exhibitions as this one a permanent feature of the cultural life of the country.

19
Dog-Day Doldrums
—1954—

The following exhibitions aroused very little public interest this year, attention being directed towards the impending Royal visit. Not that the public missed much, for the Archibald and Wynne entries were duller than usual and most of the Sulman entries were, gratifyingly, *in situ*.

Archibald Prize

Ivor Hele won the Archibald Prize with his portrait of Sir Henry Simpson Newland. Hele has been able to keep his brushwork more under the control of his vision than in entries shown in previous years. The drawing is vigorous and wiry and his statement of the figure direct to the point of brusqueness. It would not be surprising if Hele eventually eclipses Dargie's record of wins since he has most of the qualifications that go to make a popular portrait painter. What he lacks, unfortunately, are just those qualities that can lift portraiture from the realm of recording to the realm of art: a feeling for design, sensitivity in the handling of paint and colour, and the capacity to evoke by means of an imaginative sympathy the true presence of the sitter. Nevertheless, in the rugged honesty of his portraiture Hele possesses one virtue thoroughly Australian and this, surely, is a welcome change from William Dargie's simpering illusionism.

Dobell's portrait of Harry Stevenson reveals a further falling off in the quality of his work. It is difficult to realize that this is the work of the painter of *Billy Boy*, *Brian Penton*, and *Mrs. Frank Clune*. In *Harry Stevenson* Dobell is attempting to live on the capital of his idiosyncrasies.

First published in *Meanjin*, vol. xiii, no. 1, Autumn 1954, pp. 106–8.

Noel Counihan's two paintings reveal strengths and weaknesses similar to Hele's. He is a vigorous draughtsman whose ability to realize his subject in the plastic vocabulary of painting is still relatively restricted. Counihan has, however, more use for colour than Hele and has a finer insight into psychological values. Both his portraits—*Vance Palmer* and *Katharine Susannah Prichard*—have the touch of genuine artistry about them, but they cannot compare in completeness of treatment and realization of subject with his portrait of William Dolphin shown in this competition some years ago.

Among those painters who pay considerable attention to the requirements of art as distinct from the compulsion to capture a good likeness is Wallace Thornton, whose spidery portrait of Lyndon Dadswell has much to commend it; and Sam Fullbrook, whose portrait of Bernard Sahm possesses sensibility and excellent colour—qualities lacking in most of the exhibits. It is a pleasant surprise to find that an approach as individual as Fullbrook's did not cause his painting to be rejected from the exhibition, particularly as his work is not widely known. The two paintings shown by Carington Smith do not compare with work he has shown in previous years; both give the appearance of being rather perfunctory efforts.

Wynne Prize

Like the Archibald, the entries here were much less interesting than last year. Lance Solomon won the prize with *River Bend*. Solomon reminds me of those country hostesses who reach their highest flights of cookery in the cream sponge. Someone should introduce him to the virtue of a little pictorial garlic. He has invented for himself a kind of backyard Arcadia where the soft sun always filters through the trees and the air is always heavy with dew. What is all this but sweet-nothings to comfort suburbia—more than comfortable enough, as it is, in this country! The pity of it is that Solomon has real talent but he seems to lack any capacity of breaking new ground: his lyrical gift is frustrated by visual timidity.

Michael Kmit's *King's Cross Façade* is brilliantly colourful but the whole thing lacks unity. Pattern, like patriotism, is not enough. Scott Pendelbury's *The Opera House* stands out in mediocre company as a highly competent piece of work in the Sickert manner. Elwyn Lynn's *Maurice Street*, though recalling Utrillo, is full of pleasant colour and reveals a capacity to compose with greater amplitude than in his previous work. Sali Herman's *Sunrise at*

Wangi gave the impression of being rather crabbed and fussy when compared with last year's splendid *La Perouse*. Margaret Dunn's *The Fish Markets, South Fremantle* was handled with a nice sense of rhythmical freedom.

Sulman Prize

No less than twenty-five murals are cited this year as *in situ*. The interest in mural decoration seemingly is at last gaining ground among architects and their clients after being talked about for years by artists. It is interesting to note that this interest comes at a time when the number of commissions for public sculpture is also increasing. Architects, I am beginning to hope, are relaxing a little from their puritanical devotion to the plain white wall.

Eric Smith's *Convicts, Berrima, 1839* (in the Old Court House, Berrima), though still showing signs of immaturity, is an ambitious and forceful piece of work by one of Sydney's younger artists. There is nothing new-fangled about Smith's approach to the traditional problems of mural painting and he is quite capable of combining a depth of feeling with a sense of scale. It is to be hoped that he will receive more commissions to enable him to develop as a mural painter. Smith is at present primarily interested in subjects of a religious nature, so that church mural decoration would seem to be the obvious field in which his talent could develop normally. At least let us hope that the spiritual burden of his art will not be reduced to the reproduction of pretty icons for the mission to the pagans of Bellevue Hill. In this regard it is gratifying to find that Riverview Preparatory School has commissioned a *Betrayal* from Weaver Hawkins. If more schools and churches would follow Riverview's lead it would give many artists in this country a chance to do what they really want to do. Hawkins is a natural mural painter but his work has never been fashionable for two good reasons: his paintings contain ideas, and he works out his compositions in a firm linear style after the manner of the quattrocento. Most contemporary artists and critics in Australia find thinking a painful experience, which they prefer separated from the sensuous enjoyment of colour and shape. Further, Hawkins' linear style virtually contradicts the 'messiness equals sensitivity' notions unconsciously championed for donkey's years now by the *Herald* art critic. As a result Hawkins is one of the most neglected painters in Australia today. It is to be hoped that this *Two Minutes Silence* will eventually find its way into Sydney's new Anzac House.

20

The Antipodeans Exhibition: Notes for the Opening Address

—1959—

I am sure that all of you will know that the artists who have come together to form the Antipodeans—Charles Blackman, Arthur and David Boyd, John Brack, John Perceval, Clifton Pugh and Bob Dickerson—were all well known for their work long before we came together to form this new group. Let me briefly tell you therefore how we came into existence, and why. Several of us had been thinking for some time that it was high time that some group took a firm stand against the pretentious humbug that is today being put about by the champions of abstract, non-figurative, non-representative art. Accordingly, after a few brief talks between some of us, we all met at John Perceval's home one Sunday evening in February last and there decided to form a new group. We decided, after some discussion, to call ourselves the Antipodeans, and we decided too, after a good deal of discussion, to write a manifesto of our position. After a great deal more discussion, which lasted over some months, we agreed upon one. We have printed it in the catalogue. That is our basic statement. You should all buy one and read it. It will make quite clear why we formed the group.

But let me make one or two comments. We formed the group, we say, to defend the image. If you are young painter today and you want to be fashionable and you want to conform then you paint abstract.

We are opposed to abstract painting let there be no doubt about that. But let me try to make our position quite clear, because unless I do I am sure we shall be misunderstood: indeed I must say that even when I do make it quite clear I am still sure that we shall be misunderstood. Firstly then I want you to be

---

Not previously published. The Antipodeans Exhibition was held in the Victorian Artists' Society rooms, Albert Street, East Melbourne, and ran from 4 to 15 August 1959.

quite clear on this first point. There is not one of us who would not readily admit there is much of beauty and grace, and charm of colour, there is much expressiveness in abstract art. One of the best and most coherent lectures on abstract art I have heard in this country was given by John Brack, one of our members. I spent several years of my life explaining the mysteries of abstract art to children and adults both in the country and the city in New South Wales. I was directly responsible for the first purchase by the trustees of the Sydney Gallery of an abstract painting by Eric Wilson. In 1945 it was extremely difficult to get trustees to look at abstract work at all. When Wilson died I wrote an article in which I discussed the importance of his abstract art. I own some abstract paintings and I enjoy them for what they are.

But unfortunately there is an enormous amount of humbug, pretention and nonsense associated with abstract art. It has become a kind of popular secular religion which turns quite sane people into fanatics. We state in our manifesto that we are not seeking to create a national art. I want to make one or two comments on this. Each artist in the group has his own individual style, a style evolved from his contact both with art overseas and his personal experiences in this country. Although we are not nationalistic in sentiment or outlook we do think that an artist can no more avoid revealing his situation in place as well as his situation in time. A completely international art would be as dull a dishwater. Think of the whole world talking like the announcers on the BBC. Australia receives a good deal of cultural stimulus from overseas, and in the other arts, theatre, music, literature, we have been able to give something of our own in exchange. This of course is not a matter of being nationalistic. or of being regionalistic (as one of our local critics always puts it); it is simply a matter of being oneself, of being able to stand on one's own feet. Now I am convinced that most abstract work going on in Australia at the moment is a rather tame reflection of what is being done abroad. Some of it, it is true, may possess a certain rude vitality which would earn some comment if shown abroad. The tendency any-way now is to treat all abstract art sweetly rather than sourly because it is avant garde and progressive—and few people have the courage to smack that savage sacred cow on the rump.

I am convinced, however, that among the painters of this group there is work which has no real parallel in point of style overseas. This—rather than the pale copying of overseas fashions—it seems to me is truly international because it makes a genuine contribution to the total art of human society.

We are very keen that the group's work and its attitude should become known overseas. I should like to see an Antipodean exhibition abroad. We would like to show as a unit. There has I know been some talk in official circles of a big Australian show in London. I think that such a show would be absolutely disastrous for the reputation of Australian art abroad. There have been several such exhibitions since 1898 and not one of them has left any permanent mark. I am sure that any big show will meet with the same fate. It would a mixed bag selected by a committee in which each member was pushing his fancies—I have been in the art world of this country long enough to know how it works. There would be no organic unity, for the simple reason that there is no real unity in Australian art. That is why we do not want to bang the national drum—not even in a big Australian show.

Australian art has become known abroad since the end of the war solely as the result of the work of two men, Russell Drysdale and Sidney Nolan. Why? Because their work was good and it was different; it had something to say that was not being said abroad. In a modest way I was able to contribute to that development. I wrote the introduction to Drysdale's first exhibition in England in 1950 and later gave a talk over the BBC Third Programme on his work. The show made some impression. I remember for instance that the late Wyndham Lewis showed a genuine interest in it. Nolan's first shows met with little success; in more recent years his work has become widely appreciated. Now I think that the growth of an international interest in Australian art is of the greatest importance. It is only by keeping our eye on an international audience that we will raise the standards of art in this country. To do this you need professional artists, people who are prepared to spend their whole lives in the precarious activity of creating original art, not people who devote the week, for instance to commercial work, and then blossom forth as bright, abstract weekend Bohemians. As Antipodeans we are interested in painting as a profession.

Today everyone wants to discover new talent. Gallery directors love giving the new boys a helping hand, collectors like to help the young painter; all of this seems highly suspect to me. The genuine collector buys work because he thoroughly enjoys it. The trouble is that this business of discovering new talent goes on at such a pace that the average lifetime of a genuinely creative artist in the public eye is about five years—then he is considered old hat, and the talent scouts are out chasing after someone else. This is the technique of the fashion house and the sooner we get rid of it the better. The point is a very simple one, but few people grasp the full significance of it. It takes a lifetime to make an artist—but here in Australia we take about five years to train them, five years to allow them to work themselves into the public eye, and another five years to forget them. In fifteen years their effective lives as creative artists are over. Why? Because we are lovers of the fashionable rather than lovers of art. If we want our artists to produce the best that is in them we have to be prepared to support them by an active interest in their art for thirty, forty perhaps even sixty years.

Abstract painting can be a liberating force and it can be an oppressive force; it depends upon the situation. Let me give you an example. If during the next ten years it should so happen that in the Soviet Union an abstract movement in art grew up in opposition to the present officially approved socialist realism now dominant everywhere in communist countries this would undoubtedly be a magnificent triumph for the human spirit and the creative imagination over tyranny and power. I hope that I shall live to see that happen.

But in the West non-figurative art is the new tyranny which all truly creative artists must keep a vigilant eye upon. In the West today the champions of non-figuration are blown up with their own pride: they are arrogant, conceited and intolerant. They are arrogant because they wish to cut themselves off from the past. This is, and it always was, a form of cultural suicide. It is suicide because there is really no such thing as the present, it is only a frontier where the living, vital and human past battles with the dead, inert, and inhuman future. They are conceited because they claim again and again that abstract art is the only truly contemporary art, that the image is out of date. Every artist, they say, who wishes to be truly fashionable must be abstract. In the United States particularly this compulsion to be abstract assumed quite terrifying proportions, and I have not the slightest doubt that it testifies to a death of the human spirit which is as fearful to contemplate as the compulsion to be a social realist in the Soviet Union. Certainly abstract art has not assumed such dominance in Australia, especially in Melbourne. But it is going to become increasingly fashionable in the immediate future, of that we have no illusions. I notice that a new gallery, Gallery A, has just been opened in Collins Street, which informs us that abstract art is now the mainstream. Which is quite true, it is now the fashionable thing to be abstract, everybody's doing it, doing it, doing it! Isn't it true, hasn't it always been true, that in such situations the creative artist strikes camp and marches into the desert. Abstract art is now the art of the fashionable mob all over the western world.

21

The Antipodean Intervention

—1959—

First let me tell you how the Antipodean group came into existence. It should have begun in a pub over a pint of beer, but it
didn't. It began one Sunday afternoon over a cup of tea and one
of my daughter's chocolate cakes. At any rate it was a good cake.
So the birth, if you're prepared to call it a birth, was neither
Bohemian nor picturesque, but it was at least Australian in that it
began in the suburbs, from which most good things in Australian
life have sprung, though no one is ever prepared to admit it. In
short, David Boyd and his family came to visit us, and David,
who is one of the most vocal of the Antipodeans, began complaining about the current fashionableness of abstract painting and
the tendency for all young painters to jump on the non-figurative
band-waggon. 'What is needed, David', I suggested, 'is not a new
art society but a small group of professional artists who have the
guts to stand up and say outright that the image in painting is
something worth preserving—and to be prepared to keep on
saying it for five or ten years. It's going to start somewhere. Why
shouldn't it start here'.

The following day we got on the phone to a few friends. I had a
long talk with John Brack, and seven of us met at John Perceval's
home the following Thursday. After a discussion lasting several
hours we decided to form ourselves into a new group and call
ourselves the Antipodeans. Well, why Antipodeans? The name
has been criticized. Many intelligent Australians find the word
distasteful. They don't like the implicit suggestion that they stand
on their heads at the bottom of the world. Certainly Lawson,
Furphy and Victor Daley would not have taken kindly to the
word. Are we, in adopting such a word, seeking to deny our

Not previously published. Address, annual dinner, Fellowship of Australian Writers, Society
Restaurant, Melbourne, 1 September 1959.

nationality? In adopting it are we adopting a variant of that celebrated posture which your president identified, anatomized and defined magnificently some years ago? The 'cultural cringe' certainly affects the visual arts in Australia more strongly than it does any other art. Indeed the type specimen of the cringer was first identified by an Australian poet in the form of an Australian artist, none other than Correggio Jones. It begins in triumph:

> Correggio Jones an artist was
> Of pure Australian race
> But native subjects scorned because
> They were too commonplace

But ends so sadly:

> He yet is painting at full bat,
> You'll say, if him you see,
> His body dwells on Gander flat
> His soul's in Italy.

Well are we Antipodeans just a claque of C. Joneses? Certainly not. All of us were born here; only two, David Boyd and I, have ever been out of Australia, and then only for short periods. That could be a disadvantage. I think it also has advantages. I do not have to tell this fellowship that what is vital and native to our own tradition has had to battle for survival in these post-war years against powerful and at times overwhelming cosmopolitan tendencies. They have been at times stimulating and vitalizing, at times destructive. If the work of the Antipodeans possesses individuality and character it is perhaps because most of them have been able to develop as creative artists within the context of contemporary Australian society.

Having said that I must hasten to add that not one member of the group was interested in developing a new national movement of a specifically Australian character—we wanted to avoid nationalism and we wanted to avoid the word Australian. We had to settle on a word that would avoid nationalist implications, yet also announce our place *vis-à-vis* the rest of the world community, and our essential artistic unity with the world.

Let me tell you a story concerning my own reaction to the word Antipodean. Ten years ago while studying in London I was asked to write a preface to Russel Drysdale's first London exhibition, held at the Leicester Galleries, and then later make a third programme broadcast over the BBC. I wrote the talk and then found to my dismay that they had called it 'Art in the Antipodes'.

I told the young woman producer exactly what I thought of the title, so she took me into the programme department where they had thought it up. I said 'Look, you just can't use that title. Drysdale's an Australian and so am I. Don't you understand that if I as an Australian entitle my own talk 'Art in the Antipodes' I should talk about English art. Would you like me to give a talk on contemporary English art? The three young men in the programme department then gave me a rather curious look. 'No,' said one of them after a pause, 'We think it would be much better if you confined your remarks to Australian art'. 'All right,' I said, 'Let's call it "The Artists' Vision of Australia"'. And we did.

But since that time I have come to realize that the word can have its uses. You see we wanted a word that would avoid the nationalistic overtones of 'Australian' and yet define our *place* in the world. For this 'Antipodean' is quite the best, at least it is the best we could think of. It is a Greek word, of course, with an ancient and honourable history which Europeans have used in connection with this part of the world for many centuries. There is no reason at all why we European Australians, in a kind of self-centred arrogance, should sniff and sneer at it; no reason why we should regard Australia as the centre of the world. But there is no reason why artists, while recognizing their place at the 'bottom of the world' should not be able to find something worth saying both to their own community and to the world at large.

I have discussed the name at some length because it has caused more discussion in lay circles than our programme. It is centred upon a single idea: the defence of the image against the inroads of the non-figurative or, as I should prefer to call it, non-figural forms of art. Now I begin to see a look of quite logical positivist evil smouldering in some of your eyes. 'No question-begging', they seem to be saying. 'Define for us the image in art, please.' Well, I'm not going to throw myself into that aesthetico— psychological morass for any of you. We have made it as plain as we can in the manifesto. We talk about the image, the recognizable shape, the meaningful symbol. For us 'the image is a figured shape or symbol fashioned by the artist from his perceptions and imaginative experience. It is born of past experience and it refers back to past experience—and it communicates. It communicates because it has the capacity to refer to experiences the artist shares with his audience'.

It cannot be denied that so far as the visual arts are concerned the first half of the century has seen the gradual triumph of abstraction. The first pure abstract paintings were painted by the Russian artist Kandinsky, about 1910, but they came at the end of the ceaseless experimentation with free forms which developed from the Fauves and the cubists. In its earlier phases abstract art tended to be classical in its affinities. It appealed, that is, to an abstract mathematical order rather than to the inner personality of the artist for its justification. But since the war abstract art has wedded itself to the theoretical position of the surrealists of the inter-war years. Surrealism, oddly enough, adopted a highly realistic and naturalistic manner in its formative phases under Chirico and Dali. But shortly after the war, especially in the United States, the idea of automatic, accidental painting became united for the first time with non-representational painting to produce a school of accidental art. There were of course historical precedents for this. As early as the mid-eighteenth century. Alexander Cozens perfected a method of stimulating the imagination in inventing landscapes by throwing down blots on paper and gaining suggestions from them—and Leonardo has a famous passage on how the patterns on the surface of a wall can be used as stimulants to artistic invention. But it was left to an American of the beat generation, Jackson Pollock, to realize the full possibilities of an accidental art. I first saw this new art of abstract expressionism in the Venetian Biennale of 1949 where Jackson Pollock and Willem De Kooning dominated the American exhibit. With the help of a famous American patron, Miss Peggy Guggenheim, the Guggenheim Gallery and the Museum of Modern Art New York, Pollock became the single most influential painter of the post-war years.

We are taking up a position in opposition to the extreme forms of abstract art. None of us would deny that completely non-representational paintings are capable of giving a great deal of aesthetic pleasure. We think that abstract art is likely to persist, but we also think that it will persist only as one form of painting among others. What we are opposing is not so much abstract art in itself but the overweening arrogance of its champions, who maintain: (1) that it is the only form of contemporary art; (2) that it is a new pictorial language; and (3) that there is no longer any need to draw upon the art of the past. It is avant-gardism run mad with all the intolerance that is associated with it.

One point I do want to make with some emphasis, because this is a most appropriate place to make it. Painting is an art form which lies, as it were, mid-way between the arts of music and architecture, which depend far more upon abstract shape, rhythm and form than upon the compelling power of images, and literature which depends so much upon meaning as expressed in verbal images. The greatest paintings do not try to be music, architecture or literature: they are rhythmically shaped images. Unfortunately during the twentieth century painting, like some other arts, has drawn too much upon parallels with music and architecture. It began with people like Schopenhauer and Pater saying that all arts aspire to the condition of music. Notably, it was said just at the time when music was aspiring to the condition of painting. The influence of contemporary architectural thought upon painting has tended to reduce painting to the status of abstract wall decoration. What we need is a closer relation between writers and painters to redress the balance. True, a purely literary form of painting is bad, but so too are those forms of painting which depend too much upon specious analogies with music and architecture.

The idea that the Antipodeans represent the Establishment either in Australian art or Australian society makes me burst with hollow laughter. The fact is that the creation of the group has been received on all sides with almost universal hostility. The main attack of course, as always, has been upon our motives. If you are not prepared to argue with a man's opinions you can always suggest that he holds them for base reasons. One line of attack was that the image in art required no defence, least of all from a group of quite unimportant artists in Melbourne. But the image is only sustained in art by those artists who make a creative use of it. It does not survive automatically; for history is made by men, not men by history. That is a truism which needs to be asserted time and again in this age when artists continually think of themselves as reflectors of something or other instead of thinking of themselves as creators.

Not one director of any art gallery in Australia nor the critic of any newspaper in this country has told me or any other member of the Antipodeans that he considered the formation of the group to be 'a good thing'. And if these people do not represent the artistic Establishment in this country then I do not know who does.

22

The Antipodean Artists

—1959—

A new art group with a definite and vigorous point of view known as the Antipodeans was formed in Melbourne early in 1959. It consists of seven artists: Charles Blackman, Arthur Boyd, David Boyd, John Brack, John Perceval and Clifton Pugh, all of Melbourne, and Bob Dickerson of Sydney. Although the group itself is new, the artists are all quite well known throughout Australia; some of them, like Arthur Boyd, whose work was shown in the 1958 Biennale at Venice, are already known overseas.

All of them have been closely associated with the development of contemporary art in Australia during the past ten years or more, and they all work in a contemporary idiom. But they are not abstract painters. Indeed, this is the reason why they have come together to form the Antipodean group.

For the Antipodeans believe that abstract art is today no longer the work of a creative minority of artists in the western world. It is so generally and so widely accepted that it is ceasing to be of value to the creative artist. It is becoming a tyranny to which all artists who claim to be contemporary are expected to conform. The Antipodeans therefore believe that it is high time some spirited resistance was shown by contemporary artists themselves to the widespread, thoroughly fashionable, but superficial tendency to regard non-figurative art as the only truly representative art of our time. The place of the image, they claim, is still a crucial one in contemporary painting and sculpture. By the image they mean those figured shapes and symbols fashioned by the artist from his imagination's experience, shapes and symbols capable of communicating meaning by reference to an already existing body of knowledge. In practice that means the continued use of

---

First published under the title 'The Antipodeans' in *Australia Today*, 14 October 1959.

the images of man and nature in their work. To abandon such images is to debauch and degrade painting and sculpture in the scale of human values and to reduce it to the condition of a minor decorative art.

The Antipodeans are not, of course, seeking to create an Australian school of art. They are not nationalists. But they are aware that their own art is profoundly influenced by the time and place in which they live. That is the reason why they call themselves Antipodeans. For this Greek word meaning 'having the feet opposite' admirably describes their own situation both in time and place. All of them, as I said, except Dickerson, are Melbourne artists. And one of the great points about Melbourne is that it is right down at the end of the section, a metropolis at the bottom of the world. It was Einstein who first impressed upon the world the fact that the truth of a scientific observation could not be separated from the position of the observer. This is equally true of artistic observation of whatever kind it may be. And for the Antipodeans, situated as they are in the most southerly metropolis of the world, it is possible to see universal problems from a different point of view, a view that is determined neither by the West nor by the East—an Antipodean point of view. This does not mean that the group intends to follow a policy of cultural isolation and cut itself off from tradition. On the contrary, the very word Antipodean emphasizes that the group respects and seeks to defend the continuity and indivisibility of the European artistic tradition. Non-figurative artists who attempt to cut themselves away from tradition succeed only, the Antipodeans believe, in cutting their own slender aesthetic throats. The Antipodeans do not propose to join this suicide squad.

The Antipodeans are concerned above all with people, their relations to one another and to nature. This may be seen in their work. The painting of Bob Dickerson, for instance, is preoccupied with the loneliness of cities. That is not a new theme. Nor are, perhaps, any of the great themes of art. For Dickerson it arises from his own experience. Sydney today is a city of over 2 million people, a hard city and at times a ruthless one. Something of that side of the city's character is revealed in Dickerson's art. His lonely figures are usually spare of frame and stunted in proportion. They float or wander about in a space that, like Matisse's space, is often ambiguous in its dimensions, and they have no contact with one another. They express no anger, pity or fear, nothing but their own all-embracing isolation. In his painting *Man Sleeping on a Bench*, for example, the supine figure, sparely proportioned and placidly withdrawn in sleep, does not seek to evoke sympathy. It is classical in its self-containedness, and is sharply opposed to the blocky, dark, strutting figure of the woman who stares into the vacant sea. The sense of isolation so achieved is complete and the painting recalls A. D. Hope's fine poem *The Wandering Islands*, which is also concerned with the inescapable loneliness of human beings.

> *You cannot build bridges between the wandering islands;*
> *The Mind has no neighbours, and the unteachable heart*
> *Announces its armistice time after time, but spends*
> *Its love to draw them closer and closer apart.*

John Brack draws, like Dickerson, upon the contemporary urban society of Australia for his inspiration. His approach is more objective, his spatial organization more logical, and his attitude more intrinsically classical than Dickerson's. For Brack's art is an intellectual art which appeals to common sense and wit far more than to the emotions. In a country whose artists and poets have always tended to be romantic in their attitudes to art and life Brack is dry, objective, classical. Nor is it only a classicism of form in which lines and shapes are moulded into a carefully ordered composition; it is a classicism of mind which sees art as a social activity in which the artist bears a real and living relation to the society of his day. Indeed, like Hogarth's art, Brack's art is an art of social commentary. But it is not only commentary. His figures are not merely individuals, they have none of the particular emphasis of the cartoon, but are typical and representative. Brack, today, is holding up a mirror to his own times and what he is seeing may well become the accepted image of Australian society of the mid-twentieth century as much as the paintings and engravings of Hogarth have become the representative images of mid-eighteenth-century England. For our memory of the past is no mere reflex image of it but also a criticism and revaluation of it. In his *5 o'clock Collins Street*, Brack mirrors Melbourne's office workers making their evening trek towards Flinders Street Station. Here at the end of the world are the same faces, the same problems, the deserts into which the individual may sink as into sand. The figures across the street stream by in their little flat black hats and grey macks, and they have no faces. The heroes have departed. There are no wild colonial boys in John Brack's Australia. The mask-like faces pass before us like lost souls driven by a sullen wind around one of the circles of

Dante's Hell. They sweep by the fake Palladian façades of the city offices to their unknown abodes in the suburbs of subtopia. It is not a pleasant vision of the athletic young inhabitants of sunny Australia, and it seems to say, as a great poet once said, that where man is not, there is paradise. It is time perhaps that it was said of Australia.

The work of Arthur Boyd does not take its flight, as the work of Brack and Dickerson does, from the exigencies of urban life. But like Brack's art it does not lack a sense of the impending, the tragic and the apocalyptic. It is by no means always solemn, however, and often attains a lyrical beauty in which a warmth of feeling is combined with a plastic richness of colour. In its development Arthur Boyd's art has revolved about two main poles: one is concerned with painting the Australian landscape in a naturalistic and highly expressive manner, the other with figure subjects which embody a world of myth and symbol. In both manners Boyd has responded to the primitive and primordial aspects of nature in Australia. He is also an accomplished and experienced ceramic sculptor, and he has used this medium in order to create a world of animal and sub-human monsters which are in their forms and expressive gestures curiously symbolic of both man and nature in Australia. This is one of the great original achievements of his art. But by no means all of his work is concerned with such national references. Some of his finest creations, both in painting and in sculpture, are based on religious themes, such as his memorable *David Playing Before Saul* in the National Gallery of Victoria. In his recent series of paintings, entitled *Love, Death and Marriage of a Half-Caste*, exhibited at the Australian Galleries in 1958, Boyd turned his attention to the problem of the Aborigine in Australian society. In this series Boyd makes no explicit protest against Australia's treatment of her native peoples. The paintings do not represent the irritations of an angry young Antipodean. Boyd, rather, has an instinctive awareness of what is possible in painting and what is not. He sees his problem not as a propagandist but *sub specie aeternatitis*. What is so characteristic of such a painting as *Shearers Playing for a Bride* is its pathos. At the very centre of Boyd's art, and often among brutal images, there exists a quiet centre of pity. His *Shearers* is rich in allegory and symbol; the emblems of chance— love, lust and death—are all there, but no anger, only an infinite compassion. The moths playing about the lantern are also the shearers playing for their white bride. The power of such paintings depends upon the way Boyd can take a simple and obvious

Robert Dickerson, *Bank Clerk*, 1959, oil on board, 137 × 152.5 cm. The Robert
Holmes à Court Collection

group of figures and illuminate it by the warmth of old symbolic
meanings. In this regard he possesses a vision somewhat akin to
Blake's who also used a limited repertoire of figures which he
repeated again and again in a variety of symbolic contexts. Like
Blake, Boyd accepts the immanence and reality of evil and possesses, as Blake possessed, a profound belief in the healing power
of love.

The art of David Boyd is in some respects similar to his
brother's, but he is exploring a different field of interests

by bringing an expressionistic vision to the interpretation of Australian myth and history. He too is attracted by intimations of the monstrous in Australian nature. It is an attitude of mind which has been present in the country since the beginnings of white settlement. Indeed, Barron Field, Australia's first poet of any consequence, in speaking of the country, wrote:

> Of this fifth part of the Earth,
> Which would seem an after-birth,
> Not conceived in the Beginning
> (For God bless'd His work at first,
> And saw that it was good),
> But emerg'd at the first sinning,
> When the ground was therefore curst;-
> And hence this barren wood!

David Boyd's half-bird and half-human figurations in his large ceramic sculptures embody the reactions not only of Barron Field but of countless travellers who have come after him. It is to the credit of such artists as Arthur and David Boyd that they have seen that such images are not merely an aberration of a nineteenth-century colonial mentality but an essential part of a corpus of natural images which Europeans have used continuously since the eighteenth century to accommodate themselves to an antipodean world. In his recent paintings David Boyd has devoted himself to themes drawn from Australian exploration. A series dealt with the Burke and Wills expedition which attempted to cross the continent from south to north and ended in tragedy. Still more recently he has concerned himself with the fate of the Tasmanian Aborigines, who became extinct under the pressure of white settlement during the second half of the nineteenth century. In *The Intruder in the Hunting Grounds* the figure of a white settler complete with bell-topper and tails is linked insep-arably in a kind of Dantesque torment with a member of a race his people annihilated. In such images David and Arthur Boyd are giving expression to certain deep-rooted guilt feelings which the majority of Australians possess towards the contemporary remnant of Australia's native people. It is this tendency to probe into the more hidden parts of the national consciousness which is giving their art a dignity and authority lacking in the work of those local artists who are content to follow overseas fashion. In such work Australian art is acquiring a momentum of its own, already greatly developed in the work of such artists as Dobell, Drysdale and Nolan. And the issues with which the Boyds are concerned, it should be remembered, though seen in an Australian context, are issues which concern human society as a whole.

Of all the Antipodean artists John Perceval is probably the most lyrical and the most immediate in his productions. His landscape paintings are painted with a fierce joy, and with the physical energy of an action painter—but he does not obliterate his perceptions in an atavistic devotion to paint, as the action painters do. There is a rich exuberance about his colour which comes from years of experience as a potter and ceramic sculptor. His exhibition of *Angels*, held at the Museum of Modern Art, Melbourne, in 1958, was one of the most important one-man shows held in Australia since the war. It not only revealed Perceval as the master of an art rarely practised in the present century—his command of rare and lustrous glazes like the *sang de boeuf* commanded widespread attention—but it also revealed him as an artist with an observant eye and a keen wit. There was something both of the quattrocento and the rococo in these angels of his that were so like children. With their wings out of heaven and their bodies out of the earth they reminded one of Sir Thomas Browne's old vision of man himself as 'that great and true Amphibium, whose nature is disposed to dwell, not only like other creatures in divers elements, but in divided and distinguished worlds'. In their ceramic sculpture the two Boyds and Perceval have created a contemporary form of expression which is perhaps without parallel in any other country.

Charles Blackman's art is, of all the Antipodeans', the least public, the most personal. It is no simple matter to define the peculiar appeal of his strange presences. They are like dreams that break off or are only half-remembered: the deep questioning of eyes in shy faces, the pleasures of simple things, like a bunch of flowers, in a world fed on the sensational and horrific. At times he is like Dickerson—or Dickerson is like him—in his pathos. But Blackman's imagination is more lyrical and less social, more gentle, less pessimistic than Dickerson's. At times he is like Perceval—or Perceval is like him—in the personal intensity he can bring to his paintings. In 1958 Blackman exhibited a most unusual exhibition of paintings, based on *Alice in Wonderland*, at the Museum of Modern Art, Melbourne. In it he gave free rein to his peculiar sense of fantasy and produced paintings which evoked a topsy-turvy world of singular richness and charm. They were as Antipodean in spirit as Lewis Carroll's own wayward genius and may be said, in some ways, to have foreshadowed the formation of the Antipodean group.

Clifton Pugh is a painter who has achieved considerable distinction both in landscape painting and in portraiture. His work
has amplitude, energy and scale, and commands considerable
technical resources. The enigmatic and ambiguous quality of
nature, especially as it reveals itself in Australia, has attracted
him as it has attracted the Boyds. 'I want to show', he once wrote
concerning his own art, 'the soft and hard qualities of nature. . .
those great and seemingly alien powers that stirring from primeval times reach on through man who so easily succumbs to
their domination'. And in his landscapes he has often given
voice to the elemental savagery which he feels lies in the heart of
nature. But his creations are not melancholic in conception, they
are seen rather in broad formal patterns of brilliant and at times
fierce colour. The sun still shines in Clifton Pugh's landscapes as
fiercely as ever it shone in the work of those Heidelberg painters
Roberts and Streeton, but in his work it possesses a more savage
energy. Pugh's interpretation of Australian nature oddly enough
brings him close at times to Brack's interpretation of Australian
society, for though the one is romantic where the other is classic,
a pessimistic vision informs much of the best work of both
artists. And, indeed, there is nothing cosy or self-comforting in
the work of the Antipodeans as a whole. They are professional
artists who are continuing to practise an ancient profession in the
hard glare of those unpleasant facts which face the world today.
They see their art not only as a vehicle of personal expression but
as an act of social responsibility. This responsibility requires
that they should produce an art capable of true emotional and
imaginative communication. And from what they have already
produced it is clear that they have something to say both to their
own society and to the world at large.

PART IV

Pluralism in Practice: the 1960s

23
Sidney Nolan
—1962—

In this country Sidney Nolan, despite the reception given to his
Leda and Swan paintings, is still thought of primarily as an
Australian painter. But the fact that he is an Australian is not of
the first importance in seeking to understand his art. Indeed, an
emphasis upon his national origin can only lead to false conclusions, like thinking of Blake as 'English' Blake without paying
attention to his great debt to Italy, to neo-Platonic thought and
to so much more. For the courses of Nolan's art have been international from the beginning. His interest in poetry virtually
begins with Rimbaud; the influence of Klee is the earliest we can
detect in his paintings; and it should be remembered that even
his well-known image of Ned Kelly has proved to be more
accessible to the English imagination than to the Australian. In
order to understand and appreciate Nolan's art it is better to put
aside this question of national origin and concern ourselves with
something more central to the nature of painting itself: the invention of pictorial imagery. Because Nolan has concerned himself
with precisely this problem since he began to paint, and has
persisted with it throughout two decades which have witnessed
in western and westernized countries the decline, and in more
recent years the virtual disappearance, of the figurative image
from avant-garde painting. Let me illustrate my point with an
example.

Those of us who saw Kenneth MacMillan's fine new production
of Stravinsky's *Rite of Spring* at Covent Garden will recall the
magnificent tableau with which the second part begins—the
dancers motionless as votive offerings before the temple of an

First published in *The London Magazine*, September 1962, pp. 69–74 under the title 'Nolan's
Image'.

archaic god. What, surely, we asked ourselves, do they worship? The rising sun, the tree of knowledge and death, or a great Bacchic phallus arrogantly asserting the rights of man? Is it the atomic cloud which dominates the dance or that wandering moon which for an older generation of romantics was such a symbol of hope and constancy in a changing world? As the dance develops we find that the image does indeed take on shades of many such meanings and more.

For Nolan himself the image possesses another and more private meaning. Twenty-two years ago, then a young painter in his early twenties, he faced a personal crisis in his art. For the preceding two years his work had been small in scale, intimate, linear and abstract, owing not a little to Paul Klee and the early surrealists. Londoners had an opportunity to see something of this early work for the first time at an exhibition recently shown at the Institute of Contemporary Art. Nolan's first one-man show, held in Melbourne in 1940, consisted entirely of drawings and paintings of this kind. It created a sensation in Australian art circles. Someone threw a can of green paint at the exhibits. But shortly after the exhibition the artist grew restive and dissatisfied with the private nature of his art and began to search for some way to give his abstractions a wider relevance. From this search came his *Boy in the Moon*, the most controversial picture he has ever painted. It was abstract enough in itself but arose from the conflation of two images. Nolan has recalled how, shortly after his one-man show, he sat talking with a friend upon a bench at St Kilda Beach, Melbourne, how the full-moon rose behind his friend's head, and how he saw the two images as one and fashioned his painting from the double sensation. The painting created a great hubbub among artists, critics, and the public at large when shown at the Australian Contemporary Art Society's annual exhibition of 1940. Committee members threatened to resign. Some did.

Now the image which Nolan has used with such success at Covent Garden is in fact just his *Boy in the Moon* painting all over again—the same great blob of gold on a golden stalk against a blue ground. Nolan's art, we might say, has returned to its beginnings. But in a very real sense it has never left it. Beneath the changing forms a number of basic images survive: the moon-boy head—round, golden and radiant to the world; the Kelly mask—square, black and withdrawn upon itself; images of desert, of water and of crouching nudes; and those levitating images of birds, saints, and dying men. All such images have their origins in the early experience of the painter. The story of Nolan's visits to the Melbourne Aquarium as a boy to see Ned Kelly's armour and of the fascination his father's stories of Kelly held for him are well known. But it is far less known that he was attacked by swans at the age of twelve while attempting to steal swans' eggs and that the first Leda and Swan painting was completed during a period of personal tension and distress just before he began his first Kelly paintings. In thus drawing deeply upon personal experience Nolan reveals the essentially romantic character of his art. But it is not simply the origin of his basic images in childhood and youth that concerns me here. I am concerned rather with the ways in which they have come to assume pictorial form. Nolan, during the past twenty years, has evolved for himself ways of incorporating this business of image-making within the formal processes of painting which are of considerable significance for art today. Doubtless, it is impossible to discuss the complexities of pictorial invention without in some way over-simplifying the account. But I want, at least, to suggest four ways that Nolan has adopted to realize his images in pictorial form.

In the first place Nolan's images are ambiguous. One shape will evoke several meanings. But the meanings and emotions they may arouse, though ambiguous, have their origin in the artist's own imaginative processes and are limited. His paintings do not mean anything to anybody. He does not weave a rich pattern of textured colour and invite the beholder to allow his imagination to roam therein as in a kind of magic wood. A simple case of Nolan's use of ambiguity is to be seen in one of his carcase paintings of 1952 in which the dried interior of the carcase takes on the appearance of the desert landscape itself. That is an ambiguity arising directly from form. But Nolan also uses ambiguity of expression. In his first series of Kelly paintings, for example, is Kelly presented as a hero or as a clown? We can never be sure. He inhabits a world of emotional uncertainty and this, surely, is most fitting. For it is precisely the place where the Australian imagination has placed him; too much of a criminal to be given the role of culture-hero, too much like great-grandfather to be ignored.

And to these ambiguities of form and expression we must add Nolan's use of spatial ambiguity. For Nolan's space, most notably in his early Kelly paintings, again and again will open and snap shut before the eyes. At one moment the Kelly shape is impaled upon the surface of the painting, exposed like a dead fish on the sand, at another moment he is a lively shadow flitting between the trees. Spatially such figures inhabit a half-world between paint and meaning. In this, at least, he is in the tradition of Cézanne and Matisse.

Secondly, Nolan makes use of conflation: he impresses new images upon older images which have meant much to him, in his search for new significations. This is one way of stumbling upon the unexpected. Many notable examples of conflation will be found in his second series of Kelly paintings, a series which marks an important advance in his imaginative maturity. For in this series the wealth of imagery which he had evolved in his explorer, desert and convict paintings were mingled with the imagery of the first Kelly series. The image of Kelly thus became at once more personal and more generic, both the continuing symbol of the wanderings of Nolan's own imagination and the symbol of a criminal desert-prophet at once loved, feared and rejected by his people. In his fine painting *Kelly in Spring*, in the collection of the Arts Council of Great Britain, for example, Kelly has become a kind of vegetation god, a man of sorrows with a withered carcase whose old rifle blossoms like Aaron's rod.

Thirdly, Nolan makes use of transformation. One image will often take on the pattern and form of another in the same painting. In one of his earliest paintings, his delightful and witty *Catani Gardens*, painted in 1945, the many groups of lovers appear to dissolve continuously into amorous ecstasies, becoming more and more like the garden's bright lamps from which they hide. There is a fine note of wit in Nolan's work, especially in his early paintings.

Finally, Nolan has profited from the precept and example of Leonardo, Alexander Cozens and the abstract expressionists. He is aware of the value of accident in the evocation of images. As a young man he learnt with Paul Klee how to go for a walk with a line. He has recalled how he used to play a game with an artist friend in those days. Keep your pencil on the paper and draw. The first to draw a recognizable shape loses the game. Nolan learned much from that game; but today he uses accident not in order to avoid imagery but as one of the ways of going in search of it. This has became a particularly important factor in his work since he began to use polyvinyl acetate, but it has always been present.

Ambiguity, conflation, transformation, accident: such pictorial processes take us a long way from that equation of the image with conceptual thought which non-figurative painters tend to assume and seek to avoid. An image in a Nolan painting does

Sidney Nolan, *Kelly in Spring*, 1956, oil on canvas, The Arts Council of Great Britain.

not denote one simple idea nor is it amenable to interpretation simply as a symbol with a conventional meaning. His images seek to retain, or to fossilize as Nolan himself would say, personal events and memories, while finding by such processes as I have outlined appropriate contexts for public utterance. The moon-boy image married to the symbolism of Stravinsky's *Rite of Spring* is a splendid example of this. His images exist in a world of survival, transition and becoming. By such means Nolan seeks to escape from the image that is merely descriptive and the symbol that is merely conventional. He has discovered for himself painterly ways of making his shapes and meanings grow and realize themselves in a kind of vegetational process of the imagination. His imagery is achieved not through descriptive form but through what we might well call *iconomorphic* form.

The use of iconomorphic form is, of course, by no means confined to Nolan's art; one finds it in the paranoic heads of Salvador Dali, the auricular transformation of mannerist and baroque design, in the persistence of aureole and flame-like forms in Blake, to name but three well-known and distinct examples. Pater's famous passage on the *Mona Lisa* is magnificently iconomorphic even if it tells us little of Leonardo's real intentions. Certainly there is plenty of evidence for the use of iconomorphic invention in the art both of the past and the present, but I do not know of any painter of our own time whose creative achievement has depended so much upon the involvement of iconomorphic invention with the formal processes of painting. This is not surprising when we recall that so many of the most experimental painters of our time have abandoned the figurative image completely.

If one seeks for the sources of Nolan's inspiration in this matter it will be found, I believe, in the heritage of surrealism. Surrealism provided the contemporary artist with two possible roads to explore. One was the possibility of a purely autonomous art freed, as André Breton said, from 'thought's dictation'. The early surrealists, with their hard-edged realism and disquieting objects, failed to achieve pictorial autonomy. Critics quickly observed a gulf here between theory and practice. During the past decade, however, the abstract expressionist painters have achieved a kind of autonomous painting freed from the cognitive processes of mind but only at the expense of abandoning the figurative image which occupied a crucial role in the surrealist programme. For them the figurative image was the emblem of rational thought and those graphic stereotypes which inhabit the creative imagination.

The surrealists, however, were well aware that figurative images were also fashioned beneath the level of conscious thought. We dream not shapes and colours only but images whose very shape and visible form are at the mercy of feeling and signifying. The early surrealists failed, for the most part, on this score too. Their imagery belongs more to the rational analysis of dreams than to the dream process itself. It is one thing to paint the disquieting symbolic content of dreams and quite another to work out from one painting to another over a long period of years a mode of creating pictorial images analogous in many ways to the dream process itself. It is this aspect of the surrealist heritage that Nolan has continued to explore for twenty years.

That it was this aspect of surrealism which was developed by an Australian artist need be no cause for surprise. Australia only experienced the full impact of avant-garde art upon her culture with the discovery by her young painters of surrealism in the later 1930s, and the consequent effect of surrealism fell upon a firm tradition of naturalistic painting. The impact of cubism, constructivism and geometric abstraction during the 1920s and early 1930s was small and too weak to displace the local Edwardian Establishment of academic painters. There was a better reason for this than the effects of distance—or isolation as it is sometimes mistakenly called. What might have been the generation of art students to bring cubism and early abstract art back to Australia did not, like their predecessors, go to the art schools of Paris and London. They went to Gallipoli and the Western Front. Many of course did not come back and even those who did missed the crucial years of their lives as students in Paris, or had it tragically delayed. In the event it was not until the later 1930s that a new generation of artists sufficiently strong to challenge and defeat the rearguard of the academic Establishment at last arose. In the circumstances it was natural that the young artists should respond to the new possibilities which surrealism held for image-making rather than that they should abandon it in the desire for a wholly autonomous mode of creation. This is what did take place among the small group of artists gathered about the journal *Angry Penguins* during the early 1940s. In Australia we sometimes say that the Penguins are older than the Young Men. In any case, out of their state of anger with the paintings of the Establishment they began to experiment with iconomorphic processes latent in the surrealist programme. It is in Nolan's art that we find these processes developed most fully. But it was not until he had been in England for some years and about the time that he began his second series of Kelly paintings that he became fully aware of the possibilities of iconomorphic invention. Today his art points one way forward from the solipsism of non-figurative painting.

24
J. D. Pringle on Australian Painting
—1963—

Thames and Hudson, London, have chosen the London Scottish journalist John Douglas Pringle to introduce *Australian Painting Today*, the Australian volume of their Students' Gallery series of art books. This series, according to the advertisement on the dust cover, is intended to provide a concise and scholarly view of the field concerned, with an introductory text by a leading art historian.

Though Mr Pringle would be the last to lay claim to being an art historian, he is by no means an unsuitable choice for writing this particular text. For during the years in which he edited the *Sydney Morning Herald* he developed a keen and discriminating interest in Australian painting, an interest continued and deepened on his return to the London *Observer*. Furthermore, few have done as much as Pringle in recent years to develop an interest in Australian painting in England.

As those who have read his *Australian Accent* will recall, Pringle is always readable and often provocative. He is at his best when he is writing about his enjoyments, and Sidney Nolan's work is clearly one of his great enjoyments. He is always interesting on Nolan. For example:

Many Australians have laughed at Nolan's use of this [Ned Kelly] myth and have dismissed it as artificial and absurd, yet it is not difficult to find proof that the story of Ned Kelly touches a nerve in the Australian unconscious. In 1955, when the Elizabethan Theatre Trust proposed doing Douglas Stewart's play *Ned Kelly* at the time of the Olympic Games, the respectable citizens of Melbourne protested on the ground that it was outrageous to glorify a criminal in this way. For the Australian Establishment, as for the descendants of the Irish immigrants, Ned Kelly and his gang were too recent and too painful a memory to be treated as Walter Scott had treated Rob Roy in the early 19th century. Like some

---

First published in the *Age*, Melbourne, 24 August 1963.

other contemporary painters, Nolan seems to act as a psychoanalyst bringing to the surface of the conscious mind memories and guilt that had long been suppressed.

Pringle also writes with ease, grace and good judgement on the work of such painters as Russell Drysdale, Arthur Boyd and Leonard French; and his little book is happily free of the rancour and sharp tone (more snappish than biting) that has come into art criticism during the past year or so and made disinterested discussion virtually impossible.

It is in the early sections of the book that Pringle is seen to the least advantage. Although he stresses in his first sentence that the book is not a history, he plunges immediately, with more pluck than wisdom, into the solution of complex historical questions. But his interests and sympathies in this field are exclusively with the present and are therefore too temporarily parochial for the task.

He underestimates the importance of colonial Australian painting for an understanding of contemporary Australian painting, and maintains that Tom Roberts and his generation created nothing new nor added anything lasting 'to the idea of Australia'. Yet Mr Pringle's own idea of Australia, with its emphasis upon landscape as national expression, upon myth and utopian ideals, owes a great deal, in the pictorial arts, to ideas formulated by the Heidelberg school. And it was Heidelberg school propaganda which first put about the false notion that our colonial painters only painted with European eyes. Mr Pringle's highly foreshortened view of Australian art leads him to false conclusions.

Indeed he is an eloquent exponent of what might be called the London school of Australian art criticism. One might be forgiven for believing that the central tenet of this school asserts that Australian art began in the East End of London (Whitechapel precisely) during the mid-1950s. That, by an odd coincidence, she emerged armed and fully grown from the head of Sir Kenneth Clark, after it had been neatly cleft by the boomerang of Mr Bryan Robertson (chief Celtic midwife to our London Australiana), at the very moment when the London critical public were ready and willing to embrace her. Before that climacteric event there was not even a gestation. Unfortunately, the recent Tate Gallery exhibition of Australian painting tended to confirm the view that nothing had happened before Nolan. This is to be regretted.

Pringle's short view leads him to novel conclusions. Nolan leads the true way of Australian art brandishing an innocent eye in one hand and a Celtic imagination in the other as he penetrates the virgin desert. He is closely followed by Russell Drysdale, another Celt; and Arthur Boyd, yet another. Indeed Mr Pringle sees Celts everywhere. When they are not apotheosizing our convict birth-stain they are turning grass-trees into piebald leprechauns.

But it is the poets, as might has been expected, who really lead Mr Pringle into the Celtic twilight. 'It is legitimate to suppose,' he writes, 'that Mary Gilmore, A. D. Hope, James McAuley, Harold and Douglas Stewart and David Campbell all have some Scottish ancestry, while Fitzgerald's name is as Irish as it could be. This cannot be wholly accidental'. Alas, legitimacy has often been accidental in these Antipodean parts, and racial theories of national inspiration have, before this, obscured more than they have illumined. A 'Celtic' explanation of Australian art which must omit the Swiss Buvelot, and the English Roberts—guardian bulldogs of the propylaeum—were better discarded.

Nor does Mr Pringle's account of Australian art in terms of our geography and social environment come close to the heart of the problem. In the eighteenth century critics and historians like the Abbé du Bos and Winckelmann sought to explain the art of nations in terms of their geography. But little of real worth came of it. No doubt climate does have some ultimate effect upon art just as the sun has an ultimate effect upon life.

But a knowledge of sunspots is not much use to the mid-wife. Likewise, geographical descriptions, even when they are as pleasantly written as those of Mr Pringle and Mr Colin MacInnes (one more Celt does not make a twilight), will not greatly assist us to understand either the birth or the quality of contemporary Australian art. The answer will only be found in the history of art itself, for what most influences art is other art. Therefore an inquiry into the present vitality of Australian art will not lead us back to Ayers Rock and all that; it will lead us rather back to the origins of Australian art in European art itself, if we are interested in more than subject-matter. For there is no Australian tradition separate and distinct from the European tradition. The notion that Australian art is the art of an isolated island fastness in the south and perhaps the last national art to emerge into an inter-national world, is a myth fostered mainly by London critics. They should know better. Attempts to explain Australian art in terms of isolation and exceptionalism are bound to fail. There are no noble savages around here these days; and white Australians are the very last people with any claim to ape that role.

One last point. A series of art books designed to be of service

to students would surely be better served by a short book list
to take them on to other reading than by those little potted
biographies which nowadays hop from one Australian art book
to the next like a flock of rock wallabies startled by the tally-ho
of the hunter on dead man plain. Surely they could be allowed to
retire to their haunts for a season.

The book, however, apart from its curious historical explanations, is a thoroughly worthwhile addition to the growing
literature of Australian art. It has over thirty good colour plates,
though the omission of a number of important artists like John
Brack, Albert Tucker and David Boyd for the sake of some fashionable ones of, to my mind, dubious quality, is to be regretted.

25

Francis Lymburner

—1963—

Francis Lymburner's exhibition (South Yarra) is one of the finest exhibitions by an Australian painter which I have seen for some considerable time.

These paintings would stand up well in any international company and indicate that Lymburner is one of the most mature and masterly of the Australian painters today.

The exhibition came as a most pleasant shock to me. I have always regarded Lymburner as one of the finest of Australian contemporary draughtsmen, yielding place to none except, perhaps, Donald Friend. But his paintings of the 1940s—and he was one of the best-known Australian artists of that decade—never seemed to realize their potential as paintings, being rather plastic extensions of his skilful draughtsmanship and, though sure and sensitive in handling, tinged always with an unvarying and somewhat mannered melancholy. But today his paintings exist superbly in their own right.

Lymburner has lived in London now for over a decade and here, beyond all doubt, is one Australian painter who has grown remarkably in stature since his departure. The paintings which Lymburner shows are neither ambitious nor self-consciously fashionable. He has not wrenched and twisted at his style in order to make it follow the vagaries of taste. He has allowed it to develop naturally and organically out of his temperament and talent, so that today an artist who, during the 1940s, appeared as a sensitive but minor artist, is beginning to emerge as one of the major figures in Australian painting.

To those who feel that I may be the victim of a momentary enthusiasm I would ask them to examine Lymburner's *Palette*

Two articles, first published in the *Age*, Melbourne, 24 September 1963 and 1 July 1964 respectively.

Francis Lymburner, *Man Trap*, 1962, wash drawing in black and maroon ink, 48.1 × 32.3 cm. Private collection.

Table (85) and ask themselves just how many Australian painters can paint quite as well as that. I am sure that it would not disgrace itself with, say, a Soutine on one side and a Fragonard on the other.

Lymburner has gone directly to life for his material, and the old-fashioned ham has rewarded him magnificently. Here are characters from the theatre, from the ballet, from the race-track, from the London parks, caught on the very wings of their existence by paintings deft, sensitive and superbly realized. And yet, however free and fluent the colour, there is nothing adventitious about it. One becomes aware here of what one sees so rarely—the mastery of a medium.

It is no accident. A quarter of a century has gone to the development of Lymburner's pictorial skills, and the perception is keener than ever.

What distinguishes a good drawing? Exhibitions at the South Yarra, Argus, and Leveson Street galleries raise the question sharply.

One hesitates to be dogmatic. But line by its nature divides; and good drawing, it seems to me, is analytical. It is fashionable to assume these days that good drawing bears no relation to figuration. But I doubt whether drawing can remain long separated from the figure and retain the vitality and sensitivity we expect of good drawing. For line which turns away from definition and depiction becomes at best pattern, which is the result of visual synthesis rather than visual analysis.

Francis Lymburner (South Yarra) has justly been regarded for many years as one of Australia's most accomplished draughtsmen. In this city perhaps only Brack and Counihan, and in Sydney, Dobell, Drysdale and Friend, produce work of a comparable quality. For today it is an art more discussed than practised.

Lymburner's early drawings, which made his reputation, are characterized by economy, a natural feeling for interval and accent, and a sensitive arabesque line of great elegance.

His more recent work is of a finer quality. It seeks more and finds more. The economy remains: a statement swift, complete and final, scrutinizing and holding the essentials of the image. There are no afterthoughts added to finish the drawing once the statement has been made; and the calligraphy is so sure that a balance between lyricism and structure, observation and surface elegance is achieved, which is rarely seen in this country.

26
John Olsen
—1963—

Although Olsen's student art was grounded upon Cézanne, there is very little Cézannist classicism left in his art today. Since then he has drawn his painterly inspiration almost entirely from recent painting; from such painters as Soulages, Tapies, Dubuffet and Corneille. Olsen has certainly kept up with the Joneses of recent painting, but this, it seems to me, is one of the weaknesses of his art. It suffers from temporal parochialism, a blindness to most of what has happened in art before 1945. To my mind it is still insecure at its foundations, breathlessly avant-garde.

I am well aware that there are critics, whose intelligence and perception I respect, who hold Olsen's art in the highest regard. I must confess that I do not share their view. A refined and joyous feeling for colour there certainly is, and pattern-making to the point of genius. Indeed, as Hal Missingham recently observed shrewdly, Olsen's art is remarkably akin in its aesthetic quality, its ideas and expression, to the art of the late Margaret Preston. Margaret Preston's art was based upon a love of colour, a love of country, and pattern-making. These are, I submit, the principal virtues of Olsen's art.

Despite the up-to-date manner of their presentation, the ideas, the 'metaphysics', the tub-thumping, rumbustious gaiety strikes me as rather dull stuff. Olsen seems to envisage nature as a nice big flux, *élan vital* in plastic tubes. There are no snakes in his Eden. God may not be in heaven, but all's right in John Olsen's world. John is all right, Jack. In you beaut country Pippa still passes and even the animals adore living in you beaut zoo.

Of course, I am not complaining about joy and radiance in art on principle. It is simply that Olsen's joy is too forced, too

First published in the *Age*, Melbourne, 8 October 1963.

rhetorical, showy and redundant to my taste. The emotional energy is uncontrolled, diffuse. Many of the titles could be interchanged with little difference. Joy, surely, should come to us as a clear, limpid stream with defined banks, not in an ocean of pullulating amoeba. For me, Olsen's joy is a mob of little oozy-woozy people gambolling about in a haze of alcoholic euphoria, and in some ways it reflects the easy affluence of the 1950s. It will be interesting to see how it will develop through the present, more questioning, decade.

But perhaps we should not wish Olsen's art to be otherwise. Even if, in the end, it turns out to be charming rather than virile, to be the 'charm school' face-lifted by Corneille, certainly it will give pleasure to many people.

27

Leonard French

—1963—

At the Argus Gallery, Leonard French is exhibiting forty-three studies in mixed media for paintings in progress. Although studies, most are well-developed and provide a foretaste of the work to come. They also reaffirm what became abundantly clear from the Campion paintings, that French is in the first rank of Australian painters. Not that this exhibition, despite its vitality, reveals the full range of his art.

From a few elementary geometric figures, the square, cross, circle and hemisphere, French has evolved a symbolic language of great emotional force which can be yet delicate in its nuances; it is highly evocative and yet firmly structured. It is an art of balance, as much of its effects as of its foundations. When French's art reached its first maturity it was seen to be based, more or less, upon a late synthetic cubist position with affinities to Léger and Delaunay.

But in his search for a chromatic system more sonorous, subtle and evocative than cubist science provided, French turned to the vast range of medieval art and symbolism, to Celtic jewellery, Limoges enamels, and so forth. At the same time he freed his imagery from the constrictions of cubism's interlocking counter-change patterns. He went back in order to go forward. His art is planted both in the present and in the past. This, I believe, is one of the explanations of his strength.

Certain stylistic changes are worth noting. From these studies it would appear that the softening of the geometric rigidity of his early work, already apparent in the Campion series, continues. On the other hand, many of the studies reaffirm his basis in geometry.

First published in the *Age*, Melbourne, 8 October 1963.

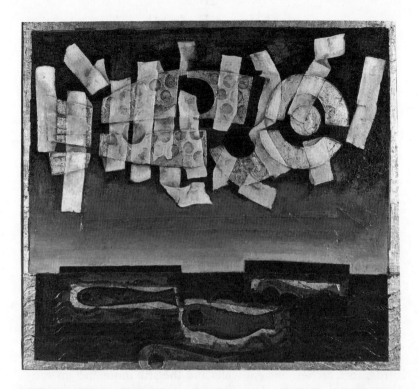

Leonard French, *Death and Transfiguration*, 1961, enamel on canvas on hardboard, 122.6 × 137.9 cm, Sir Charles Lloyd Jones Bequest Fund, Art Gallery of New South Wales.

There is a particularly fine series of studies for the *Creation—from the First to the Sixth Day*. Most of the studies suggest a chromatic change from the Campion series. Earth colours, black, browns and ochres predominate, alleviated by white, purple (that difficult colour which French handles with such assurance) and blue. There is a splendid balance, too, between organic and inorganic motifs. It is apparent that French is beginning to explore more carefully than hitherto ambiguities between shape and meaning, as, for example, in *Turtle over Temples* (43).

Like Olsen, French is much occupied with imaging the processes of generation, but this is not orgiastic immersion. In French's noughts and crosses there are also pain, power, honour and evil. He has built a strong bridge between the past and the present.

28
Norma Redpath
—1963—

Norma Redpath is without doubt one of the most impressive Australian sculptors at work today. She has been able to commute for some years between Italy and Australia with obvious value for her development as a sculptor.

There is nothing thin, mean of cramped about her work. It now has a largeness of conception, a baroque amplitude, a feeling of controlled power. The two large bronzes cast in Italy possess a monumental sculptural presence of a kind rarely seen here. *Horse, bird and sun* (17), in its compact and flattened forms, is like a weathered outcrop of slaty rock. Her work evokes the effects of geological, residual forms.

Although she makes use of an impressive range of images—birds, rock arches, ancient walls and the still more ancient sun—they do not intrude. And she can, like César, create the most compelling contrasts between rough and polished surfaces, between dark and light.

It is still, however, the work of a young sculptor, for all its power and promise; international and almost anonymous, in the best sense. Redpath, wisely, has not yet allowed her work to set into a personal style. At the moment it is still assimilating an international idiom, and what is personal about the work is here of much less importance than what is sculptural.

I find the large works more impressive than the bronzettes, the niggardly forms of many of which can only be justified as maquettes, not as finished sculpture.

First published in the *Age*, Melbourne, 15 October 1963.

29
Robert Klippel
—1963—

Although Robert Klippel has lived in the United States during the past few years, studying, practising and teaching sculpture, he had already made a reputation for himself as one of the most promising and original sculptors at work in Sydney during the early 1950s. Indeed the resurgence of interest in sculpture which took place in Sydney ten or more years ago owed not a little to Klippel's work and activity.

His present exhibition at the Australian Galleries is one of the most unusual and arresting exhibitions of sculpture that we have seen in Melbourne for some time. Although quite different in its approach, it may be compared favourably with the recent exhibition of Norma Redpath's sculpture for its assurance and maturity.

Klippel is concerned with abstract form and, like many sculptors of recent years, seeks his raw materials in junk yards. There can be no doubt that his steel junk sculpture, if approached with an unprejudiced eye, will be seen to take on a formal beauty of its own quite distinct from the character of the discarded material out of which it has been fashioned.

Klippel in this exhibition reveals less interest than he did in the past in the exploitation of open-space sculpture. It now consists in general of massive encrusted forms compactly welded together and stood upon one or more legs. From the central mass angular rods radiate like antennae. They wear the hard but sensitive beauty of delicate precision instruments. One of the finest of all these junk pieces is *Steel Junk Sculpture* (no. 9), a tall, slender thing in which line answers line, and mass replies to mass in visual counterpointing of great beauty.

First published in the *Age*, Melbourne, 2 December 1963.

Robert Klippel, *Steel Junk Sculpture, no. 16*, 1963, Collection of Janet Dawson.

Junk sculpture is still a novelty in Australia and it is fortunate that a sculptor of Klippel's ability is here to introduce it. By contrast, his large bronze-relief wall sculpture, with its radiating frond-like forms, although thoroughly professional, echoes the work of that versatile American Herbert Ferber a little too closely.

The lighting and display reveal the delicate rhythms of junk sculpture to advantage.

30
Twenty-Five Years of Contemporary Art
—1963—

The Contemporary Art Society of Australia (CAS) was established in 1938 to combat the academic, the conservative in art, to oppose art having no other aim than representation. 'When you cease to find in the Annual Exhibition of the Society any new thought or feeling or any urge to explore the possibilities of the unknown, then you may be sure that the Society no longer carries the banner it was intended to bear.' So wrote Mr John Reed in the introduction to the catalogue of the second Contemporary Art Society Exhibition in 1940. These are wise and courageous words, but they raise deep problems for the society after twenty-five years of existence.

For the fact of the matter is surely that the CAS has, to a very large extent, won the battle it was created to fight. The Australian Academy is long since dead, the academic is most unfashionable, art having no other aim than representation is out. So what, precisely, are we fighting against today? It has often been said that revolutionary bodies (and the CAS is certainly a revolutionary body), begin by attacking and defeating reaction and then proceed to devour their own children. Can the CAS, I should like to ask, survive only by attacking and destroying the art of its founders? Must it devour its children to survive?

Let me come back to that point later. At the moment I want to stress what seems to me to be one of the cardinal facts about the art situation today, and that is the virtual disappearance of an avant-garde. George Heard Hamilton, Professor of Fine Arts at Yale University, and a specialist and protagonist of contemporary art, pointed this out with great clarity a year or so ago when

Opening addresses given at the Contemporary Art Society's (Sydney Branch) annual exhibition, held in Farmer's Blaxland Galleries, 23 October 1963. Published in *Broadsheet of the Contemporary Art Society of New South Wales*, December 1963, pp. 6—10.

writing on contemporary American art (*Burlington Magazine*, May 1960). When any signs of innovation are accepted by critics, dealers and galleries as soon as they appear there can be no longer any genuine avant-garde.

What I am saying is that during the past twenty-five years a fundamental change has taken place overseas and in this country among the art-loving and the art-buying public. Today they too, as well as the artists, are committed to innovation, to contemporaneity. To a very large extent they have been convinced by the argument of modernism. Let us consider the historical facts briefly. The fundamental break-through into the idiom of twentieth-century painting took place between 1906 and 1918. These were the years in which cubism, abstract art and futurism were pioneered. The idiom of twentieth-century art was virtually complete by the First World War. Surrealism was perhaps the one radically new idiom which emerged later, but even that was implicit in the *pittura metafisica* of De Chirico. What has happened since has not so much been radical new departure but rather the exploration of the possibilities implicit in the new idiom. Abstract expressionism, for example, is a mingling of abstract art, expressionism and surrealist principles. It is not a radically new style but a working out of veins discovered earlier in the century; neo-Dada is, well, neo-Dada; assemblage is a natural development of collage; pop, an intriguing movement, is a kind of marriage of Dada to the social comment of the 1930s. It is fifty years since the creation of modernism. Today we no longer live among the pioneers of modern art, we live among its mannerists.

Meanwhile the principle of innovation, of contemporaneity, of permanent revolution in the arts has shifted from a few pioneers to society as a whole. Perhaps, as you will leap to remind me, Australia has been a little slow. But I can remember a time barely twenty years ago when it was impossible to get the trustees of the Sydney Gallery to buy a cubist painting. Indeed I played some part in getting the first cubist painting into the Sydney collection in cohort with the late Sydney Ure Smith. We managed to convince a sub-committee for travelling exhibitions that an Eric Wilson should be purchased for educational purposes only. The Trustees allowed the painting in by the back door of a strictly educational programme. They would never have bought it straight out. Times have changed. Today, not even the Commonwealth Art Advisory Board can be depended upon to stand fast as a sturdy opponent of change. I hear that Mr Laurie Thomas has been asked by the board to prepare an exhibition to represent Australia overseas. Mr Thomas will certainly uphold the principle of contemporaneity. The Establishment, even in Australia, has come to accept contemporaneity as a principle.

Now under these circumstances can the CAS do anything but become, during the next twenty-five years, as important a part of the artistic establishment of this country as the Museum of Modern Art in New York has undoubtedly become a part of the artistic establishment of the United States. Frankly I doubt whether it can. There may even be knighthoods awaiting the most successful innovators. Once a nation becomes committed to innovation the most successful innovators are also the most honoured; the pace-makers of change, not the die-hard conservatives, become the status-men in the society committed to change.

Is there any way out of this dilemma? I think that there is but I doubt whether the CAS is institutionally capable of taking it. It would consist simply in facing up to the question: are all kinds of change desirable, or is it possible that some kinds of change are undesirable?

Now I believe that change is fundamental to the arts, that the history of art itself is largely the history of the avant-garde, but I believe also that change should never be accepted at face value; change must be questioned and questioned. One must accept at once the reality of change and adopt an attitude of criticism towards it. Innovation has to be made to answer for itself, to stand up for itself and state just what it proposes to add in terms of human spiritual value to the whole tradition—because the tradition itself is not dead, it is a living tradition built by innovators who have stood the test of criticism. All original art is contemporary art, and the original mind draws upon the whole tradition of art, not only upon the recent past. This is where art is radically different from science. The scientist may discard the work of earlier scientists and build upon the recent past which contains within itself the living past. Ptolemy is ousted by Copernicus but Masaccio is not ousted by Sam Francis. (On this point see A. Boyce Gibson, 'Works of Literature and Work in Philosophy', Australian Humanities Research Council, Annual Report No. 7, 1962—63.) In art, originality constantly draws upon the whole tradition which is a tradition of innovation. Critics like Harold Rosenberg, who talk about a tradition of the new, try to explain progress in art as though it were progress in science. This is always a fertile source of confusion. Art is not a self-destroying process; it is not symbolized by Jean Tinguely's self-destroying machine knocking itself to pieces in the sculpture court of the

Museum of Modern Art. Destruction is mechanical; growth, genuine change, is organic.

So let me come back to my first question: must the CAS devour its children in homage to the god of mechanical change, the *deus ex machina*.

An artist who exhibited in the first exhibition of the CAS in this city in 1940 at the age of twenty would be forty-three today, still a relatively young man by today's standards. If he has been an original artist his work has changed and matured. It is considerably different from what it was twenty-three years ago. But the changes which have taken place in his work, to the extent that he is an original artist, have depended more upon the inner, organic changes of his own temperament and personality, than the changes that have taken place in the world of art outside of him. True, he will have reacted to these changes, but he will have reacted in his own way. Artistic development, artistic originality, is a personal development and its curve is related to the life cycle of the human organism. Now in being true to himself an artist may have to resist changes which are inimical to him. The crucial point is this: will the CAS accept such resistance to innovation as natural to an organic development, or will it turn on its own members and describe them as reactionaries and conservatives?

This is a real question because today, with everyone accepting change, the cycle of change is speeding up; the changes are not from generation to generation, or decade by decade, but from year to year. Somebody once said that time was a river without banks; today time is much more like a freeway without lanes in which the minimum speed is being constantly increased, in which the smog thickens hour by hour and the suburbs are getting further and further away. What a pity if one is compelled to go so fast and then only end up in the outer suburbs of originality!

I am critical you see of change that is external and mechanical. Genuine change in the arts is not geared to seasonal changes like changes in dress and fashion, nor is it geared to technological and market changes, such as styling for obsolescence; it is organic and related to the life-cycle of the artist.

The recognition of this fact is particularly important for art in cities like Sydney and Melbourne. Art is, to a large extent, a product of urban man. A city is provincial when it accepts external, mechanical change, change from outside, from some distant metropolitan centre. It dances to a tune that is played elsewhere. But when a city becomes truly metropolitan, as

Byzantium, or Rome or Paris became metropolitan, its change is developed out of its own inner development, it gives out more than it takes in. In this the original city is like the original artist; it knows itself, it does not have to dance mechanically and involuntarily to tunes invented elsewhere.

During the next twenty-five years the CAS could help to turn the art of this city from a provincial into a truly metropolitan culture, if only it brings a more sophisticated approach to the problem of change at a time when everyone is becoming committed to change as the normal condition of art.

A metropolitan as distinct from a provincial art delves inwards as well as outwards. A metropolitan culture is one that has learnt to have some respect for its own past, it does not seek to destroy it in a fury of self-abasement for being merely provincial. In practice this would mean, for example, that the present generation of younger Sydney painters might even learn that they them-themselves, having been born out of a similar urban situation, have more in common than they know or would perhaps now admit with that 'charm school' which their own art has replaced. Because originality and achievement are products of continuity as well as change. This truth is at least borne out by the history of this branch of the CAS. It has had the good fortune to maintain over the years since its foundation the loyalty of a few good artists for whom the principles for which the society stood were of more importance than elevation to the status-conferring societies.

Some at least of the society's first children remain; too tough perhaps to be devoured. But of how many shall we be able to say that their art developed organically and in response to an inner need and not under the breaking stress of external change and in fear of the *deus ex machina*?

31
Charles Blackman
—1964—

At the South Yarra Gallery Charles Blackman is holding his first one-man show in Australia since his departure for the United Kingdom in 1960.

The imagery for which he is now so well known both here and abroad—women bemused by memories, dreaming, seeking comfort or simply lost in a twilight loneliness—remains. But the manner in which he presents his world has undergone considerable stylistic change since his exhibition at the Matthiesen Gallery, London, in 1961.

Then he was depending upon firm, blocky shapes and dramatic contrasts of light and dark to figure forth with his tender images and used a minimum of colour. In the present exhibition he appears to be seeking a new synthesis between that dark, dramatic, tonal style and the still earlier and more colouristic style of soft, dreamy transitions characteristic of his Alice in Wonderland series of paintings of the mid-1950s.

This exhibition, therefore, represents both a development and consolidation. Now he is seeking to develop a more colourful and painterly style without losing the telling and dramatic chiaroscuro of recent years. The new painterliness is seen at its best in such a work as *In a Glass Darkly* (P6). A recurring practice in the exhibition—and it is a feature of some of the best works shown, such as *The Drama* (1), and *Dream Image* (6), purchased by the Castlemaine Gallery—is to contrast a compact shock of bright and singing primary colours against a soft tonalism of greys and blues and at times, and more dangerously, against rose reds. The exhibition reveals Blackman's style in transition. There is less dependence now upon the dramatic silhouette; the painter is seeking surfaces more sensuous and painterly.

First published in the *Age*, Melbourne, 18 March 1964.

Charles Blackman, *Tryst*, 1959, oil on board, 118 × 91.44 cm. Private collection.

It is a tender and eloquent exhibition, the kind of achievement we come to expect from an artist as personal in manner as Blackman, but it does have weaknesses. *Remembrance* (8), for example, lacking the cubic austerity of earlier work, teeters dangerously upon the edge of sentiment, and the experiments with double images and ambiguity, as in *Transformation* (5), are awkward. There are, however, some splendid Conté drawings which reveal Blackman at his best, among which the *Duenna* (27) is outstanding.

32
Arthur Boyd
—1964—

The Museum of Modern Art has enterprisingly secured for Melbourne the drawings and paintings from the Arthur Boyd retrospective exhibition originally shown at the Adelaide Arts Festival, and has added some rarely seen works not shown there.

It is the most representative show of Boyd's work yet seen in Melbourne. Here we may study his early buff-grey and blue landscapes, which owe something to both Van Gogh and local tradition and are yet already sure in touch and tone. We may examine those crucial drawings and paintings of 1943 when his personal style, violent in gesture yet strangely tender in mood, asserts itself.

After the nightmarish fantasies of the war years when Boyd first revealed his rare capacity for transforming, like the Greeks, reality into myth, a new synthesis was established between his early pastorals and his vision of the curse of Cain, a synthesis which culminated in the magnificent religious paintings of the late 1940s, such as *The Mockers*, *The Golden Calf* and *The Burning City*. There followed the exquisite landscapes in tempera and oil, quiet and lyrical in temper, of the early 1950s.

But that moment of peace was shattered by the artist's moral energy, which revealed itself again in the allegories of the Half-Caste and Bride series, a masterpiece of pictorialized emotion which foreshadowed those remarkable studies in doom and transience, the Diana and Acteon paintings of 1962.

Of Boyd at least we shall be able to say that he could paint love and death, neither furtively nor cynically, but like a mystic, seeing love as a kind of death, a death of self; and like a biologist, seeing death as the price of love, and be able to say that he was one of us; one of our generation.

First published in the *Age*, Melbourne, 2 May 1964.

33
Carl Plate
—1964—

Carl Plate is without doubt one of the most accomplished of the many abstract painters busily at work in Sydney today.

In his exhibition at Gallery A the full resources of painting are directed towards genuinely abstract goals. They are not, like so many abstract paintings, visual metaphors; his graphs and segments do not stand for this or that feeling, this or that piece of nature. They are paintings seeking an aesthetic utopia in which painting may be enjoyed purely as painting and for no other reason. Any associations which they arouse are likely to be the spectator's, and irrelevant.

By any standard they are good paintings, especially the big ones which have been so carefully related and thoroughly worked out. By contrast, the studies and many of the smaller pictures appear crowded and muddled. For this is a highly conscious art of the most careful judgement and discrimination.

The construction is essentially tonal. Segmented and blocky shapes, confronting one another in asymmetrical and disjunctive relationships, are built up upon green, ochrous and brown grounds, the colour being subdued and the painting thick.

Plate avoids the perils of pure decoration by depth achieved by means of tone and colour, and the tension established between the blocky shapes all loosely interlocked with tenuous ribbons of paint. It is good, serious, abstract painting: no bombast, no exhibitionism. Its instincts are classical, though it is never serene. If the show has weaknesses, the weaknesses are perhaps inherent in abstract painting.

So much careful weighing of shape against shape, tone against tone, in this private world where only paint is king can dull the eye rather than stimulate it, and depress the spirit. The finer the balances, the smaller the weights.

First published in the *Age*, Melbourne, 27 May 1964.

34
Art Criticism
—1964—

Why do I write art criticism? Why does anyone write art criticism? Some artists—the more naive ones—have a ready and simple explanation. He must have failed to make the grade as an artist. This explanation of criticism as a kind of revenge taken by the uncreative upon the creative may help to explain the psychological origins of a lot of poor criticism, sour, bitter, censorious and jealous, but it fails to explain criticism at its best which is rather a kind of advocacy, a faith in certain artists or kinds of art, the desire to help win a public towards a new vision, a new way of seeing. The revenge theory does not explain Ruskin's criticism of Turner, Baudelaire's criticism of Delacroix, Fry's criticism of Cézanne, Clement Greenberg's criticism of the abstract expressionists. All were enlightened acts of advocacy in which criticism itself might fairly be said to have become a creative art. It is that kind of criticism in which I am interested. But it is a much more complex thing than simply saying nice things about your friends.

Most critics begin with some creative experience of the art they criticize. For my own part I drew and painted from the age of seventeen to twenty-five before I first ventured into criticism. And for me the switch was abrupt and final. I had painted a biggish picture for the first exhibition of the Contemporary Art Society held in Sydney; it had taken months to paint. Then in the middle of the show I simply decided that I did not want to be a painter, and symbolized my decision to myself by leaving the picture with the society. They must have destroyed it years ago, or scraped it down and put it to better use. But I did not cease painting out of a sense of frustration or failure; I had become more interested in painting than ever but not my own. Who were

Not previously published. A talk for the Australian Broadcasting Commission, given on 16 July 1964. One of a series entitled 'On the Critics—by the Critics'.

we, we Australian artists? Where had we come from? What were we trying to do? I became interested, and the interest has never ceased, in the Australian artist's situation; in what made him what he was. It was a historical and critical problem. It fascinated me. It still does.

Our society is still pretty young and naive, and few people realize that it is possible to obtain a sense of fulfilment and satisfaction from such unpopular pursuits as history and criticism. That is not surprising. Philistinism has been so rampant in our society that it is only in recent years that a reasonably large public has been won over to accept the most obvious forms of personal expression, like the art of painting itself, as an acceptable social goal. But that one should find history or criticism creative is met with incredulity. People so often say, 'But wouldn't you like to return to painting?', as if to say 'Surely criticism is a rather stultifying activity'. Heaven forbid! There are too many art critics in Australia painting poor pictures for high prices as it is anyway.

But, you say, what is the value of art criticism? Well I believe that criticism is an integral part of the mechanism or psychology of creation. When an artist persists with a sensation, a mood, an idea, until a work of art is born from it, a process of critical selection has been going on from the very beginning. I am well aware that some artists believe that art can be reduced to pure automatism in which no choice is exercised. But surely being creative without the exercise of choice is a kind of rape. After all, even the simple business of picking up a paintbrush is an act of choice, or a critical judgement of a simple kind. Some artists have great difficulty in deciding whether they should pick up a paintbrush or a mug of beer.

Criticism, then, begins as a dialogue between the artist and his work. It may continue in his studio among his friends. But if he decides to exhibit his painting for all to see, discussion of his work becomes a public matter. In a free society this discussion may be carried on verbally or in writing. It must be remembered that art criticism is only one specialized aspect of the whole body of criticism which is the very life of a free society, in which neither religions, governments, nor—and this is most pertinent to our subject—the artistic process itself should be regarded as sacrosanct and beyond the reach of criticism. In other words criticism is the price artists pay for the right to live in a free society. It is no accident that the first professional art critic was Denis Diderot, one of the intellectual architects of the French Revolution. We may disagree with many of Diderot's judgements today—a taste of Greuze is much too sweet for our bitter century—but there can be no doubt that his criticism helped to dislodge French painting from its identification with the state.

The most a critic can do then is to begin a discussion. If the art work is of true originality the discussion will never end. Critics are still discussing the aesthetic merits of the Nessos Amphora, a pot thrown and painted in Attica over 2600 years ago and now in the Metropolitan Museum, New York. The genuine artist need not fear criticism; if the judgements are wrong so much the worse for the critic, they will be revised. What the artist need fear is the lack of discussion, silence, apathy: the crowds at the official opening chattering over their cask riesling with their behinds pointed symbolically towards the paintings.

I think that the first thing a critic should endeavour to do is show that he does thoroughly enjoy the art which he criticizes. If his criticism is going to err it should err on the side of generosity. If he places too much score upon the importance of his judgements he will only succeed in being pompous. In the field of the arts and humanities no judgements are final judgements, and it is foolish therefore to present them with an air of finality. The most the critic does is to initiate a public discussion.

I do not think that a critic should attempt to be impartial; I think that he should write from a point of view. It is this point of view which always makes him, when the chips are down, advocate rather than judge. But it must be a point of view which provides him with a civilized and tolerant view of the whole divers field of art and of the whole range of human behaviour. Christianity, socialism, humanism, the doctrine of art for art's sake, have all provided critics with points of view from which criticism of quality and distinction has proceeded. On this very point Baudelaire, one of the greatest of art critics, has written with wisdom. 'Criticism,' he says, 'should be partial, passionate and political, written from an exclusive point of view, but a point of view that opens up the widest horizons'. If a critic does not have a point of view fashion will quickly reduce him to being an opportunist. On the other hand he has a special duty to understand points of view which differ markedly from his own. This is not as difficult as it may sound. Although critical vitality springs from advocacy it is not confined to advocacy. De Tocqueville writing on America, John Pringle writing on Australia, Baudelaire writing on Ingres, have all written perspicaciously about their subjects without identifying themselves with them. A critic must learn to live with other points of view, but needs to have one of his own.

But, you might say, 'It's a poor lookout for the artists who don't share the critic's point of view'. The only answer to this is other critics with other points of view. The critical health of a society depends not upon multiplying so-called impartial points of view, but the interplay of real differences of opinion.

That, indeed, has been the historical reality of criticism. The good art critic is one for whom art is a crucially important function of life, and it is the way in which he sees art related to life which provides him with his point of view, and from this he operates as critic. If he tries to be impartial he will not succeed, he will only substitute a set of external criteria, an intellectualized notion of value in the place of his whole experience of art and life. Of course a critic should try to be fair; but if he really believes he can be impartial I doubt very much whether art means very much to him.

The desire to be impartial is a kind of inverted arrogance, a belief that one can be above the issues which are constantly fashioning and changing art.

And yet however important art may be for his own life the critic's final responsibility is not to art but to his own craft of criticism. He is not the artist's spokesman. He represents, rather, that small section of society for which criticism is important. There are of course art critics and art critics; from the newspaper critic's hasty and snap judgements to Panofsky's extraordinary interpretation, say, of the mind and art of Dürer. But damage one and you damage, in the end, the other. The most a newspaper critic can do is to initiate a public discussion, to give some idea of the work under review and offer some kind of judgement. Often he will be only stating the obvious; but it is proper that it should be stated in public as well as whispered in private. Of course he must be prepared to judge to the best of his knowledge and feeling. And the most that can come from that activity is a prompting of others to consider and judge too. In this he may help to develop an informed critical opinion in his community; I do not believe that art can today flourish without it.

Although the critic must judge, he should not offer the artist gratuitous advice. He is critic, not art teacher. Nor should he seek to mould opinion. The expression of his own opinion as clearly as he can put it is his concern, not its effects on other people. Too great an interest in the effects of his judgements will turn him from criticism to manipulation. And the less he knows about sales from the art shows he reviews the better. He should, it seems to me, avoid promoting individual artists as artists. What he advocates is his own position, which may well draw him more favourably to the art of some artists than to others. But that should be the product of his position, not the product of his personal relationships. It is to be remembered that it is his position, his attitude to art and life which has made him a critic in a way similar to that in which the artist's attitude to art and life has made him an artist.

The most any critic can do is to speak as well as he can for his generation. It is supremely difficult to do even that. And he should write, therefore, as if his cause were a lost cause; it will improve his tone if not his judgements. And in the end, after all, it will not be the quality of his judgements but the quality of his enjoyments which will determine whether his own work will stand.

35
William Dobell
—1964—

The Art Gallery of New South Wales is displaying in Sydney what is probably the most important exhibition held during the eighty and more years of its existence. It brings together the most comprehensive collection of the paintings of William Dobell yet assembled. It has taken more than two years, and over £6000 to stage, but both time and money have been wisely spent. When I visited the exhibition in the middle of the week a steady stream of people of all ages was moving four deep slowly from painting to painting. It was, for Australia, the rare spectacle of a populace engaged upon understanding and enjoying a master.

The exhibition will remain open throughout August, and it looks as though Sunday afternoon at the Sydney Gallery during the next four weeks will be like Sunday afternoon at the Louvre in late summer. The response to the exhibition is a remarkable tribute to an artist widely regarded as the finest the country has produced.

The exhibition itself provides further evidence of Mr Hal Missingham's capacity to present exhibitions of a new kind in this country. I mean the kind of exhibition which takes many months to prepare, is mindful of the deeper currents of public interest, and advances, by careful presentation and adequate cataloguing, the real understanding of an artist while providing a display of high aesthetic quality which can be enjoyed by all of normal intelligence and sensibility.

There are weaknesses in hanging and presentation; there are inaccuracies in the catalogue. A few more rooms would have made for a less cramped display and catered better for the crowds. The separation of the artist's work into categories—portraiture, the figure and landscapes—has little to commend it.

First published in the *Age*, Melbourne, 1 August 1964.

If all the works had been brought together according to a plan which revealed the artist's development from year to year and was applied loosely enough to satisfy the aesthetic requirements of presentation, a more wholly satisfying exhibition would have been mounted. To gain a real understanding of an artist's development and total achievement is, after all, the great objective of a retrospective exhibition.

Despite these weaknesses the arrangement is sufficiently good to provide a better general picture of Dobell's development than has hitherto been possible. But the specialist rash enough to be interested in, say, the relation of Dobell's portraits and landscapes at each stage of his development will be involved in miles of extra walking from room to room because of the categorial presentation.

Even so, the whole exhibition is so much better than anything we can normally expect in this country that one hesitates to criticize points of detail for fear of detracting from the unquestionable achievement. The Adelaide Festival, for example, though very well hung, achieved nothing like the same standard of cataloguing.

And when the National Gallery of Victoria—or is the correct title now the National Gallery in Victoria?—next stages an exhibition with the same degree of professional competence we shall have to hang a garland of forget-me-nots around the neck of Jeanne d'Arc or fly a pennant of rosemary from the tower-to-be of the new Cultural Centre. The trustees of the gallery have, however, shown good sense in acquiring recently (though somewhat late in the day) the best version of the several fine portraits of Helena Rubenstein.

To coincide with the exhibition, Thames and Hudson have produced a lavishly illustrated monograph written by James Gleeson. It contains 32 colour plates (of uneven quality) and 118 black and white illustrations. Gleeson's text is admirably lucid, often quite penetrating in its perception, and is always closely related to the paintings under discussion, so that his words, instead of becoming rhetoric, assist us to understand and enjoy.

His consideration, for example, of that little early Dobell masterpiece, the *Dead Landlord*—the painting around which Patrick White wrote his play *The Ham Funeral*—is most illuminating:

The picture rings with clear echoes. The curving rail at the foot of the bed repeats the curve of the mirror above the fireplace. With a touch of strange humor the sprightly bow of the pyjama cord, perched like an insect on the dead man's stomach, mocks the formal tidiness of carved gilt bows on the top of the mirror. The lines of the pillow ape the woman's curving buttocks.

Even the clock on the mantelpiece and the bedhead are first cousins. Everything is precisely calculated and placed according to a classic formula. He uses tight reins to hold the mood in check.

By extraordinary insight amounting almost to an identification with the woman's state of mind, he has felt that only the strictest controls could prevent a collapse into hysteria. How clearly the composition echoes the woman's feelings!

Its artificial formality is a pictorial counterpart of the instinct that urges the woman to brush her hair. They both represent a desperately forced attempt to hold on to normality in a situation that could easily get out of hand.

Dobell's gift for finding the right mode of expression for each subject he paints is well discussed by Gleeson. And it is marvellously revealed by the exhibition.

To trace the emergence of the artist's original genius from the exquisite tight-grained Constable-like landscapes, such as *Village in Somerset,* painted in 1930, through to dark, leaping forms of the *Mural for the Savarin Restaurant* of 1947 is alone a delight worth a visit to Sydney.

Yet Dobell remains a major problem for most Australian critics. They respond readily enough to the quality of his work, but the work itself challenges deeply cherished beliefs. So critics hasten to explain that he is not a modern artist, that he belongs more to the nineteenth century than the twentieth, that his work has had little effect upon Australian art. A close study of the situation will, I believe, reveal all these assumptions, in good time, to be false.

Gleeson succumbs to the same generalizations, so that his criticism, despite its penetration and sensibility where individual works are concerned, fails to elucidate the quality of Dobell's achievement as a whole and for its time. The failure comes from trying to fit Dobell's work into an essentially nineteenth-century view of history which personifies the historical process as a time-spirit or *Zeitgeist.* This leads him to assert with confidence at the very beginning of his book that Dobell's 'contribution is of a kind that will not affect the subsequent course of art'.

Against such confident assertions the history of art provides many warnings. There is the case, for example, of Federico Zuccaro, who flourished in the second half of the sixteenth century. Zuccaro inherited a 'modernistic' tradition of mannerism which for over fifty years had stressed the importance for the artist of responding to the 'inner vision' rather than to the external stimuli of the every-day world. How easy it was then for Federico to scorn the art of his contemporary, Caravaggio, as painting in a naturalistic manner which was then, as Federico thought, so hopelessly out of fashion. And yet the future lay not with Federico's late mannerism, but with Caravaggio, whose revolutionary art pointed towards a path which the greatest masters of the seventeenth century, Velasquez, Rubens and Rembrandt, were to follow.

The point of this historical parallel is that Caravaggio's sixteenth-century naturalism was not the same as fifteenth-century naturalism, and one of the tasks of criticism is to discover and understand the differences.

Similarly with Dobell. It is not enough to point to his resemblances to Dickens, Goya and Soutine, nor to point to possible sources of his inspiration, such as that of Bronzino operating first through the portraiture of Lambert. It is, rather, to elucidate the peculiar quality of his achievement, to show how it differs from the achievement of Dickins, Goya and Soutine. Because it does, and it is this difference which makes it modern, makes it of our time, and yet not only of our time. But such an elucidation cannot be undertaken while critics approach Dobell's art prejudiced by notions such as 'the spirit of the time' and 'the avant-garde', for these are little more than personifications with which the cunning cloak their own particular choices and fancies.

Dobell's art is often uneven and sometimes embarrassingly ragged, but the best of it possesses the authority and presence of the masters. The exhibition will help us to appreciate this better in Australia. The Thames and Hudson monograph should help to make it better known abroad.

36

Jean Bellette

—1964—

Jean Bellette's exhibition at the South Yarra Gallery should lift the heart and rouse the spirit of all who love good paintings. I cannot recall an exhibition in Melbourne of this quality since I began to write this column.

It is, in the first place, from a technical point of view, painting of immense authority. The lessons of the great classicists, of the painters' painters, Giotto, Masaccio, Poussin and Cézanne have been learned. That is to say, there is expressive force and power here to an unusual degree but, more importantly, there is always control, genuine pictorial control. This is not painting trying to be literature, or trying to be music, or trying to be the twentieth century, but painting employing the full resources of the art and, again and again, succeeding.

Jean Bellette was born in Tasmania, but this landscape is Mediterranean and the vision is classical. It is, however, a classicism which does not lie along the surface of the mind but has been torn out of the heart. The land is time-worn and exhausted, borne down with yielding its vines, olives, almonds and corn; and every root and rock surprises some threatening archaic presence. The mood is heroic and melancholic: the gods are dead and man is dying. The superbly painted pictures, which recall at times the deft and sculptural authority of Daumier, act out their parts with slow grandeur and elaborate rhetorical gesture. But they tell no story; the narrative is frozen into a timeless icon.

There are many passages of pure virtuoso painting, such as the two magnificent acolytes in that memorable painting *Eastern Procession, Palma*. And on either side of them there are other figures, painted with a combination of command and sensitivity that is quite breathtaking.

First published in the *Age*, Melbourne, 19 August 1964.

Jean Bellette, *Acheron, c.*1944, oil on paper on board, 31.7 × 41.3 cm. The Joseph Brown Collection.

Jean Bellette, of course, had a considerable reputation before she left Sydney with her husband, the artist and critic Paul Haefliger, but these paintings are of a quality never reached by her Australian work. Her brushwork and colour are now far more free, far more capable of indicating subtle transitions and delicate passages between figure and figure, and figure and landscape. Her paintings Electra II (and Acheron *c.*1944) are remarkable examples of this, figures, buildings and landscape all being interlocked with great subtlety. In such paintings we become aware that metamorphosis is not a fashionable trick, but a vision of life well known to the ancients.

This exhibition also reminds us that the Mediterranean and its classical language, contrary to all the theories of the self-expression pundits, continues to liberate Australian artists from the poverty of pure self. In recent years, even in recent months, Sidney Nolan, Arthur Boyd, James Gleeson, Leonard French, have all drawn in their own personal way upon the heritage of ancient

Greece. Why it seems to mean more to Australian artists than
to their European (except some Italian sculptors) and American
contemporaries is a difficult question. But it is one of the questions
worth asking.

37
Mike Brown
—1964—

Originality is an elusive and capricious virtue, and harder than ever to find today in the visual arts with everybody so formidably equipped to search for it. But I would say without hesitation that Michael Brown's show at the Museum of Modern Art is the most original Melbourne has seen this year.

It is not, of course, an exhibition like Jean Bellette's, in which a personal style reached a masterly maturity after years of development, but a show in which it is possible to feel the present as something active and alive.

Brown is not unknown to Melbourne. In 1962 his work appeared at the Museum, together with that of Colin Lanceley and Ross Crothall in the Annandale Imitation Realist Exhibition, the exhibition which for all practical purposes introduced pop art to Australia. Later he came into the news when his painting *Mary Lou* was accepted and then rejected from an exhibition sponsored by the Commonwealth government to tour Europe. More recently he flew a kite in a Young Contemporaries Exhibition in which he castigated most of the critics and many of his fellow Sydney artists. Now he has brought that kite to Melbourne.

All this might well suggest a young man making a disturbance in order to become known. This explanation will suit those who endeavour to interpret every new movement, every new talent as a kind of conspiracy. But it just will not explain Brown's art at all. He means it.

The paintings are bright, flat, posterish and apparently naive; and they are as bracing as a fresh wind on a spring day. Brown's art, and his thinking, have embarked upon an exciting journey towards simplicity. And he has had the courage to write an

First published in the *Age*, Melbourne, 14 October 1964.

Mike Brown, *Mary Lou as Miss Universe*, 1964, mixed media on plywood,
84.0 × 48.0 cm. Destroyed by artist, 1970.

introduction to his catalogue which states a position without ambiguity, mystification or paradox. The paintings possess a similar clarity. Purely as paintings they possess without exception a bright, showy radiance; but behind the radiance there is a mind prepared to satirize, burlesque, and scarify. Gently at times, not too gently at other times.

The strength of Brown's art lies not in his adoption of a prepared moral position but in the highly skilful use of innocence. This calculated innocence ranges from the lyrical immediacy of such delightful hard-edge works as *Sunrise Through my Window* to the hilarious devilry of the *Pleasures of Smoking*—the poster to end all smoking posters. It is an innocence which Brown has had to fight for, and learn how to use. This is what distinguishes his work from most avant-garde painting in Australia today. A personal voice is beginning to come through. And a personal voice is better than echoes.

38
Sam Fullbrook
—1964—

Marked improvement is seen in the work of Sam Fullbrook (South Yarra) since his last exhibition. Colour is more sensitive, construction more assured. The poster-like awkwardness of the earlier paintings is gone.

Fullbrook draws his inspiration from the interior: its landscapes and peoples. But he is aware that the images of Drysdale and Nolan have become visual clichés, as have the earlier images of Streeton and Heysen. So he has put droughts, carcases and monolithic Aborigines to one side, seeking a more personal approach through colour.

It is almost as if Fullbrook were seeking to emphasize the truth of a remark made by the literary critic A. G. Stephens at the turn of the century. Stephens, at that time combating the melancholy and melodrama which writers like Marcus Clarke and Adam Lindsay Gordon had brought to the interpretation of Australian nature, turned away from the flood, fire and famine school and invoked, instead, the intimate and refined poetry of Verlaine. 'Verlaine's cult of faded things,' wrote Stephens, 'extolling the hinted hue before the gross color finds a natural home in Australia—in many aspects a land of faded things—of delicate purples, delicious greys and dull dreamy olives and ochres'.

Fullbrook's paintings are a fine illustration of Stephens' point of view, and when we recall how much in common Nolan and Drysdale have with Clarke and Gordon, the paintings become even more interesting.

The wheel of vision turns more quickly than the axle of environment.

First published in the *Age*, Melbourne, 28 October 1964.

39
John Brack
—1965—

John Brack is one of the best-known artists in Australia. But he works slowly and exhibits rarely.

His current show is certainly his best yet, so that Gallery A has wisely decided to keep it open until 1 May; a genuine tribute in these days of quick reputations and ready sales, to an artist whose originality is unquestionable.

The first point to be stressed is that the paintings are extraordinarily well made, abstractly and structurally self-sufficient and at ease with themselves. Which is, I believe, an advance on his earlier work. In those the formal elements were so tensed towards their expressive purpose that they became anonymous. Here structure is relaxed sufficiently to act as a foil to the artists' mordant perception. Beauty just manages to escape, screaming down the back stairs, though pressed to within an inch of her life.

It is to be noted, for example, that the scissors which recur in so many of his paintings are executed with exquisite brushwork and colour; blue-green, rose, purple, against olive. The painting continues to glow even when the image consumes.

The position from which the artist approaches life has changed also, moving from the confident position of the satirist to a closer personal identity with the bathos of daily living. In his well-known *5 o'clock Collins Street* he is observing the fatuity of other lives; in this exhibition he is much more involved with the fatuity of his own. The normal self-confidence of the satirist has gone. The imagery is deliberately banal, a microcosm of scissors and rubber surgical instruments, artificial limbs, wheelchairs and tailors' dummies. In another part of the city Brack's scissors

First published in the *Age*, Melbourne, 13 March 1965.

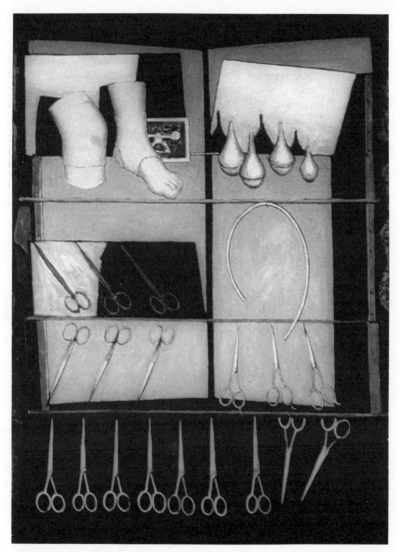

John Brack, *Still Life with Self Portrait*, 1963, oil on canvas, 149.2 × 78.6 cm. Private collection.

might well win a prize for industrial design; here they confront us blandly as the sterilized and efficient symbols of a half-sterilized world.

The artist is always there in the picture, separated from pain and mutilation only by a glass window. Wheelchairs, transfigured by blue and crimson lights almost supernatural in their radiance, spread their arms to embrace him tenderly and passionately. But he leaves them, dejected that his own vision can offer less comfort.

Matisse wanted his art to be as comforting as an armchair. Brack's art is about as comforting as an operating theatre. But it is a thoroughly contemporary and adult art in a world in which far too many artists are playing the phoney game of being fake children.

40

Gareth Sansom

—1965—

Gareth Sansom's paintings (South Yarra) are deeply involved with the social and sexual lives of pederasts and transvestites. They are, therefore, this country being what it is, acts both of provocation and courage.

Australian artists, when they have concerned themselves with sex at all, have confined their interests largely to the more common forms of that widespread activity. Even this has presented problems. Back in the late 1870s those grand old men of Australian art, Tom Roberts and Douglas Richardson, were temporarily dismissed from the Gallery School for demanding the establishment of one of those pits of corruption, the life class.

True, things have changed a little since those days. But most Australian artists, frontiersmen to a man, have preferred a ruggedly masculine view of sex to immersion in the deeper sensualities. They could take Norman Lindsay but not Charles Conder. There was, they said, something unhealthy about him.

Indeed it was Norman Lindsay, the wowser-killer, who was the local expert in these matters. In 1912 Lindsay came back from Paris to inform the readers of the *Lone Hand* that more female couples danced together at the Bal Tabarin than couples of 'assorted sexes'. But it was all done, he assured them, to charm the males, only another example of Parisian innocence. But the innocence was all Lindsay's, with his view of sex as a creative detergent, a kind of purifying fun.

That it is much more difficult for Sansom his paintings bear witness. Anyone who takes homosexuality for a subject must find an aesthetic position from which he can paint without conveying the impression that he is moralizing, acting as a licensed voyeur

---

First published in the *Age*, Melbourne, 21 April 1965.

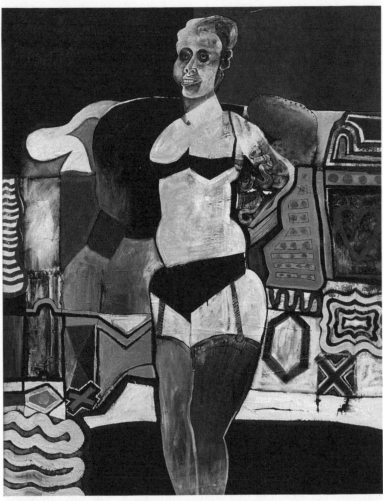

Gareth Sansom, *The Blue Masked Transvestite*, 1964, oil and enamel on board, 166.0 × 135.5 cm. The artist.

for art lovers, or indulging in self-pity over the memory of a lost innocence.

The subject is so emotionally explosive that it leaves little room for the artist to move safely: an inch one way and he becomes a moralist dispensing the Wolfenden Report, an inch the other way and he becomes another kind of moralist reluctantly uncovering sinks of iniquity.

True, in the *Phaedrus* Plato succeeded in taking homosexuality and wringing from it everything from sadistic aggression to divine love. But then he knew very well where he stood in relation to his subject.

Sansom reveals less certainty. But the effort to come to grips with a difficult subject has been worth it. By means of a vigorous, at times brilliant, palette and by cubist, collage and pop-art devices he has created a series of challenging paintings. Perhaps the *Blue Masked Transvestite* is the best; firmly drawn, convincingly painted.

Altogether an important exhibition by a talented young painter. If there is a weakness it lies, in my view, in the ambiguities which lead too often to a confusing rather than to an enriching of the expression. This is probably due to the fact that Sansom clearly wants to say something in paint about the nature of homosexuality, but is not at all certain what it is that he wants to say. Perhaps we should be thankful that anyone wants to say anything at all in this good-thinking city.

41
Kevin O'Connor
—1965—

Kevin Connor has wrestled more vigorously and committed himself more completely to a figurative art than any other Australian painter of his generation. His painting remains pure in the sense that he does not seek to contract out of the central problems of painting by resort to collage, assemblage and similar quasi-pictorial devices. Painting is here seen very much as the significant image expressed in the terms of brush, plane surface and paint.

Connor works on white grounds, painting primal areas and dominant motifs into them while they are still viscid, by means of long, dragging glazes of scumbled and translucent colour, which have been given elasticity and fluency by dammar resins. All this is traditional enough. But it works.

It gives his preference for the red-purples and acid-greens resonant luminosity. The stark and grotesque presences are transmuted by the radiance of the paint and the growing mastery and control of the brushwork. A particularly fine example is the small nude (38), in which flecks of crimson animate the pellucid flesh tones of mauve, pink and rose.

Connor's work is significant in another way. It is assimilating both local and overseas experience. The quotations from such artists as Bacon and Kokoschka are still a little obvious, but have clearly been of the greatest importance to the artist's development.

His links with recent contemporary Australian painting are strong, but depend less upon individuals.

Only when artists begin to draw upon national roots as well as the so-called international tradition, do they cease to be provincial. One of the reasons so much of the work in Australia which derives its inspiration predominantly from overseas sources, looks

---

First published in the *Age*, Melbourne, 28 April 1965.

tired and second-rate is that overseas art is still accessible here largely through reproductions, whereas local work carries, at least, the full impact of the original. And inspiration through pictorial reproductions, though always important, proceeds more effectively at the level of ideas and image than at the level of technique and material.

42
Andrew Sibley
—1965—

It is sometimes claimed that the decision between figurative and abstract is no longer relevant to contemporary Australian painting. Those who make such claims either do not visit the galleries or are incapable of interpreting what is going on in the pictures.

For there is most certainly an intense struggle between the claims of figure and form, which is more central to painting here today than, say, the exploitation of accident or the exploration of optical ambiguities and conundrums. Indeed, so central that artists prefer not to talk about it.

These comments are prompted by Andrew Sibley's fine exhibition at Georges. The feeling of intensity, of personal involvement, of the brush speaking lucidly for the man, is achieved here because Sibley has kept his art directed towards that burning point of the imagination where form and meaning wrestle.

Sibley's paintings are intensely calligraphic, saturated with high-keyed refulgent colours yet economical of line and mass. They remind one of the spirit of Matisse at times, but not irritatingly, and are more ecstatic and less epicurean in their sensuousness than Matisse.

The paintings are structured by means of a sensitive but vigorous calligraphy of scarlet brushwork to which lambent masses of floating colour are attached. But this is not colour disembodied; it brings with it the authority of memory and experience.

Union and acceptance, rejection and isolation are problems at once pictorial and human. And Sibley's art still seeks an adequate symbol for both in the processes of painting. In this way it reaches beyond mere cleverness and the flaccid unities of decoration.

First published in the *Age*, Melbourne, 19 May 1965.

Andrew Sibley, *Bound*, 1965, oil on canvas, 68.5 × 63.5 cm. Private collection.

43
John Perceval
—1965—

John Perceval at his best is the master of an expressive arabesque which brings delight in colour, light and flesh to a tremulous danger-point of ecstasy and hysteria.

The English mists and damps, represented in his current exhibition at the South Yarra Gallery by four Hampstead paintings in dulled greens and black and depressing horizontal hatchings, lit only by flickers of orange and red, have introduced a leaden and ominous echo into his *oeuvre*.

The Kathy and Aspendale paintings, however, return to subjects which he had made his own before leaving Australia. The first group assail the pictorial problem of painting the nude—usually with a mirror—in highly lit and multi-coloured interiors with an expressionistic vigour which rises to the melting point where the image liquifies into pure, heavily encrusted paint. When he successfully brings them off, his paintings of nudes become bouquets bursting into a multi-coloured radiance of flowers and petals. But it must be admitted that he often has difficulty in relating the figure to the whole painting. Too often the expressive energy disintegrates the painting. Of the Kathy group it is the small painting (no. 6), pink, salmon, yellow and white, in ceramic richness against a plain orange-red ground, wherein the pictorial problem, native to this kind of art, is most fully resolved.

But by far the finest painting in the show is the *Yellow Boat at Aspendale*. Here the alla prima slashings of paint are right on target—a radiant and ecstatic vision of yachts, sand, sky and sunshine achieved in a breathless moment in which we see Perceval again at his best.

First published in the *Age*, Melbourne, 21 July 1965.

44
Donald Friend
—1965—

Donald Friend's exhibition at Gallery A would be a refreshing experience if it were only for the chance to look at good drawing again and see modest prices plainly set down on the catalogue. But there is more to it than that. His gallery of fun pieces, to begin with, his Australian-way-of-life ready-mades; it would be humorless indeed to ask him to stop that side of his art—as insensitive as handing over Edna Everage to Professor Higgins.

The best of the work, however, consists of figure compositions utilizing three or four nudes beautifully drawn and composed on backgrounds of free, luminous washes of colour.

Over the years Friend's drawing has become a personal language which responds subtly to his intentions and intuitions. In *Puppeteers* (5), for example, the blue, sepia and sanguine contours embody a world poised delicately between reality, wit, and fantasy.

There is nothing in this show but which reveals Friend's wit, intelligence, skill and sensuality.

His art has been compared to that of the mannerists, but it has little in common with that neurotic, guilt-ridden age. His kinship rather is with Praxiteles, the Donatello of the Cantoria, the young Michelangelo, and Titian. There is a very quiet centre to his art, and his satire is aimed at those who would separate him from it. It is Apollonian, sensual, instinctively but not intellectually classical.

Norman Lindsay's drawings excited him as a youth and, despite the obvious differences in temperament and outlook, Friend has to a considerable degree enacted in his art and life what Lindsay talked of, wrote and dreamed about. Running through the art of Lindsay, Friend and Olsen, then, is a firm thread of primitivism

First published in the *Age*, Melbourne, 27 July 1965.

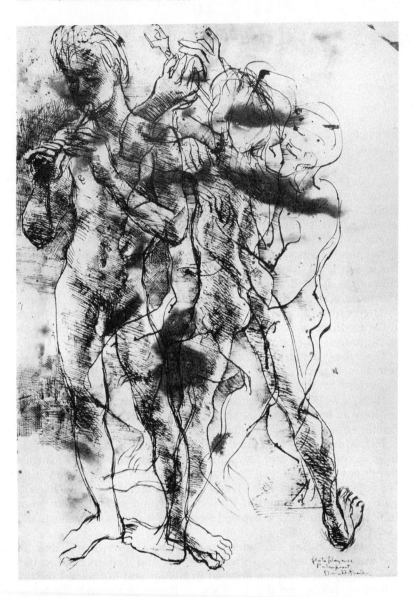

Donald Friend, *Flute Players palimpsest*, c.1965, pen and wash drawing. Private collection.

and vitalism which is not uncharacteristic of art in Sydney in general and has given it a certain continuity. The sources are not so much in the climate as the artistic tradition.

Yet Friend's art is complex, avoids easy simplifications. Of the generation who began to exhibit around 1940 he seems today better equipped than any to stay the distance and produce his best work towards the end of his life, because he has avoided becoming an institution, given few hostages to fortune, and retained a healthy fear of fame. A not-so-young artist still worth watching.

45

Arthur Boyd

—1965—

At the Australian Galleries the vitality of Arthur Boyd's work continues unabated. The faltering and weariness of the artist in middle age is not here. The imagination still transforms; the challenge of a different medium still delights and refreshes both artist and beholder.

A voracious curiosity about the possibilities of untried materials helps to sustain him. It has always been there from his early experiments with oil and tempera to ceramics in all its forms: as pottery, as painting, and as sculpture, to his recent brilliant series of etchings. Now it is pastel.

And as soon as he takes to a new medium his own voice is heard. He is never dominated by traditional procedures so that the artist is submerged by the craftsman; yet he respects the innate character of materials, not forcing, rupturing and breaking them in an angry effort to induce them to express what they cannot naturally express. So that Boyd the pastellist speaks to us with the same authority and tenderness as Boyd the painter, sculptor and etcher. It is an achievement in range and virtuosity which few have equalled in this country, none surpassed.

The present exhibition is devoted largely to a recreation, within the artist's own symbolic language of forms, of the story of St Francis of Assisi. It is a narrative cycle which comes easily, almost inevitably, to the artist.

It is no exaggeration to say that, where most of his generation have chosen anger, anger with the society which is not good enough for them or anger with the materials with which they work, slashing and destroying in a petulant or apocalyptic impatience and disgust with the idiocy and futility of life, Boyd has

---

First published in the *Age*, Melbourne, 28 July 1965.

chosen to be gentle. Or, perhaps, I should say that for him there was no choice, no other way. Gentle without being genteel. Man is a beast, and like the beasts, good. Evil is an aberration. For Boyd there is something holy at the centre of life which he refuses to kick in the guts in order to assert the power and freedom of his legs.

St Francis, naked and defenceless, embraces the lepers and the wolf of Gubbio. In the confrontation identity is lost.

Boyd's art today is mature enough to give tongue to this language of holiness wherein the simple ceases to be naive and becomes eloquent at all levels: in the eyes, the gesture of hands, the clumsy misshapen bodies of the saint and his brother disciples, and in the transforming touch of the chalk upon the paper.

Boyd's work has one thing in common with the best and most characteristic Australian art and literature of his generation: it is based upon a discursive mode. It takes up a traditional theme and impresses it into new service. The retention of traditional form, the exploration of myth, legend and allegory has much in common with the poetry of A. D. Hope; the metamorphosis of the good in its defenceless immersion in evil brings him close to Patrick White.

Needless to say there are differences; but perhaps the kinship is more important than the differences. Because the reassertion of moral imperatives within symbolic form has given some artists and writers here an old and deep well to draw from.

That is why Boyd's art continues to command respect without needing to be propped up with highly publicized jaunts to the South Pole or visits to Timor heroically perched upon the top of an oil drum. Undoubtedly it is one of the most important exhibitions of the year.

46
Ian Fairweather
—1965—

The Ian Fairweather retrospective exhibition assembled by the Queensland Art Gallery, now showing at the National Gallery, provides a rare opportunity to enjoy the art of one of the most naturally gifted artists at work in Australia today.

Now seventy-four, Fairweather, the son of an officer in the Indian army, studied art at the Slade, and Chinese at the School of Oriental Studies, after release from a prison camp at the end of the First World War. Since then he has lived and worked in Canada, China, Indonesia and Australia.

The exhibition covers some thirty years of his association with Australia. It reveals him as a master of the arabesque and a colourist of unusual sensitivity. It is an art of beautifully interlaced linear rhythms and matt surfaces; the colours blond yet earthy; chocolate-browns, ochres, dull pinks and warm greys, with much use of lacunae to keep the surfaces open and vibrant.

The titles of Fairweather's paintings matter. He has genuine themes and he realizes them. His paintings are visual equivalents which present the idea in a new and original way, often quite ravishing in its unity and clarity.

In *Mangrove* (51) a spiky black tangle of interlace is set against a ground of pale cream mud; in *Raindrops* (61) lines curl and wilt in liquefaction; in *Epiphany* (55) the design recalls Chartres glass, the gothic woodcut, and the squat fetish forms of West African sculpture, but the result is masterly. And this is only to mention some typical paintings, rather than select the best. We do not often see an exhibition of this quality.

Fairweather is one of those happy people who has succeeded in creating a wholly personal style from the idiom of twentieth-century art. It is useless to trace influences here. Most of the

---

First published in the *Age*, Melbourne, 15 September 1965.

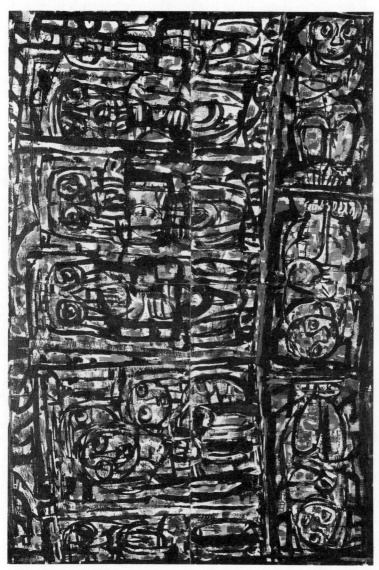

Ian Fairweather, *Epiphany*, 1962, polymer paint on board, 139.6 × 203.2 cm.
Queensland Art Gallery.

twentieth-century masters of flat pattern and arabesque from Matisse to Pollock are involved and, of course, Africa and the East. It is an art complete in itself; and to criticize it is to criticize a type of sensibility, or a period style for its inadequacy, like criticizing the rococo. But some will, I believe, rightly see an inadequacy in the fluency and easy perfection (yet distilled from a lifetime's absolute dedication to his art) of these visual melodies. That is to say it is a late art which makes magnificent use of proven ground; not the work of a man who works at the frontiers of vision, or even of sensibility.

A better painter surely than the American Mark Tobey, whom he in some ways resembles, Fairweather is a kind of latter-day Gauguin; a man for whom China is still Cathay; a beachcomber is search of the Terrestrial Paradise, and who has found it, almost, on Bribie Island. A good man who still believes in the noble savage, in Buddhists before they incinerated themselves in sacrifice to the western god, Nationalism. In short, an art which for all its lyrical beauty is at heart somewhat escapist, a trifle sentimental. Not the kind of art to withstand Cézanne's withering comment: 'Gauguin was not an artist, only a painter of Chinese images'.

But that is to invoke a standard which only a few pathfinders can possibly face. If Fairweather is a little lower than such angels his life's work does reveal a sensibility rare in this, and in most, countries.

47
Sidney Nolan
—1965—

There are some fine paintings in Sidney Nolan's exhibition at the Australian Galleries but the show as a whole is disappointing.

Nolan's imagination seems to falter when confronted by the spectacle of virgin nature: desert, jungle or Antarctic waste. A painter of heroes and myth, his landscape functions best as a background to myth. But landscape untramelled by man or hero troubles him. He either forces it into over-expressive gestures, as in this exhibition, or reproduces it with passive realism from unusual angles, as in the Australian desert paintings of 1949–50.

Many of the paintings do little to enhance Nolan's reputation. *Icebound Ship* (2) retains something of the folksiness, but little of the lyrical immediacy, of Nolan's early work. *Explorer and Pony* (12) over-exploits a somewhat hackneyed image. Far too many of the landscapes, despite the initial visual impact of their hard blue and white surfaces, are unhappy combinations of illusionistic tonalism and expressionistic techniques. An integrated and personal image just does not emerge. Perhaps it is the result of seeing too much too briefly, a kind of picturesque expressionism which does not penetrate beneath the surface.

The exhibition is redeemed by some of the explorer paintings. The reappearance of the hero figure gives Nolan's paintings some coherence. He presents us with a kind of Voss figure of the explorer driving himself stubbornly into a cold, black waste of nothing. There are several memorable and effective images. But even here one feels that Nolan is exploiting a stock image rather than creating one as genuinely personal as his Kelly, his Mrs Fraser, his Leda and the Swan and his Gallipoli paintings.

Occasionally, however, the old magic comes through. The deft

First published in the *Age*, Melbourne, 22 September 1965.

mastery with which Nolan has painted the explorer's flag in *Camp* (11) is a splendid example of the way in which he can make use of the ambiguous symbol while relating it indissolubly to the act of painting. Such passages of pure painting do much to cheer one through an otherwise disappointing show.

48
Edwin Tanner
—1965—

Much contemporary art concerns itself with asking aesthetic questions. That and little more. Much is best understood as diagrams for textbooks in aesthetics.

Optical painting, for instance, directs its attention to relations between colour and space, and asks: What aesthetic status shall we give to those spatial ambiguities which colour and shape, by their very nature, create?

Edwin Tanner (South Yarra) is such a composer of aesthetic riddles; a philosophical carpenter and joiner who designs neat problems for lookers. He is preoccupied with the problem of mark and meaning. How do marks become signs having meanings? It is all very dry, bright, exceedingly well made and cerebral. References tend to be obscure, erudite. Two paintings entitled *Dark Ages* and *Middle Ages* look like the cosmological diagrams of Ramon Lull. Or he affects a wry humour, feeding his engineering colleagues gently into their computers or constructing teaching aids for Wittgensteinians.

Tanner is certainly an unusual artist and an original one. His weakness, it seems, is in his cleverness, his propensity to be arch, his patent scepticism about symbolic communication. Occasionally he ceases taking the mickey out of meaning and works more traditionally. In one painting little pearl shirt buttons become the eyes of the dead peering from their graves (spaced with Tanner's precision). This is an effective work inspired by Prospero's speech on the power of his magic, and one of his few paintings which does not carry a suppressed snigger.

Yet Tanner is a significant artist who should be better known. He is an artist for those who still think and argue about the nature

First published in the *Age*, Melbourne, 24 November 1965.

of painting in these art-dealing, art-loving, art-wallowing days.

But he is no cosmetician. So it is not surprising that several of these works were hidden in a dull corner upon the occasion of Sydney's last big cosmetics prize.

49

Rapotec, Rose and Gleghorn

—1965—

Gallery A is showing an exhibition, small, modest and catalogue-less, of the work of three Sydney painters: Stan Rapotec, William Rose and Tom Gleghorn.

There is a period flavour about it, and it is difficult to avoid the conclusion that the work of all three was more challenging in the mid-1950s than it is today in the mid-1960s.

Of the three, Rapotec has certainly achieved a kind of completeness; his work has an air of unity and finality about it. For him neither problems of pure colour nor problems relating to the figurative image have any importance. He limits his art to tonal construction, freely but effectively ordered by means of brushwork gestures. What you might call an apotheosis of finger-painting.

Rapotec's art is often said to symbolize tension. But these strokes and whorls of dark paint are all too deftly placed, too exquisitely adjusted to the pictorial space to become telling symbols of tension.

The weakness may well be in abstract paintings itself. Tension seems to bleach out of it with the years. When I first saw Jackson Pollocks in the Biennale of 1950 they all looked tense enough. But when I saw them again in American museums in 1962 they were beginning to look like wallpaper designs after nature.

And Rapotec's paintings, it must be admitted, look uncommonly well as handsome, demure, and restful backgrounds to teak furniture in modern architectural settings. Quite an achievement really; but more an achievement in decoration than expression.

William Rose paints open, spidery patterns, radiating and rather geometrical, in blue, white and yellow upon pale, flat grounds. He calls them—invoking the musical analogy all too common since Kandinsky—symphonic paintings.

First published in the *Age*, Melbourne, 1 December 1965.

Rose's work in its slim, precise way possesses a kind of drawing-board charm. But access to his art has not been assisted by his admirers. His work as a student and young artist was so patently and obviously inspired by the work of the Portuguese painter Maria Vieira da Silva that for some strange reason they have felt it necessary to adopt a curious critical device with a murky history. Rose's work, his champions assure us, is utterly unlike that of Vieira de Silva. They protest too much.

To the extent that Rose's symphonies are simply a 'sounding together' of colours and shapes he is only invoking qualities similar in music and painting. But they cannot recreate the experience of music or effectively symbolize it.

Indeed the results obtained by those who have sought to make painting adopt the aesthetics of music have, for the most part, been so disappointing that it is wondrous to find so many artists still fascinated by this late-nineteenth-century ideal. Painting, surely, should aspire to its own conditions, which are not the conditions of music or of architecture. And in this show it is Rose's large (and nameless) painting that invokes visual rather than auditory associations, which is the most effective.

Tom Gleghorn's *Epitaph for Spanish Lovers* combines an interest in allegory with landscape motifs and textural devices painted in acid green, crimson and deep red-browns. An ambitious and melodramatic painting, which none the less faces pictorial problems of tone, texture, colour, symbol and image squarely instead of avoiding them by omission.

His semi-abstract landscape themes are less successful, and I cannot help feeling that Gleghorn's art loses a certain vitality when he turns from the human figure to landscape as a source for his compositions.

50

Art from Czechoslovakia

—1966—

The exhibition from Czechoslovakia at the Argus Galleries is well worth a visit if only because we see so little visual art here from eastern Europe. But one should not expect too much.

It is a modest exhibition. Half consists of small-sized graphics, drawings and gouache paintings chosen, one suspects, partly because they present no major problems in packing and transporting and partly because many might be expected to command some market among former Czech nationals in Australia.

With these reservations in mind and remembering that it is not intended to be a representative cross-section of contemporary Czech art, one can succeed in gaining, even if a little indirectly, a glimpse of the existing situation.

Doctrinaire socialist realism is little in evidence. The bricklayer's assistant is no longer climbing up the ladder of progress with the hod of the revolution upon his happy back. Perhaps he slipped and fell. Only two paintings in the show, Baros' *Guitar Player*, a rather drab echo of Picasso's *Guitarist*, and Sutera's *Porter*, a comment on Asian poetry in which colour pulls against mood, invoke the iconography of socialist realism.

The general impression is not so much one of political direction, as a certain timidity, a lack of zest and adventure in the work, despite the fact that it varies from Kunc's functional landscapes to Malich's informal abstractions. One gains no impression of a bouyant Czech market for present-day art, but of painters and patrons content with a slightly old-fashioned and provincial situation. Are pigments, one wonders, so expensive that they must be used with such circumspection?

And yet, within these limitations, there is much that is pleasant

First published in the *Age*, Melbourne, 16 March 1966. (An exhibition organized by Mr O. F. Polasek, Melbourne.)

and sparkling. Nikl's highly abstracted *Red House* against a grey ground, for example, is sensitive both in its colour and spacing; Veselka's *Still Life* possesses the kind of competence one associates here with the George Bell school. Paur shows well-structured linear abstractions derived from townscapes; Gajdusek, a dark and well-designed *Motif* reminiscent of both Gromaire and Léger. By contrast, Malich's essays in informal abstraction possess a tentative and perfunctory air. Perhaps the best abstract work of all is to be found in Hovadik's darkly textured graphics.

Czech humour and good nature make their appearance. Soldier Svejk, of course, is there; a series of colourful children's book illustrations by Fuka; and an uproarious image by Horanek of two lovers.

Prague exiles will experience a flutter of nostalgia for paintings of the Charles Bridge, Manes Café and the little Golden Street. But it seems a pity that Czech painters do not seem to be able any longer to gain inspiration from their own fine medieval masters such as the Master of the Třeboň Altar and the portraits of Master Theodorik.

51
Charles Blackman
—1966—

A slack week has followed the recent concentration of shows around the Moomba and Adelaide festivals. Fortunately it provides an opportunity to discuss Charles Blackman's forthcoming exhibition at the South Yarra Gallery, which opens on Wednesday next and remains on view until 22 April.

No less than a year ago some of us had begun to fear that Blackman had reached those unhappy middle years when the zest for painting so often languishes and an artist is forced to depend upon his accumulated technical and spiritual resources to get by.

The present exhibition shows our fears to have been groundless. It is nothing less than a personal triumph won at a critical stage of the artist's development, and must be numbered among the most original exhibitions I have had to review in these columns.

In the first place it must be stressed that this is a rich and varied exhibition, not simply a few crumbs which have fallen from an expatriate's table. A new group of lithographs is also being shown.

Blackman's art is so evocative and tender in the way it touches upon the intense and yet ineffable moments of experience, that all who write about it are tempted into impressionist criticism, seeking, in bursts of fine writing, to evoke some shadow of what they have experienced before the paintings.

Such writings have value. They can prompt the sluggish to feel with the aid of words what should best be felt without words. Indeed in the hands of poets like Ray Mathew, in his recent book on Blackman, and Barry Humphries, in the catalogue of the present show—his comic mask slipping as he lays his little bunch

---

First published in the *Age*, Melbourne, 23 March 1966.

of gladioli at the feet of his friend—they become the poignant and expressive tributes of poetry to painting: *Ut pictura poesis*.

But the quality of Blackman's achievement lies in a delicate synthesis between picture-making and meaning. At the heart of it there is something desperately simple and desperately human. Blackman's people have learned how to live upon the other side of nothing. The soul reaches out nervously from its dark bed of loneliness in exhausting but never-ending encounters. His art has grown around the desire to elucidate, in contemporary visual terms, more about the nature of these encounters.

In early work he restricted his motifs and shapes with great severity. But from those schoolgirls, dark, blocky and cubic, of the 1950s, he has evolved an expressive vocabulary of gesture and colour which is remarkably flexible and capable of the most subtle nuances of feeling. He has become various without turning from the source of his strength.

A year ago one would not have imagined possible the range of expression which extends from the dramatic and firm umbrous calligraphy of *Thoughts* (13) to the roseate luminosity of *L'Interieur Rouge* (12); from *Park Bench* (4) with its virtuoso brushwork to *Window Shadow* (3) with its dream world of frail presences.

Most typical of all, perhaps, is his *Illusion of Children* (19) in which one can study Blackman's language of pictorial gesture in all its complexity and watch how a sturdy group of youngsters are made to melt, in a passage of symphonic richness and beauty, into the faintest suggestion of a white head and the ghost of a rose-pink hand.

And the miracle is that sentiment does not cling. The paint which is so evocative everywhere continues to work in its own way. Partly, I suppose, because wherever we look we can see Blackman making judicious use of avant-garde experiments.

52
Udo Sellbach
—1966—

Udo Sellbach's series of etchings and aquatints at the Leveson Street Gallery—entitled *The Target is Man*—concerns itself directly with what so many Australians are, at the moment, thinking about: man as sacrificial victim.

Sellbach's etchings gain relevance from the Vietnam War, as Dr Hoff has pointed out, and from the conscription issue. They should hold a special interest for the art lovers of Kooyong.

A few days ago a correspondent of the *Age* wrote: 'The elders of the tribe have decreed it to be expedient that some should die'. That in a way, is Sellbach's theme too. Goya has said it before. Sellbach says it again, yet with a difference. Art is like that: timeless when the timeless issues are in question. Not time's victim. And there is a contemporary edge to this particular piece of moral disgust.

The American artist Kenneth Noland has given currency to 'target' paintings, brilliant concentric coloured circles which contract and dilate as we stare. But Sellbach, like Goya and Picasso in similar situations, has discarded colour and put Noland's targets into another context, using them not to evoke a visual *frisson* but to ask questions.

In Sellbach's eyes man is a target, a target to use, persecute, humble, chain, exhibit, scorn, sacrifice, execute, dump, ignore and forget. These are the very titles of his etchings. Not nice words, but he is not thinking nice thoughts. Indeed he's thinking dangerous thoughts—rocking the boat.

Most philosophers from Plato down, most politicians and priests, detest this sort of thing. Stick to beauty, they advise, and leave morals to us.

First published in the *Age*, Melbourne, 30 March 1966.

Sellbach trained among some of Germany's most important graphic artists and has developed a masterly command of his medium. It is good graphic art, good anti-conscription art; like Goya's.

In the best tradition of etching he is offering both single prints and folio sets.

53
Roger Kemp
—1966—

I doubt whether there is any senior artist permanently resident in Melbourne who is held in greater respect by the artists of the city than Roger Kemp, now showing at Gallery A.

Kemp has always been very much a painter's painter and the growth of his reputation has been remarkably free from the more vulgar forms of publicity so frequently resorted to by dealers and artists alike in the promotion of an artist's public 'image'. Neither his art nor his personality lends itself to the gimmick.

Although he has recently won two of Australia's major art awards, the Georges Invitation Art Prize and the Transfield Prize, Kemp's work has remained largely inaccessible to the art-buying public. His intensity and dedication may be more than they can bear. This is to be regretted, for his limited repertoire of repeated forms is the element from which he has fashioned a pictorial microcosm; a world view traditional, yet very personal in its expression, to the painter himself.

There is one small painting entitled *Greek Drama* which provides a pathway into the meaning of Kemp's art. Small, dispersed figures, classically draped and deftly painted, are gazing away from us, the spectators, towards a dark, red-brown sphere set against the deepest blue. The painting seems to pose Kemp's central metaphysical problem. How can man, Lear's 'bare forkt animal', be harmonized with that perfect geometric form, the sphere? Everywhere in Kemp's painting this problem presents itself: how to relate man to the sphere.

Kemp's art, that is to say, is preoccupied with a problem central to western metaphysics. His paintings may be read as pictorial presentations of problems which occupied Plato and

---

First published in the *Age*, Melbourne, 6 April 1966.

Plotinus, Leonardo and Dürer: how to express man as one function of a Divine Geometry.

Indeed, as one passes around Kemp's exhibition it is possible to find a remarkable parallel with Plato's explanation, in the *Timaeus*, of the origin of man:

First then, the gods, imitating the spherical shape of the universe, enclosed the two divine courses in a spherical body, that, namely, which we now term the head, being the most divine part of us and the lord of all that is in us; to this the gods when they put together the body, gave all the other members to be servants, considering that it must partake of every sort of motion. In order then that it might not tumble about among the high and deep places of the earth, but might be able to get over the one and out of the other, they provided the body to be its vehicle and means of locomotion, which consequently had length and was furnished with four limbs extended and flexible.

Bound always to the cosmic order Kemp's man is at times Icarus, the aspiring humanist; and at times Christ, the crucified God. But whether rising or falling they always seem to remain emanations of the eternal wheel and sphere of things.

Kemp is beginning to express his metaphysic with a greater richness and variety than hitherto. A particularly fine example is *Philosophy*, a dynamic and animated construction in which the lights, with a beautiful feeling for space and placing, give movement and intensity to the rich reds, purples, blues and ochres beneath.

Experience with Orchestration is another splendid painting, magnificently animated around a blue sphere placed off-centre. And at times Kemp will discard his intense red, purple and blue palette for the pale greys and salmon pinks of *Plastic Concept*, or the tender, lyrical surface of *Phantasy*.

There are some excellent drawings which provide a further guide to the nature of the man's work. Taken together, it is an exhibition which hangs well and is of a remarkably even quality.

In the past year or so his style has become free, more painterly, somewhat more relaxed, with greater variety in colour, construction and movement. All this has helped to soften the element of prophetic stridency in his work, rendering it more civilized, but without diminishing its undoubted originality. A painter's painter and a prophet worthy of more honour in his own country. Some of these footnotes to Plato should find their way into our universities, where they would shine much more handsomely than effigies of professors emeriti.

54
Elwyn Lynn
—1967—

The texture paintings by Elwyn Lynn now showing at Kym Bonython's Hungry Horse Gallery, Sydney, reveal a development within a now well-established personal style. Two years ago Lynn's work was more lyrical, that is to say his surfaces were essentially harmonic in their continuities: the colours muted to neutral greys, buffs and red browns; the textures, for the most part evenly wrought, rarely disrupted by intimations of violence. What was evoked, and evocation is close to the heart of this kind of painting, was not only the signs of age but also the signs of continuity. Visual flow was all.

And to some extent it still is; for the basic structure of the style remains. But now there is a greater stiffening of the forms, more compositional thrust, more direct and static confrontation between beholder and image. We are no longer permitted to absorb the pictorial harmonics in peace and accept them as an image of cosmic or human order.

The exhibition testifies to the transition. The 'earlier' manner is present in such paintings as *Charybdis*, *Drift*, *Battle Plan* and *Hungland*. Here the continuities and rhythmical flow dominate the structure. But paintings such as *Shore*, *Mandala*, *Motonaga* and *Sealed Land* confront the beholder square-on, and more statically. Tones are more contrasted, forms more symmetrical. An emblematic, heraldic, at times almost hieratic presence occasionally emerges, as in *Sealed Land*.

One of the effects of the change is to assert more firmly than before the physical existence of the materials and not prevent them from disappearing in an even flow of seductive visual undulations. Lynn builds up his evocative pastes by mixtures of

First published in the *Bulletin*, Sydney, 27 May 1967, p. 40.

plaster, sand, grit, rice-paper and polyvinyl acetate. These are then sun-dried and pressed, kneaded, torn or cut, further texturing being attained by scouring, rubbing and painting to create effects of time akin to 'under-cleaned' paintings.

Textures of this kind create highly evocative surfaces. Such means have been employed of course for their own expressive purposes by Dubuffet, Tapies, Burri and others. And what is evoked, however caried, wayward and apparently irrational it may be, tends to find a focus in the ideas and experiences associated with age. For that which is new and young tends to be smooth, firm-edged and clear; age is corrugated, roughened, textured. Edmund Burke first pointed to the aesthetic effects of the distinction and it still holds, even if a little muddled by the manneristic cosmeticians of today.

Time's cracks and erosions, then, are simulated by these paintings. The sun itself works the changes more delicately, more rhythmically, than where Lynn the artist works directly upon the material. And this metaphor of man as dominator and intruder is surely built into these paintings: in the firm gashes of red which disrupt the gentle nuances of a picture like *Posted* in a manner akin to Burri's bleeding sacks, or in those recurrent little seals in such paintings as *Sealed Land*, which strike one at once as so absurd and so final.

To enlarge upon the evocations of Lynn's paintings will seem highly irrelevant to the purist. But paint is only paint when it is in the pot, can or tube. To paint is to intend to paint; and out of intention, and often despite conscious intention, expressions and meanings emerge which are an inalienable part of the very stuff of painting.

Altogether a handsome exhibition by an accomplished artist.

55
Whither Painting?
—1967—

Some of you will have read the letter published by the artist John Ogburn, in criticism of what he regards as the uncritical enthusiasm with which Sidney Nolan's retrospective exhibition has been received by Sydney's art critics. Now although I have a high regard for Nolan's achievement, which I believe to be considerable, one must admit that it is an eccentric rather than a central achievement in twentieth-century painting. He has, in other words, developed against the grain rather than with it and his achievement may have to be considered in the future as essentially a regional or national achievement. This, certainly, is Ogburn's view:

The greatness of paintings during the last 100 years especially has been the supreme effort made by painters such as Cézanne, Matisse, Picasso, Mondrian, Klee, Pollock, etc. to do just this—to reduce the sentimentality in their painting to a minimum and increase the visual reality of their work to a maximum.

With a minor change, the substitution of the words, say, associational values, or literary values, or symbolic values for the pejorative term 'sentimentality', I would find myself in general agreement with the statement, although I should prefer to describe the central movement in the twentieth century more as a single-minded pursuit of purity for painting, rather than greatness. But what has occurred—the desire to create a purely visual reality—is certainly of central significance for twentieth-century painting.

Mr Ogburn, however, does note that the pursuit of a purely visual painting presents grave difficulties and cites Braque: 'I have never been able to resolve the fact that a painting is a

---

Not previously published. Paper prepared for the Arts Council Weekend, WEA, Newport, 30 September 1967.

self-existent thing with the other fact that it is always about something'.

Now I think we can best approach the question 'Whither Painting?' by coming to grips with this conflict between painting which seeks towards a pure visuality and painting which is associational or referential.

We might begin, if I might use an incongruous medieval metaphor, by drawing a long bow or, shall we say, taking a distant panoramic survey of the situation—from the seventeenth century to the present day. We might compare a Velasquez with a Jackson Pollock. One feature is patently obvious: paintings today look flatter than they did in the seventeenth century. If we go three centuries further back, to the fourteenth century, we again meet with paintings which look flatter, more two-dimensional than those of the seventeenth century. Now, although I can here demonstrate my point with three paintings only, the general point could be backed by an overwhelming mass of visual evidence. There is, we might say, a curve of illusionist painting, with a peak at the height of seventeenth-century baroque painting, and a falling away on either side.

What significance shall we attribute to the curve of illusionism in painting? Shall we view it as a growth, materialization and decay curve? If we take this view we are taking illusionist painting as the painting most characteristic of, or an analogue of, the energy of western society.

It is usual to date this movement towards flatness from the time of Paul Cézanne and the impressionists; yet it can be shown that the movement back to the surface, as we might call it, begins much earlier: for Boucher, though three-dimensional, is at heart more two-dimensional, more decorative, flatter, than Rembrandt and Vermeer. So too is Blake, Goya and Ingres, and even the champion of realism, Gustave Courbet, was accused by contemporary critics of flatness, of making his pictures look like playing cards.

The importance of flatness, of design in two dimensions rather than in illusionistic third dimension lies in its universality. All twentieth-century painting, whether figural or abstract, traditional or avant-garde, tends to be flatter than the art of the past. It is a much more general quality of twentieth-century painting than, for example, abstract or non-representational art.

The historical movement towards flatness is the visual or formal sign of an inner change. The seventeenth-century artist creates a world which, though a visual illusion created by perspective and chiaroscuro, is like the real world; the twentieth-century painter has rejected this self-consistent illusory world and turned picture-making into the making of objects which refer less and less to the world outside their frames. The picture, in other words, has become increasingly an autonomous object, to be seen as it is in itself and not as it refers to any other thing. As Maurice Denis said at the beginning of the century: 'A painting before anything else is a system of tones and colours'.

Now art as three-dimensional illusion has created since the Renaissance a system of categories of painting based upon the kinds or types of nature represented: portraiture, the representation of faces; landscape, the representation of natural scenery; still-life, the representation of food and flowers. The decline of illusionist painting has brought with it the decline of the categories associated with illusionism and the emergence of categories which are based upon the painting as an autonomous object. Let us consider some of these categories in turn.

First there is geometric abstraction. The most rigorous of the geometric abstractionists of the first half of the century was Piet Mondrian, who reduced all colours, in his doctrine of neo-plasticism, to the unmixed primaries red, yellow and blue, and the monochromatic scale, black, white and grey. In natural succession from Mondrian is a painter like Josef Albers who keeps to a strictly reduced formal grid, usually the square, but allows himself to experiment with subtle nuances, interactions and diffusions of various hues and intensities of one colour. Art of this kind, though very much an important aspect of the avant-garde, does possess traditional features. Western artists have used geometric grids and constructions for the creation of harmonious compositions in all ages. Again, geometric abstraction is a deliberate, planned, highly conscious art. It was revolutionary, on the other hand, in extricating itself from the symbolic, the referential, the narrative. In Albers the coloured squares set up their own world of forms, that and no other.

In sharp contrast to geometric abstraction might be placed texture painting. Texture avoids geometry and hard linear outline; places the emphasis upon the working up of the surface. Theoretically, of course, a texture painting could be as much pure object as a Mondrian. In practice, it rarely if ever is. The worked surfaces of things arouse association just as shapes do. Wrinkled surfaces suggest age; torn surfaces, violence; jagged surfaces, brute strength. In a texture painting, then, like the Spaniard Tapies, or Dubuffet, the ideal of the painting as pure object is not consummated. We are brought into close contact with the material, the physicality of the paint, but that physicality tends more often than not to suggest surfaces other than itself, creates its own symbolism, becomes allusive if not illusive. Yet texture-painting is very much a twentieth-century style in its emphasis upon the surface; what we enjoy in texture-painting is the visual enjoyment of a surface. For if we see it as illusion, that is as depth, we cannot see it as surface and texture.

A painting is made up of a succession of disjunctive acts; each act of the brush might be compared to the notes played upon a musical instrument, although the painter is able to create his own scale, if need be, each time he works. Indeed, he creates his scale to suit his piece. Now a modern painter may emphasize the fact that a painting is a series of separate acts or blows of a brush or knife on a canvas or board; the canvas becomes an arena. Thus we have action painting, the finished canvas serving as a historical record of a series of movements, like a camera with an open shutter tracing out the movements made by a dancer. Such a painting possesses traditional qualities, for ever since the time of Titian and Giorgione the quality of the brushwork, the facture, has been treasured as a sign of the personality and style of the master. Indeed brushwork is, of course, often one of the main means of attribution and identification. One usually sees an action painting as pure object, but it is not so purely art as object, as is a Mondrian or Albers, for to the extent that it is a record of a personal activity it also is a symbol, a referent of that activity. We tend, that is to say, to interpret it as an expression of the artist's personality. Action painting indeed is the theory of expression reduced to its limits, a kind of vestigial romanticism whereby the pure enactment of the pictorial process, shorn of any other references to the outside world, becomes the artist's own sign.

Yet another approach to painting as pure object is the French development known as *art visuel* or op art. This is akin to geometric abstraction in its impersonal and predominantly linear character. But it takes into greater account the interactive effects of colour—the spreading effects of colour, after-images, and so forth. This form, too, has historical roots. Since the Renaissance artists have been interested in the recessive and advancing effects of colour in the treatment of atmospherical perspective. During the nineteenth century the great French chemist Chevreul, employed at the Gobelins to establish fast dyes, worked out the law of the simultaneous contrast of colour, whereby a colour will modify an adjacent colour by the after-image of its own complementary, a rule which Delacroix made use of and after him

Seurat and the neo-impressionists. Among Americans, Kenneth Noland and Larry Poons might be cited.

A logical extension and at the same time a reduction of *art visuel* is colour-field painting, in which pure colours are floated onto unprimed canvas to gain great intensities of hue like dyed fabric, the visual effect depending upon the gradation and intensity of the hue.

Now all these contemporary modes—geometric abstraction, texture-painting, action painting, *art visuel*, colour field-painting —are attempts at pure painting as distinct from referential, representational, symbolic painting.

All of these avant-garde forms have their roots in some particular aspect of traditional representational paintings. They are not so much innovations as attempts at the extensive analysis of specialized aspects of the formal side of traditional painting. It is as though the formal structure of traditional painting were divided up into fragmented parts and within each part highly intensive research activities were in progress. The new categories, that is to say, are formal categories, not representational categories, and specializations drawn from the old formal structure of representational art.

Now up to the present I have been approaching the work of art as a finished object, from the point of view of the spectator, the critic, the art historian. This is a legitimate process because it is the finished work only which faces outwards towards the community.

An attempt to answer the question 'whither painting?', would require us to consider also the theoretical and philosophical presuppositions within which artists have worked.

The height of illusionistic painting in the seventeenth century marks a moment when religion and science in western society still maintained a single world view. The fragmentation of that world view, what T. S. Eliot, in a famous phrase, once called 'the dissociation of sensibility', led science to back intellect, and the arts to back feeling. The idea that the artist was not a man of intellect but a man of feeling, though prefigured in Plato, does not begin to dominate the western view of art until the time of the third Earl of Shaftesbury, whose theory of sentiment influenced Rousseau, and through Rousseau the romantic movement which has operated with continuing power right down to our own time. It is perhaps only in the past ten years that the romantic assumption that art is before all else personal creative activity first looks like being seriously questioned with any chance of success. If art was feeling, the business of the artist was to ransack his emotional repertoire from ecstasy to suicidal desperation; and that is what romantic art from Blake and Goya, through to the surrealists and the abstract expressionists has done. Freud supplied depth to the romantic emotional range by his theory of the unconscious. It was the Greek theory of inspiration in a novel form: the artist worked best when possessed, not by the gods, but by his own subconscious drives.

This reliance upon instinctual energy was reinforced by the philosophies of Nietzsche and Bergson. Nietzsche emphasized that the artist must destroy the past in order to create anew by the strength of his creative will, his power to will and create; Bergson seeing reality only in the temporal flow of things, stressed the life-force of which the artist was only a part.

Vitalism has been the main theoretical prop of much twentieth-century art up to and including abstract expressionism. Vitalism emphasized action, immediacy, spontaneity, the personal genius. It was not in itself hostile to representational and illusionistic painting.

The new drive towards an art devoid of figural and literary associations was strengthened by the decline of Christianity in Europe. Nietzsche had declared that 'God is dead'. The new spiritual force which began to activate the crucial painters for the twentieth century—Kandinsky, Klee, Mondrian—came from the East. It should be noted at this point that oriental influence, notably in the Japanese print, in the work of Degas, Van Gogh, Bonnard and so forth, played a significant role in the movement towards flatness. The new spiritual force came largely from the United States and India: in spiritualism. The first spiritualist church was founded in New York in the 1870s by Colonel Olcott and Madame Blavatsky, and spiritualism was linked with theosophy and the anthroposophical church of Rudolf Steiner. It is significant that all the creative forces in the development of abstract art were deeply touched by theosophy or anthroposophy during the creative periods of their lives: Kandinsky, Mondrian, Klee, Gropius, Robert Delaunay, the orphic cubists and many more. It is likely that long before Kandinsky the first purely non-representational paintings of modern times were produced by spiritualists.

Theosophy and anthroposophy exercised their appeal because they did not emphasize a God who was like man, and who revealed himself to man in the image of a pure man—that kind of God, as Nietzsche said, was dead. Instead spirituality, the inner voice, the creativity demiurge of man was seen as a function of hidden cosmic forces; man had to get in tune with the infinite in order to work creatively. Since man was a tiny part of the spiritual infinite he must seek to understand it and work in harmony with it.

The vitalism of Bergson and Nietzsche, the theosophy of Madame Blavatsky and Rudolf Steiner and others, the psycho-analytic theory and Freud and its variant in the idea of primordial archetypical imagery of Jung, probably have been the leading theoretical, philosophical, psychological and religious presuppo-sitions which have given abstract artists their ideological world-view.

I want to attack the problem now from a slightly different angle. Our subject is painting, but painting is only one art among many—music, architecture, theatre, ballet, poetry, sculpture and so forth—in which the creative spirit of man seeks to express itself. All the arts are related to one another, but their respective relationship changes from century to century. They are, we might say, like the stars in a planetary system sometimes drawing closer, at other times becoming more distant, one from another. The influences which they exert upon one another are thus not constant but varied. Now from Greek times down to our own there has always been a particularly strong relationship between poetry and painting. It was noted first in the sixth century BC in a statement attributed to Simonides of Chios 'that painting is mute poetry and poetry a speaking painting', and it has come down to us in Horace's phrase *Ut pictura poesis*. What struck these thinkers was the element of visual imagery which poetry and painting hold in common.

But painting from Greek times has also been closely linked with architecture, through the theory of harmony, number and proportion deriving from Pythagoras. Architects and painters were often trained in the same workshop in Renaissance times and what we might call the aesthetic of architecture has influenced the art of painting through the ordering and composing of the work.

During the twentieth century, however, the link between poetry and painting has been weakened. Those painters who gain inspi-ration from poetry are the exception rather than the rule and are likely to be charged with being reactionary or sentimental. Con-versely, the link between poetry and music has grown in strength. In the nineteenth century Schopenhauer remarked that 'all art aspires to the condition of music', and most twentieth-century avant-garde artists would agree with him. And whereas in

Renaissance and baroque times sculpture deeply influenced the art of painting, in our own time sculpture has been directed more, I should think, by developments in the art of painting.

The links between painting and the other arts are, I would suggest, always unstable and uneasy, breaking down and re-forming from century to century. This is highly relevant to any consideration in 'Whither Painting?'. Associated with the problem is the desire to create a total art which would embrace all the others. This was first illustrated in Baudelaire's doctrine of cor-respondences, of synaesthesia, the interaction of the senses; and in Wagner's ideal of the *Gesammtwerke*, the total opera which would embrace all the arts. This has led to a breaking down of the categories which divide the arts, so that today the division between painting and sculpture becomes increasingly difficult to draw. A work like Claus Oldenberg's *Hamburgers* is only one attempt to combine the world of painting and sculpture; the shaped canvases of Col Jorden or Richard Smith are other examples of the way artists are seeking to escape from the limitations of traditional painting.

What we might call the ultimate in pure painting has been asserted several times already during the twentieth century: Malevich's *White on White*, Alexander Rodchenko's *Black on Black*; these have had their more recent manifestation in paintings like Ad Reinhardt's. Even Reinhardt with his crosses introduces, of course, symbolic overtones.

Is the wholly pure painting a genuine goal or the twentieth-century painter's myth? It is I believe closely bound up with the realism of the innocent eye, the belief that we can see, if we try hard enough, as James Gleeson put it poetically a week or so ago, as Lazarus might have seen at the moment of his resur-rection. Is it possible to achieve this goal of pure visual inno-cence; or is it a rare state like the mystic's moment of ecstacy, when the essential unity of truth confronts him as a blinding white radiance?

I do not want to make out that progress towards a pure art is impossible. During the last fifty years there can be no doubt that the art public has been educated to see paintings increasingly as pure form, and not concern itself with referential or symbolic meanings.

Now any answer to the question 'Whither Painting?' will depend upon whether this movement towards a purely visual art represents a permanent break in the western tradition, a tradition of the new, as Harold Rosenberg has described it, or whether it is something less than that. Will the search for pure visual values be regarded as the characteristic feature, perhaps the peculiar delusion, of twentieth-century arts or will it be seen as the birth of a new language of vision? I don't think we can know the answer to that question.

Those who believe that we are at the threshold of a completely new era of art will find many to support them. There is much in our age which is unprecedented. Rene Huyghe, for example, the French art theorist and historian, argues that all art until the nineteenth century was grounded upon what he calls the agricultural cycle, which was basically repetitive and conservative, but that the Industrial Revolution has brought into existence a world motivated by power and energy, which does not promote cycles, recurrences and conservatism, but continuous change.

Before we accept such positions too readily, however, we must ask ourselves to what extent painting is really equipped as an art to sustain itself in such a world. It is an ancient art, not a technology; it is also a handicraft, something still made by hand in the ocean of industrialism.

I myself have always felt that sculpture as an art form was much more amenable and more adaptable to the requirements of a pure abstraction, to art as object, than painting. The recent tendency of painters to shape canvases, to break out of the rectangle, use very high pastes like Dubuffet, reveals a certain impatience with the limitations of painting.

Some serious objections can be raised against painting as a pure two-dimensional object without symbolic associations. The critics of illusionist paintings have pointed out that the depth achieved by perspective and chiaroscuro is an illusion. But is not the ideal of a purely flat surface an illusion too? Place any mark on a white or coloured ground and we at once establish two planes: a mark and a ground. Our vision is stereoscopic: colours on a flat surface advance or recede, create visual illusions, ambiguous planes; the painter must work out his constructions within these illusive planes. The illusive nature of painting may well be one of the central characteristics of painting as an art-form. Shapes too take on symbolic values and colours: blue cannot be ever entirely divorced from our experience of the sky and sea, red from blood. A symbology, not necessarily archetypical, but deeply built into the personal experience of all of us, stands between us and the contemplation of pure shape and pure colour. The idea of the painting as a pure object may be as much a myth as that of the innocent eye.

There is another curious point about painting. Paint itself is a plastic, highly viscid material which can be thinned and thickened, drawn out and dabbed on. This is true whether we are thinking of gouache, oil, polyvinyl, the acrylics and so forth. It consists of pigment and a gluey vehicle; and it is the best thing in the world to use, apart from a camera, to make visual illusions with. Paint is the illusive material *par excellence*; and to use it only to colour surfaces may be regarded as a drastic reduction of its inherent possibilities.

Even so the attempt towards abstraction may have been worth it; but if the goal is unattainable it may be abandoned for others more attractive. In this regard we must remember that, as John Ogburn says, the search for a pure visual reality has been the striking feature of our century. There have been at all times rivals waiting in the wings to take over from Matisse, Mondrian, Klee, Pollock and company. There have been periodical outbursts of figural painting during the twentieth century; the surrealist verism of the 1920s; the magic realism of the 1930s; the pop painters of the 1950s and 1960s; which cannot be explained as the inertia of traditional painting.

I am a historian not a prophet and I do not believe that historians can make predictions. The most I can attempt are some very general observations. The first is that the values which we ourselves give to the art of our time will not be the values which the twenty-first and twenty-second century will ascribe to it. What is done now will be seen differently and judged differently. Again, it is true that each century does produce an art which is characteristic of it. The early baroque, for example, emerges around 1600 with Caravaggio and runs a cycle of about 150 years. It was replaced by a return to classicism around 1750, from which painters did not break free until the 1870s and architects still later. Every indication of style suggests that the formative period of twentieth-century painting was between 1895 and 1914, and that we have now reached high noon if not mid-afternoon. At sixty-seven the century itself has reached we might say retirement age. The end of each century in western art usually brings with it old radical restlessness and questioning of the central values of the century. Will Mondrian, Klee and Pollock go down in such a revaluing as men seduced by impossible myths, like the creative unconscious, the primordial archetype and the innocent eye—or will they be seen as the pioneers of a new millenium of painting? Who can tell?

56
Elwyn Lynn on Sidney Nolan
—1967—

Elwyn Lynn's *Sidney Nolan: Myth and Imagery* (Macmillan, London, 1967) is a welcome contribution to the growing literature on Nolan. It is probably the best general introduction to Nolan's work which has yet appeared; certainly the most comprehensive. Although it does not live up to the promise suggested by the title, it does shift the discussion of Nolan's art from the boring polarities of nationalism versus internationalism to the formative processes of his art. Much of the strength and most of the weaknesses of the book lie in the fact that it is written in the tradition of descriptive, impressionistic, and evocative criticism, in which the author seeks to convey in words something of the effects produced by the painter. There are, on the other hand, many perceptive and illuminating discussions of the relation between Nolan's technical innovations and his art as a whole. The book, in short, is a good introduction to Nolan's art for the general reader.

But as a serious consideration of the role of myth and imagery in Nolan's work it leaves much to be desired. Discussion remains at a discursive, descriptive level, comment is disparate, the treatment episodic; there is no attempt at a systematic analysis of the way in which Nolan employs image and myth, or of their role in the formal development of his art. In short, a case is not argued through; no coherent theory of the role of myth and image in Nolan's art emerges.

The failure results, it seems to me, from several factors. The first is a problem of evidence. Elwyn Lynn obviously has been in no position to examine all the evidence, both pictorial and verbal, in existence but not available to him. For one thing we need a

First published in the *Bulletin*, Sydney, 7 October 1967, under the title 'Nolan as Mythmaker'.

definitive catalogue of the artist's work, especially his early work; one based upon a study both of the artist's own presentation of its chronology and such external evidence as is available. Until this is completed, any attempt to provide an account of image and myth in Nolan must remain highly speculative and be based upon shifting sand. Even with such a catalogue the problem will remain extraordinarily complex. The second problem is one of interpretation. Lynn fails, it seems to me, to present Nolan as an artist possessing a singularly unified temperament and personality. He does not ask himself what Nolan wanted of art, what art means to him, the role he has made it play in his life. These, admittedly, are exceedingly difficult questions, but they are contingent upon any real attempt to explain Nolan's use of image and myth.

Lynn accepts without much examination, for example, the current but, I believe, misleading view that Nolan began as an abstract painter and gradually turned more representational. At a broad, descriptive level, this appears to be true enough; for Nolan's early work is more formalized, employs a more elemental, more rudimentary symbology than his later. But that is not to say that it was abstract in any strict or sustained sense. The real truth of the matter will not be revealed until a greater body of Nolan's early work becomes, if indeed it ever does, available to the public. Certainly it seems clear that in the climactic months of 1937, when Nolan was discovering the modern movement for himself in a condition of intense involvement, passion, and speed, he experimented widely. But I am not convinced after reading Lynn that Nolan ever occupied a position in which he regarded the work of art as pure object.

The point at issue revolves around the fact that Nolan intended first to be a poet, and the imaginative energy of his early, highly formalized works are to be found in Rimbaud, Verlaine and Blake; in Klee, Miro, and the surrealist assertion that the real source of inspiration lies in the subconscious mind, true locale of personal and primordial myth.

To stress an early abstract phase in Nolan's development may lead to confusion, unless that phase is carefully defined. This, surely, is what has happened in Lynn's analysis of the first plate in his book, a free drawing of 1937, which is compared to drawings by New York abstract expressionists of the 1940s. The implication is that Nolan was here a man before his time: informally abstract prior to the masters of informal abstraction. But to read the drawing as anticipatory of abstract expression is, I would suggest, misleading. Its natural ambience is to be found rather in the art of Gaudier-Brzeska, whose supple and flexible line drawings delighted and excited the 1937 evening classes which Nolan attended at the National Gallery of Victoria.

Even a monotype like *Lovers* (1940), the second plate in Lynn's book, is not to be read, surely, as pure abstraction but as an intensely personal document, a private world of elemental symbols: the crosses are not marks only but kiss symbols; the tearful eyes owe something to Picasso's drawings for *Guernica*. It belongs to a sequence of drawings related to a line in William Blake's first Book of Urizen: 'the eternals closed the tent', at the point where the poem deals with the passion of Los for Enitharmon and the birth of Orc. It is related to *Tent* (1940), exhibited as No. 2 in the current Nolan retrospective, at the Art Gallery of New South Wales; to a large painting in Mr Peter Bellew's possession; to designs for the ballet *Icare*, and other paintings of this time. Here, in short, is an iconographic cluster of drawings and paintings at the outset of Nolan's career, the analysis of which is of the first importance for any rigorous examination of Nolan's iconography. The fact that he developed a highly personal manner of painting *en serie*, which has become a cardinal feature of his work, renders a close study of these early image-linked clusters highly relevant to an understanding of his later development.

The stress upon Nolan's early abstraction leads Lynn also to a misinterpretation of the Wimmera landscapes. Certainly, in his experiments with collage, Nolan moved towards a more abstract position. But even here the real interest lies in spatial ambiguities between two and three dimensions; it is, that is to say, Cézannist and cubist rather than purely abstract. The crisp, stereoscopic image confronting two tonally distinct and spatially varied edges—what might be called the Ned Kelly-gum-tree motif—has remained with him all his life. But such devices are not to be equated with the notion of painting as pure object. For Nolan made such devices work as symbol.

Lynn's inclination to see Nolan's landscapes as pure objects leads him to assert that they are 'not a repository of a variety of human feelings'. Yet in *Dimboola*, plate six, the only Wimmera landscape illustrated in colour, an irresistible lad is offering some great smacking kisses to a coy maiden in the middle distance. The kiss symbols we have already seen in *Lovers*; doubtless they are to be found in his wartime letters. And are not the silo and moon in the background a Freudian analogue of the love idyll of the foreground? The attempt to interpret Nolan's landscape as devoid of human feeling, as 'landscape as object', has little to commend it; the author himself abandons his case in his discussion of Nolan's Antarctic landscapes.

Elwyn Lynn throws little if any light on the way image is transformed into myth in Nolan. One path towards a solution may lie in Nolan's link with Rimbaud, often commented upon but never closely examined.

This could be important, for many of the early works, especially the St Kilda paintings, are close in mood, atmosphere and setting to passages in *Les Illuminations*, to which Nolan was introduced by a close friend, Howard Matthews, at the National Gallery School. Lynn underestimates the importance of that school, and the friends Nolan found there, upon his art and life.

But Nolan owes more to Rimbaud, surely, than a primitive, hallucinatory clarity of image. For Rimbaud, the absolute nonconformist living outside and beyond conventions, became for Nolan something of a persona; and the poet who abandoned his poetry for a life of violence and gun-running in the Red Sea prefigures that second persona, Kelly, whose life of criminal action, sanctified in myth, has woven its dialectic, in the realm beyond good and evil, around the artist's development.

Nolan's identification with these two amoral men of action deserves a closer analysis than Lynn provides. A clue may be found in Nolan's interest in Kierkegaard, to whom Max Nicholson introduced him during the war and whom he read extensively. In Kierkegaard, Nolan may have found his answer to Freud and André Breton. For there is indeed a change during the war years, from a stream-of-consciousness outpouring of personal symbol with its ideological roots in Breton's unconscious modes of integration, to an art in which choice and decision will play a larger part.

In this movement from an art owing much to psychic automatism to an art which is, among other things, an act of conscious choice, Kierkegaard may have been the catalyst. And this shift, to be distinguished clearly from a shift from abstraction to representation, finds its mythical correlatives in Rimbaud and Kelly. If my analysis is sound, it might provide us with one explanation of how personal myth gave Nolan the courage to develop his art against the grain of the century.

What I have called elsewhere Nolan's iconomorphic use of myth and image has made it possible for him, I would suggest, to create a private world within which he can operate and develop as an original artist without his art becoming a reflex of dominant trends, the fate which awaits most artists born, as Australians are, into culturally insecure, provincial societies. Because from his *Moon-Boy* of 1940, to the astounding Michaelesque imagery of *Gallipoli* of 1963, is an eccentric path indeed for a creative artist of the twentieth century.

Not that Nolan's work is to be discussed wholly in terms of choice; far from it. The constant exposure to new sensations in world travel, the stimulus of new materials and techniques, the role of accident must also occupy an important place in any full discussion of his art. But choice is there; Nolan chose Kelly, even if he only stumbled upon him at a propitious moment for his art, as he has later chosen Mrs Fraser, Bracefell, Leda and the Diggers of Gallipoli, interweaving, transforming, and conflating them into a personal mythos. It has not been fully appreciated how this personal mythology has made it possible for Nolan to develop a far greater range of style and technique than artists whose development reveals itself primarily in stylistic and technical terms. Myth has given him ambience and span as well as a personal focus. In drawing so continuously upon a personal iconography he may be compared with his own enigmatic little figure of Narcissus who succeeds in looking at himself while looking at the world.

The presentation and layout of the book leave much to be desired. A great many of the paintings discussed in detail by the author and crucial for his argument are not illustrated, and references from text to plates are difficult in the extreme. More often than not even quotations lack quotation marks, so that is it difficult to know, except by the change in voice, whom one is reading.

There is no bibliography and, although many other critics are quoted, Mr Lynn makes no serious attempt to assess what earlier writers have written. This is an endemic weakness in Australian art criticism. The critic presents his views in isolation without any serious attempt to relate what he has to say to what has been said before. Mr Lynn seems to view criticism, except presumably his own, as 'reactions' to works of art rather than as a corporate and unending attempt at clarification. It is not enough, surely, to quote Robert Melville on Nolan's Kelly image; one should be prepared to consider to what extent Melville has succeeded in interpreting the imagery of the Kelly paintings. 'Nolan', Melville writes:

had to invent a figurative system which would go beyond appearances without altogether dispensing with them. He found the prototype for such a figuration, as his own reference to Henri Rousseau indicates, in the art of those simple, untrained painters who, in 19th-century New England and 20th-century France, produced stiff, solemn incorrect versions of the human figure oddly and intensely imbued with human presence. The unreal realism of the naive painter is the visual counterpart of Kelly's illiterate eloquence.

Melville's analogy is attractive but inadequate; a too-mechanical and over-simplified version of what, I believe, actually occurred. Nolan, for one thing, did not invent a figurative system to accord with Kelly as folk-hero. His *faux-naif*, figurative manner had already developed considerably in the Wimmera landscapes and St Kilda paintings before he began to paint Kelly; and that manner was primitivistic and highly sophisticated, not primitive, *faux-naif*, not naive.

It is necessary to stress, as indeed Elwyn Lynn does, that Nolan's primitivism was not the product of an 'innocent' eye, a naive colonial boy of painting in a country which lacked an artistic tradition. That, perhaps, was the artist's stance, but not the reality. And it was the fashion in which London critics first approached Nolan's art; but the innocence was, in this case, in the eye of the beholders. Robert Melville certainly avoids that early, extreme position, but he is still, I would suggest, too ready to accept Nolan's explanation of his sources—'Kelly's words, Rousseau, and sunlight'—at their face value. There is much more to it than that. In these matters the heart feels more than the mind knows, and hand and eye retain more than memory recalls.

Nolan's style has tangled roots. Elwyn Lynn indicates how Nolan's primitivistic manner originated at a time when primitivism in a variety of forms was making a powerful impact upon the Australian art scene, and Nolan was, from the beginning, the most uncompromising and thoroughgoing of Australian primitivists. And the sources of Nolan's primitivisms are various: initially there was the psychic primitivism of surrealism, which provided the theoretical justification, the *raison d'être*, of all the rest: children's drawings, French naive painters like le Douanier Rousseau, Australian colonial primitives and the art of primitive peoples.

The complex heritage of Nolan's apparently naive style may be appreciated by a study of some of the possible stylistic sources of the painting entitled *The Defence of Aaron Sherriff*. It is likely that the wallpaper and bright patchwork rug derive from personal memories, but the style adopted suggests the influence not of Rousseau so much as Matisse around 1910–11; Matisse-like patterns and Matisse's play with perspective are also present in other paintings of the Kelly series. The way in which the patch-work of the rug is made to pass across the reclining policeman is certainly a Matisse-like device, plus a witty emphasis, doubtless, upon camouflage, so much a part of many an Australian artist's life during the war years.

The enchanting trio who emerge from beneath the bed have their pictorial origin, I would suggest, in quite a different source. There is nothing, to my knowledge, in the verbal sources which Nolan used to account precisely for this engaging and memorable image, but there are two likely visual sources. Nolan, at this time, was interested in early colonial painting. The idea of a figure emerging, rather ludicrously, in a condition of fright from beneath a bed was probably inspired in part by the well-known colonial broadsheet which depicts *The Arrest of Governor Bligh*. Nolan might have seen this either as illustrated in Dr H. V. Evatt's *Rum Rebellion* (1938) or my own *Place, Taste, and Tradition* (1945). But the painting appears to have other roots also. Nolan has called upon, it would appear, the art of archaic Greece. Does it not incorporate his recollections of a photograph of the charming triple-headed monster from the limestone pediment of the Old Hekatompedon on the Acropolis at Athens, which Frank Medworth used as the head-piece to his article on 'Greek Art of the Sixth Century', published in *Art in Australia* of March 1942? It is not, of course, a deliberate borrowing but the vestige of a visual experi-ence embodied and recreated in a new situation. Yet the curious moustaches of the monster, the bright, whimsical archaic smile (why should they be smiling, one might well ask, with murderers at the door of the hut?), the elbow-resting position, and the con-vergent bodies melting into a kind of tail, all find a source in the ancient Greek monster.

When Nolan, years later, came to envisage the Gallipoli campaign as a kind of re-enactment of the Trojan wars, his imagination, it seems, had already been prepared by an earlier marriage of Greek and Australian myth.

It is into such questions that a book like Elwyn Lynn's *Sidney Nolan: Myth and Imagery* must inevitably lead us. They will be considered irrelevant questions only by those who pretend to no interest in the processes of the creative mind, or try to identify myth with nationalism. The book, therefore, whatever its weak-nesses—and it has been more to the point here to stress its weaknesses rather than its strengths—is more than a personal reaction to Nolan's art. It is an attempt to understand it and clarify our notions about it; a contribution to a continuing discussion. It brings a sophisticated breadth of reference and technical knowledge of the subject to do the artist some justice. An attempt is made to see Nolan's art in its multiformity instead of impaling it upon the polarities of nationalism and internationalism.

57
David Boyd
—1969—

The David Boyd Exhibition represents a personal victory over fashion. For ten years David Boyd has painted against the current of the mainstream and for ten years Australian critics subjected his art to severe criticism. But during the past twelve months or so the hostility has weakened; revised opinions are beginning to appear. What was really at issue was not so much the quality of his paintings as the validity of his position. Moral values, the human condition, might well have inspired, so it was argued, great art in the past. But painting had now exhausted these positions. They were no longer available for the artist of the 1960s.

The criticism has not mattered much. Boyd has continued to paint in his own personal manner and to find an audience and a growing market for his art in Australia and Britain. He has found that there is still a place for a moral painter. Indeed those who constantly proclaim the death of the moralist in painting occupy a position not dissimilar to those who constantly proclaim the death of abstract art. In Blake's words, 'They throw the straws against the wind and the wind blows it back again'.

The quality of Boyd's art is not readily accessible. Neither composition nor painted surface immediately impresses as inevitable nor provides instant visual pleasure. There is an awkwardness of structure, a coarse rhetoric, especially in the early works, which occurs in the art of visionaries such as John Martin and (more often than is admitted) William Blake; a rugged vitality which draws more upon moral than upon aesthetic energy. Such qualities have always been unsettling to the gentlemen of taste but they are capable of producing highly memorable and durable

First published as the catalogue introduction, David Boyd Exhibition, Commonwealth Institute, London, May 1969.

imagery. And in the end, if one is patient, the rhetoric turns out to be an inalienable part of the image.

Boyd's personal victory has not, of course, depended upon purely personal resources. His art occupies, whatever its personal idiosyncrasies, a fairly central position in the development of an Australian tradition in painting which, while strongly affiliated to the art of western Europe, has sought to put down its own roots into the Australian society and become a valid expression of civilized values in Australia. That he has been able to contribute to this Australian tradition more fruitfully from London during the past decade than he could possibly have done from Melbourne or Sydney is itself an indication as to how thin, hesitant, and self-conscious are the very factors which make for culture and civilization in Australia, a country in which criticism, caught between the pressures of national conservatism and the international avant-garde, is only now beginning to find a place for free-wheeling, eccentric genius.

But not purely personal resources. As a member of a family perhaps more famous than any other in the annals of Australian art, Boyd has been close to the grass roots of Australian culture since childhood. The family milieu combined the Christian faith and morals with a routine of creative activity in potting, painting and music. Both his art and his moral values have grown in him since childhood. Again the art of John Martin, William Blake (and Odilon Redon also) come to mind; all eccentric, provincial and visionary.

The real strength of David Boyd's art lies, in short, in the fact that there is a grass-roots quality about it, a kinship with folk art. Nor is it surprising that those artists who have moved him most deeply should have themselves drawn deep sustenance from folk tradition: from Bosch, who drew upon popular tales, alchemy and mystical literature; from Brueghel, who like Bosch, turned to popular parables and proverbs for his didactic material; from Goya whose deep moral pessimism drew upon popular superstition and witchcraft.

It has been asserted from time to time that this folk quality, which has manifested itself both in a recourse to local history, legend and myth and a certain crudity and naivete of presentation is rather in the nature of a fraud. 'Mere' this and 'pseudo' that, have flourished in any discussion of the place of myth in twentieth-century Australian art. But the facts are not obliterated by abuse. And the historical fact is that for a highly creative generation of Australian artists who began to paint just before the beginning of

David Boyd, *Judges in a Landscape*, c.1962, oil on canvas. Private collection.

the Second World War, the legends and myths which they drew, fabricated and transformed from their own young society meant more to them than the archetypal myths which they might have drawn, in another country, out of Jung. Doubtless analytical psychology did blend with the geographical predicament, but Ned Kelly, Burke and Wills, Ludwig Leichhardt in their wandering came to mean more to them than the nocturnal peregrinations of archetypal images. This preference for men of action rather than for the mythos of an introspective psychology is to be found in the attraction—unusual in mid-twentieth-century painting—for the heroic. A penchant for the heroic is to be found in Nolan and Drysdale, Arthur and David Boyd, and Leonard French. And in David Boyd the heroic element, as in Poussin and David, assumed a distinctly moral tone. Furthermore, Australia's heroes, as Max Harris and others have pointed out, have been almost invariably losers. Their heroism has always worn, even more than is usual to the type, an attitudinizing and histrionic air. So that the true genre by means of which they have been depicted is mock-heroic rather than heroic, and their end comic, or ludicrous, or pathetic rather than tragic.

Boyd's imagery in this way combines hero and anti-hero in a benedictional gesture of pity. In an early painting, *Bass and Flinders* (1958), bearded old men with the wide innocent eyes of children, sail in a toy boat onto a wild lee shore as tangled as human folly. In another, the explorer Burke, buried to the neck, clutches at dead stumps and curses the desert sky. The explorers are drawn as slightly impossible, obsessed and star-benighted men drawn to the edges of the known world by their heroic vanity. A similar theme informs later work. The young pot-smokers of London, painted in *sfumato* technique, are moved by the same obsessive drives to experience the limits of the known which moved their Victorian grandfathers, and at the crisis confront the unknown with the same wide-eyed innocent wonderment. *The Frightened Child* of 1967 is but another version of Truganini bemused before the skulls of her ancestors. Man, in Boyd's art, is the ceaseless explorer and victim of his own nature. For his Australian nature is clearly not topographical but an allegorical sign in his moral universe.

And this universe can be easily misunderstood. A superficial glance at his works has suggested to some the ardour of the reformer. But Boyd is no moral optimist. The paintings express no great faith either in man's natural virtue or his capacity to improve himself. A Manichaean dualism informs the work. Evil is as real and as omnipresent as good; man is a victim of eternal moral antinomies, a lost, pathetic creature who reaches with opened arms (how frequently the motif occurs) into an implacable universe and finds no comforter. In the *Spearing of Gilbert* (1958) naturalist and Aborigine find a temporary reconciliation only at the moment of death. But in life there is no enduring union. Even the Boschian *gryllos* introduced in the left corner of the painting— a kind of comic fun-figure of evil—opens its arms like the dead trees in the vain search for union and understanding. There is no continuing warmth or solace in union. *The Betrayed* (1962) are united by the cold guilt of the betrayal; the prodigal is united with the father, but the mood of the initial rejection lives on in the union; the judges are lost souls wandering in a wasteland of moral uncertainties in which the only landmarks are monoliths raised to the iniquity of the law. Everywhere man is held fast in the grip of his dual nature. Boyd, in short, is a moralist not by exhortation or preachment, but in his relentless presentation of the moral predicament of man.

Because his universe is a moral universe it can exist only through and by means of the depicted reality of man. A representational art is just as essential to him as it was to the art of Michelangelo: but it is one thing to work with the human figure in the early sixteenth century when everything is working for you, and to work with it in the late twentieth century. That scientific and amoral universe of energy and motion which has laid such a hold upon the imagination of twentieth-century man does not concern him. The moral law, the act of judgement, duty and responsibility, obsession and redemption, charity and love concern him—not the vacant, interstellar spaces. Not the space age, but its children.

The exhibition reveals a development which has been dialectical, not unilinear. The early Explorer series grow from an active family tradition which includes the work of Boyd's brother Arthur and his brother-in-law John Perceval. These early pictures are often awkward in composition, the handling worried and turgid, the colour full and often melodramatic. It is the rhetoric of a visionary at odds with taste. The Antipodean Exhibition of 1959 brought a considerable reduction on all sides: the images were reduced in number, simplified and given a cubic monumentality which may have owed something to the monoliths of Easter Island and to Mexican art. From this reduced cubic manner Boyd might have moved towards increased abstraction, but he turned after the Trial series (1960—61) to a more painterly, less sculpturesque technique, in the Church and State series (1965), using colour with more *élan* and assurance.

If Boyd's art is approached from the standpoint of the international avant-garde it can only be misunderstood. But seen for what it is, an art with its roots in the ubiquitous moral tradition of Europe, a tradition successively betrayed and successively renewed by church and state, it is an impressive, as well as an eccentric and unusual, achievement.

58

Architecture in Australia

—1969—

Here, in J. M. Freeland's *Architecture in Australia* (F. W. Cheshire, Melbourne, 1968), is a major achievement in Australian historical writing. It is now possible for the first time to read a considered synoptic view of the history of building and its social ramifications in this country from the beginnings of settlement to the present day. The discussion is conducted upon a consistently chronological base over a wide range of building types: domestic, civil, commercial, ecclesiastical, rural, industrial and so forth. The grasp upon historical explanation is firmer and more sophisticated than in Professor Freeland's earlier books, *Melbourne Churches 1836—51* and *The Australian Pub*.[1] His explanations, at times convincing, at times plausible, at times arguable and at times frivolous, are always worth reading.[2]

How, for example, a style such as that stilted, exposed structure style of Northern New South Wales and Queensland, rural, vernacular and functional, emerged, persisted, declined and then caught the attention of perceptive architects in recent times. How the techniques of an art such as plasterwork should be transformed under the combined pressure of economic change and competing building methods from work run on the site to pre-cast modelling, from gypsum to fibrous; and how the immigrant Italian plasterers, following the slump of the 1890s, should turn from their craft to cafés and market gardens. How such laws as the 1837 Building Act and its interstate derivatives should have left such a lasting effect upon Australian architectural design. To read the book is to be provided with a new path into Australian social history. For building brings a society into the most direct contact with available materials and skills, climate, and traditional concepts about building and architecture.

First published in *Historical Studies*, vol. 14, no. 53, October 1969, pp. 85—92.

It is to Professor Freeland's credit that he has been the first to look at the subject in its entirety and to have extracted a pattern from the tangle of building activities in Australia over almost two centuries. Subsequent historians will be able to refine and qualify where he has, more broadly, got it right, and will be able to check back to his sources, and scrutinize them with greater care and better judgement, where he has got it wrong. Most will be able to pick up an error or two from their specialized reading. But Freeland has opened out the subject in a way that no previous book has done, and Australian architectural history will develop in no small measure by testing the validity of his explanations.

It has, of course, been built upon the work of several predecessors, and it would have been a better, and a more scrupulous piece of scholarship, had Professor Freeland provided us with a clear track back to his sources, so that we were informed what was Freeland, what was from previous publications, and what was from the almost anonymous labours of architectural students. Of these predecessors, Morton Herman is undoubtedly the most important. Herman confined himself to colonial architecture and, largely, to New South Wales. Freeland's span is greater and his grasp upon historical interaction more firm. Yet in some respects Freeland shows up poorly against Herman's narrower, more antiquarian approach. In catching, at times breathlessly, 'the main crest of each architectural wave as it had flowed across the surface of Australian society' (for such is the aim of the book), he paints such a broad impressionist view of things that one misses Herman's more detailed and better documented account of individual buildings.

More serious is the complete absence of plans. Indeed, it says much for Professor Freeland's verbal felicity that he has been able to write such a good book without providing any plans at all. He has benefited, too, from the more popular, but seminal books of Robin Boyd and has, less fortunately, inherited many of his verbal mannerisms. When Freeland, for example, describes the lantern of St Matthews, Windsor, as a pepper pot, or Sydney town hall as a 'lollipop' building we are back with the old Boydian archness, excellent devices no doubt for capturing the wavering attention of students but as architectural explication fundamentally unhelpful and—all too often on the long view—Philistine.

For in such cases one is offered in the place of analysis a cute analogy which at once amuses and obfuscates, tells us nothing about the objective character of a building, but much about the author's visual prejudices, offers us a stone (or a lollipop), not bread. It would be easy to forgive such small lapses in a book obviously designed for the general public as much as the specialists, were not the private jokes of 'experts' turned so quickly into justifications for demolition. How sad it would be if Professor Freeland's apparent incapacity to enjoy a highly ornamented style should lead the City Fathers of Sydney to demolish one day what is probably the finest and certainly the most elaborate example of Second Empire neo-baroque in the country!

All too often when Professor Freeland's taste and sympathy are not engaged the cute verbal analogy is offered in place of objective analysis. Closely related to this is his tendency to describe buildings which he finds distasteful as expressions of human behaviour. Carthona is 'a castellated pile of bombast', the architectural tone of the three decades after 1860 is 'hypocritical', the buildings of the 1880s are 'pompously ostentatious', High Victorian architecture in booming Melbourne is 'imbued with the excessive love of voluptuousness', art nouveau is 'narcissicistic' and so on and so forth; all of which tells us much more about Professor Freeland than about the architecture. All such attempts to describe buildings as expressions of human qualities must fail, for human qualities are perennial, but architectural styles temporal. Roman, Gothic, Renaissance, baroque, rococo, and High Victorian architecture, to name but a few styles, have all been derided as 'ostentatious' at one time or another. But what is significant for the history of architecture is the way in which they differ.

In this and in other ways *Architecture in Australia* is something of a battleground between Professor Freeland's historical judgement and his architectural taste; between the concepts with which he seeks to structure his material and the material itself. We are informed, for example, in the preface, that Australian architecture is 'largely the story of rapid disintegration under the steadily growing impact of machines'. But the story which Professor Freeland does tell, and it is to his credit, is not like that at all. True, ever and anon he does get out his archaic hold-all and pop in a declining craft or two; in go the joiners, the plasterers, the glaziers, *et al.* and we are asked to sit down with William Morris, the Arts and Crafts Movement, the walrus and the carpenter, and greatly sympathize. But the real story he tells is not, of course, a story of 'increasingly rapid artistic disintegration' at all. It is the story of an emergence, which the note of Gibbonian woe cannot fit.

Greenway's Convict Barracks, certainly, was very good of

its kind—Bristol provincial and Sydney colonial; but William Wardell's St Patrick's Cathedral is better, and the Sydney Opera House better still. And at the domestic level, the theme which is spelt out, to take some typical examples, by Elizabeth Farm (1793), The Rectory, Windsor (1825), Carthona (1836), Como (1847), Royal Terrace, Fitzroy (1858), Highlands, Waitara (1891), Purulia (1912), and the Seidler House, Turramurra (1950), cannot, on the basis of Professor Freeland's own exposition, be remotely described as 'artistic disintegration'. It is no criticism of Greenway's undoubted achievement to suggest that it is time that Australian architectural historians, and their camp followers in the national trusts, abandoned the concept of Australian architecture as a steady falling away from the purity of colonial Georgian until the rehabilitation of architectural ideals in recent years.

Such primitivistic presuppositions, what Arthur Lovejoy called the theory of progressive degeneration, give Professor Freeland's book an old-fashioned air. In his explication of architecture as distinct from his explication of building techniques, ruling concepts rise to vitiate empirical analysis and empirical judgement. But in speaking of building techniques rules of taste are not directly engaged. We gain invaluable accounts of brickmaking, the evolution of the veranda, of building ordinances, of plaster work, cast-iron work and glass in Australia, such as have never before been brought together within one book. But just at the point where the ebb and flow of constructional techniques coalesce into architectural form, analysis is largely abandoned and buildings are described as expressions of behaviour.

This, it seems to me, is the central weakness of an admirable book. It is surely unnecessary to describe Mortimer Lewis' architecture as 'schizophrenic' when he was simply working in the accepted mode of his time, as common to the greatest architects of the day, such as Schinkel and Soane, as to minor men. There was nothing unusual in taking the view that it was appropriate to build ecclesiastical buildings in Gothic and civic buildings à la grec. Surprisingly, Professor Freeland provides no indication that he is aware of the creative factor in historicism; that it provided the architect with the power of choice, broke down the monolithic rule of taste based upon the classical tradition, and thus acted as midwife to the modern theories of functional and organic architecture.

Furthermore, it must be stressed that historicism is endemic to almost the whole tradition of nineteenth-century Australian architecture, except that sub-architecture of the vernacular from which, on the primitivistic hypothesis, all blessings flow. Poor Lewis can hardly be blamed for it. Professor Freeland views the tremendous neo-classic debate between the virtues of the Greek and the Roman, the classic and the Gothic, as no more than academic pedantry. He does not appreciate, as Emil Kauffmann and his disciples have so convincingly shown, the significance of that debate for the emergence of modern architectural theory.

The paradox of the book, then, is that old-fashioned concepts are working against the elucidation of the material in objective terms. Nowhere else can one find such a complete account of Australian architecture during the second half of the nineteenth century, but it is presented from the viewpoint of the Georgian Rule of Taste pioneered in this country by Hardy Wilson. And an old-fashioned terminology likewise tends to blunt the precision of the architectural analysis. Much of the narrative naturally concerns itself with the post-Renaissance tradition, an architectural language rich in stylistic dialects: Palladian, mannerist, baroque, neo-classic, and their sub-varieties. But Professor Freeland inclines to describe it all as classic which, of course, in a generic sense it is. And to the classic he opposes the Gothic.

But such primal co-ordinates provide far too broad a grid within which to place, with any precision, local work in respect to its British, Continental or American exemplars. Dawes' plan for Parramatta is said to be 'a fine Renaissance scheme in the best classic manner'. But Renaissance planning is above all centralized planning, involving the reassertion of agora and forum in what has been neatly described as 'the extroversion of the cloister'. Dawes' plan for Parramatta is axial, centred at one end upon a Government House, closing the vista at the top, and with an open square at the water's edge. The first plan for Sydney is drawn in the same spirit, featuring a central avenue and a broad plaza at the waterfront. These plans have their source neither in antiquity nor in the Renaissance but in baroque vista planning, the finest English example of which Governor Philip knew in person from his schooldays at Greenwich naval college. It may have influenced him.

The British sources of early Australian architecture are given, in general, little attention. Professor Freeland is centrally concerned, and quite rightly so, with tracing the roots of a local tradition. Such a programme, one would have thought, demands a much closer attention to overseas sources. It is most disappointing to find Greenway's style still presented in such simplistic terms as 'traditionalist', 'classical in foundation but the total expression ... English'. Such broad categories throw little light upon the *nature* of Greenway's originality. What of his relation to Inigo Jones, to Wren, Soane, and to his master Nash? Was he, indeed, stepping out of his 'accustomed architectural manner' when he designed Macquarie's stables in 'battlemented Gothic'? Assuredly not. Greenway's associations with the picturesque tradition have worried a generation of Georgianophiles in Australia because they have chosen to interpret him in the light of their own neo-Georgian tastes rather than in the light of his tradition. It is disappointing to find that no use has been made of Franz Philipp's incisive discussion of Greenway's sources in his review of Morton Herman's *Early Australian Architects and their Work*.[3]

The neo-Gothic styles fare worse than Greenway in Professor Freeland's discussion. Carthona is described as a 'castellated pile of bombast'; Mortimer Lewis' quite pleasant use of timber on the gables and veranda of Richmond Villa, Sydney (1849), is described as a visual trick. The author's attitude to the Gothic Revival suggests that he gives no credit to that movement for the role it played in reviving an interest in the frank, natural and expressive use of materials. Had he done so the line of theory and practice which leads through the Gothic of Lewis, Blacket, Barnet, towards Horbury Hunt and modern functional ideals might have taken on a new light.

The story which leads to the acceptance of modern architecture in Australia still remains to be written. Certainly it did not, as Professor Freeland is himself well aware, spring ready-made out of Desbrowe Annear's Broceliande, like Athene from the head of Zeus. Professor Freeland has drawn attention to the roles played by Hardy Wilson, Robin Dods and Walter Burley Griffin. But a full account will involve a far more sympathetic treatment of nineteenth-century Gothic, and the debates which it engendered, than Professor Freeland has brought to his narrative. It looks as though it will involve, for one thing, a trenchant re-appraisal of the limitations of the neo-Georgian tradition within which so much Australian architectural history has been written.

The rehabilitation of neo-Gothic in Australia, the leavening of ideas and ideals in local architectural circles consequent upon the work of Pugin, Ruskin and Morris is essential, surely, before any adequate discussion of 'an Australian style' becomes possible. But these men are barely mentioned in the text. Theory is not given its full place. The discussions of the second half of the nineteenth-century are taken too lightly. One of the most rewarding features of Professor Freeland's book is to be found in his relentless search for the indigenous and the original. But there is a strong tendency to assume that arguments about style are irrelevant to the emergence of originality. Professional architects assume far too often that ideas issuing from the profession itself yield only eclecticism and self-consciousness, that originality is to be found only in unselfconscious building, in the vernacular: the slab-hut, exposed structure, oast-houses, silos and so forth. A less primitivistic view of originality might find it written, in letters too large to be easily focused, across the face of the country.

By which I mean that a more sympathetic account of late nineteenth-century practice and theory should lead to a more acute analysis of that style, so inadequately named Queen Anne, which flourished from the late 1880s until the First World War. The historical sources, of course, as in the case of all deep-rooted and vigorous styles, are many: a congeries of local materials and techniques, Gothic asymmetry and picturesqueness, the survival and transformation of the veranda, structural polychromy, the ideas of Pugin, Ruskin and Morris at work in the minds of men like Blacket, Wardell, Barnet, Kemp, Hunt and Sulman. Out of it all there emerged a house which is not quite like anything else in the world.

Concerning Horbury Hunt's buildings, crucial to the emergence of the style, Professor Freeland writes.

Hunt's red-brick buildings had all the hall-marks of Queen Anne architecture with their irregular massing, broken gabled roofs showing exposed trusses and latticed struting, polygonal bay windows, turned timber verandah posts and cowled chimneys. ... conditions were such that only this one style was both economical and acceptable.[4]

But the Australian house called Queen Anne has little in common with the English domestic brick architecture of the first decade of the eighteenth-century, and much which distinguishes it from Nesfield, Stevenson and Shaw's revival of it during the 1870s. The local tendency to discuss it within the terminology of Queen Anne is surely as old-fashioned as Bannister Fletcher's discussion (still influential in schools of architecture in the mid-twentieth century) of the baroque under the heading Renaissance.

The style in question is an Australian style if ever there was one, and deserves its own name. My own nomination would be Federation style. For it was born within the context of a discussion about the nature of an Australian style which parallels the political discussion that led to the foundation of the Commonwealth, and its decline parallels that loss of national energy consequent upon, as Professor Crawford has elsewhere suggested, Australia's human losses in the First World War. During the last decades of the century architects such as Barnet, Hunt, Kemp, Sulman and others, seriously discussed the possibility of creating an Australian style of architecture. Perhaps it is time that we began to take that debate more seriously, because it is just possible that they succeeded in producing what they had set their minds to: a style, that is to say, with characteristics as marked and definable as any domestic style within the tradition of western architecture. Like the Australian accent this style has been discussed for too long in terms of its derivatives. But to call it Queen Anne tells us as little about it as to call our accent Cockney. Perhaps we have not grasped its originality because it has so often offended our architectural tastes. But we need to remind ourselves that originality is often offensive until it becomes the new small talk.

Professor Freeland very rightly stresses at the outset the great value of the study of a country's architecture as a part of its general history. But he presents a description of the nature of architectural history so naïve that one must doubt whether he holds it seriously:

Buildings are original historical documents. Unlike the original sources on which most historical fields depend, those of architectural history, in the main, are not buried under the ground or locked up in closely-guarded libraries and archives and cautiously made available to a few crusty scholars. The documents and evidence of architectural history are everywhere around us, openly and freely available and readily accessible to anyone who has the skill and the mind for it to study, to read, to interpret and to understand. Buildings carry more history than a library of books—and it is not second-hand.[5]

Nice rhetoric, but how misleading! One would have enjoyed the spectacle of Professor Freeland maintaining his thesis in a seminar conducted by the late Dr J. L. O'Brien,[6] who cogently warned against the dangers of taking the visual and material evidence of buildings on trust. Buildings require the constant support of written and visual documents; alone their evidence is veiled and often enigmatic. Often they are a palimpsest of reconstructions and alterations. And architectural history itself is even less of a material study *per se* than the parallel studies of paintings, sculpture and antiques, which are smaller, more transportable and, relative to size, more precious; whereas buildings occupy valuable land and are much more prone for that, and other reasons, to be destroyed. So that a history of architecture confined to the evidence of surviving buildings is likely to provide an account even less true than comparable histories of the other visual arts.

That is one of the reasons why the policy of the National Buildings Record of Great Britain has been to give first priority to the compilation of photographic records of buildings threatened by destruction. While much can certainly be learned simply by looking, it is misleading to underplay the importance to architectural studies of written documents, plans and visual materials. Certainly Professor Freeland's book could not have been written without his constant access to all three.

In a review of this kind, and for this journal, it has been appropriate to concentrate upon points of interpretation and method which seem to be relevant to further studies in Australian architecture. It should not be read as an attempt to detract from the very considerable achievement of the book itself, as the pioneering history of Australian architecture. The subject is complex and exacting, demanding many differentiated skills, both of a historical and professional kind. Professor Freeland is as well equipped as anyone to write the history of Australian architecture, and has come closer than anyone else to writing it.

Notes

[1] Melbourne University Press, Melbourne, 1963 and 1966 respectively.
[2] But, in fairness, I can find only one, of pure frivolity. His explanation for the High Victorian style of buildings like the Federal Hotel, Melbourne, and Queen Victoria Building, Sydney: 'The successful man could not adorn his wife, let alone himself, with jewels, furs and brightly coloured silks when a touch of grey or muted lavender was the only relief permitted to the universal and gloomy black or brown suits and dresses. He found the answer to his frustration by dressing his buildings in a way which in other times he would have dressed his wife', p. 171.
[3] 'Notes on the Study of Australian Colonial Architecture', *Historical Studies*, vol. 8, no. 32, May 1959, pp. 405−21.
[4] *Architecture in Australia*, p. 202.
[5] ibid., preface.
[6] See Peter Balmsford and J. L. O'Brien, 'Dating Houses in Victoria', *Historical Studies*, vol. ix, 1961, pp. 379−95.

PART V

Reviews, Revisions and Revisitations: the 1970s and 1980s

59
Arthur Boyd
—1972—

The art of Arthur Boyd is one of the central and most universal achievements of that generation of Australian artists whose work first came to maturity during the years of the Second World War. Although it is grounded closely upon personal experience, and does not seek at any time to deny or avoid the face of the regional and national environment in which Boyd grew up, it is an art which aspires beyond the personal and regional towards a universal expression of man's place and man's dilemma in the universe.

Boyd began as a landscape painter at the age of fourteen shortly before the Second World War. His early landscapes are naturalistic, highly competent in technique, and painted with a natural sensitivity for the painted surface. They are pastoral in their vision and mood: sheep grazing in bright fields, harvests warm in the autumn sun. Or beach scenes: long stretches of sand and shore where children play the endless hours away. These pre-war Peninsula landscapes, as they have been called, depict an age of innocence. Boyd experienced a childhood into which little deeply-felt bitterness entered, having been born into an unusual household of artists and writers: it included his father, a studio potter for whom the arts were a kind of natural religion; and his grandfather and uncle, both well-known landscape painters. Indeed the young Arthur Boyd and his uncle Penleigh were among the last of those artists who might be said to have made a personal and creative contribution to the naturalistic impressionism of the Heidelberg school, Australia's most authentic school of painting which was itself, for the most part, a kind of celebration of Australia's age of pastoral innocence when sheep upon sunny

First published in *Hemisphere*, April 1972.

pastures became a literal symbol of the young country's prime source of material wealth.

The war shattered the precarious beauty of this pastoral dream. The troubled future was foreshadowed in Boyd's art by a group of grimacing heads, painted in 1938—reminiscent of the expressionist art of Oskar Kokoschka. Contact at this time with the young Polish Jew Yosl Bergner brought him into contact with expressionism, politics, and the tragedy of the Jews in Hitler's Europe. By 1940 his art had moved away from its pre-war innocence to become more primitive, turbulent, expressive. He deliberately discarded the considerable technical skills he had developed in naturalistic landscape painting, and began to paint his first images of tormented man, of Adam expelled from his Eden. During 1942 and 1943 he laid the foundations, within an energetic and expressive manner, of the imagery which was to embody the elements of his vision.

Boyd sees life as an endless movement between the material and the spiritual, that is to say, as cyclic. In this of course he belongs to a mystical tradition of thought which reaches back to the Jewish cabbala, and beyond that to the most ancient East. This is one of the reasons why we feel so often in Boyd's work a spiritual kinship with Blake—though the style is so different.

His painting *The Seasons* is typical. The four ages of man are depicted around the tree of life. The setting is no longer rural, but industrial and suburban, drawn from experiences of St Kilda and South Melbourne, where he lived at this time. A Hobbesian pessimism prevails. Life is ugly, brutish and short. But even the cripple clings screaming to the apple of life: to pain and experience.

These strange figurative fantasies have their source in a vividly experienced personal reality. Franz Philipp, in his splendid book on Boyd,[1] describes him as a 'literalist of the imagination': images drawn from his own life become characters for a universal yet personal myth. For the cripple in *The Seasons* he drew upon a vivid personal experience of two close friends, both victims of a polio epidemic of the 1930s. The prone figure, aged and bearded, in the foreground, so reminiscent of one of Blake's Gothic *gisants* in its stiff lifelessness, is drawn from a memory of his father, an epileptic, lying prone on a suburban nature-strip as he awaits the onset of an attack. The strange goanna-like creature which dances with the children in front of the menacing factory is the transformed image of the family dog—a Skye terrier—which in its countless transformations becomes an emblem of the life-force

that returns frequently throughout Boyd's art. Here Boyd differs
from Blake. For where Blake drew upon earlier art for the proto-
typical emblems of his art—on Roman carvings of Jupiter, for
example, for his symbol of the authoritarian father-figure—Boyd
drew his symbols directly from early-life experiences.

The cyclic vision may also be seen in Boyd's painting *The
Shepherd*. Here man may be seen as man lost and returning to the
vegetable kingdom, an image possibly inspired by Blake's illustration of Canto XIII of Dante's *Inferno, The Wood of the Self
Murderers*, which was available to him in the original in the
National Gallery of Victoria. Boyd greatly admired and studied
the Melbourne collection of Blake's illustrations to Dante. In *The
Shepherd*, too, man may be seen in his vitality and sexuality,
aspiring to escape from his vegetable condition and become,
like the birds, a free spirit. Here the memory of the family's
Skye terrier has become transformed by a memory of the famous
offering-stand discovered by Sir Leonard Woolley at Ur, in which
a ram is depicted among a flowery thicket—a Sumerian symbol
of the fertility gods.

There is, in these paintings of 1944 and 1945, of life thrusting
itself up out of the earth or returning back into the earth in both
natural and monstrous forms, something that recalls to mind the
early evolutionary vision of life expressed in the Roman poet
Lucretius' philosophical epic *De Rerum Natura* (*On the Nature of
Things*). For example, Book V (ll. 836–45):

> *Many a monster, withal, then ventured the Earth to produce, forms*
> *Springing with marvellous features and limbs: man-woman, a thing the*
> *Twain 'twixt, nor one sex, nor the other, remote from them both; some*
> *Lacking of feet, some widowed of hands, and again, of a mouth reft,*
> *Some found dumb, some blind for the want of their eyes; and were*
> *things, fast*
> *Bound by adhesion of members o'er all of their bodies, so could they*
> *Nor aught do, nor anywhere go, nor evil avoid, nor*
> *Take what had they need of. And others besides of the kind, both*
> *Monsters and prodigies, would she produce...*[2]

During the years immediately after the war, Boyd turned to
a series of Biblical paintings. In place of the blind fecundity
of nature imaged by Lucretius, and the hybrid little monsters
of Hieronymus Bosch (whose work had deeply impressed him
during the war years) Boyd now turned to the humane pessimism
of Brueghel and the gentler humanity of Rembrandt. Both his
technical methods and the range of vision were greatly enlarged.

Venetian colour and the more spacious energy of Tintoretto began to appear in his paintings. *Jacob's Dream* is typical of the new mood. At this time casein tempera and oil techniques, often painted over chalk grounds, provided the artist with beautiful, mellow surfaces and fine gradations of tone. It was not so much a mood of blind thrusting and often cruel vitalism which prevailed; rather it was the moral world and its dilemmas which concerned him: blind authority and the free expression of sexual passion, guilt and betrayal. This we may see in such paintings as *Susannah and the Elders* and *The Kiss of Judas*.

Boyd's paintings have alternated continuously throughout his whole career between landscape painting, which is direct, personal and naturalistic, and symbolic, figurative painting by means of which he has given expression to his vision of life. This vision has always been expressed, however universal its expression, within the context of classical and Christian myth—and within an Australian landscape setting usually gained from his experiences of bush landscape either in the environs of Melbourne, or the drier, sparse open woodlands of the Wimmera. It was not until the later 1950s that he turned to life as lived in Australia (apart from the direct figurative emblems from family life already discussed above) for inspiration. On a visit to Central Australia in 1951 he had been seriously affected by the squalid degradation of the life of the detribalized Aborigines and half-castes whom he saw living in shanty towns along the railway line. About eight years later he turned back to these memories, and gave them embodiment in the series of paintings, *Love, Marriage and Death of a Half-Caste* (1958). It is a theme, close to that of many of his Biblical paintings, of love frustrated and betrayed. It is, expressed in simple terms: 'the story of a half-caste wooing a half-caste bride while haunted by the image of a white bride and a fear of white society'. His moral vision of the world was thus given a more secular and regional mould. It was, not surprisingly, the series by which he first became widely known in Australia and then, during the early 1960s, in England.

We have been concerned mainly with Boyd's paintings. A closer study of the development of his imagination would require, however, a detailed study of his drawings. And he has ranged widely and prolifically in many other fields. Trained by his father in ceramic techniques, he produced a large number of ceramic tiles during the early 1950s, many devoted to classical and Christian myth. The smaller area of the tile provided a problem of composition comparable to that of the Greek sculptors in carving metopes for Doric temples, and he often solves the problem in a similar fashion: by using two or three figures interlocked and struggling. The interest in two figures in a summarily rendered landscape is developed further in the pictures painted in England during the early 1960s of nudes and beasts, of Actaeon torn by his dogs, or fantastic butterfly-people levitating through deep pools of colour. The colour is streaked across the surface, thinly and flatly, like raking light in a darkened room.

Boyd's work of the early 1960s is centred upon love myths drawn from classical literature and Renaissance painting. Lovers, blown about like leaves in the wind, coupled or confronting, are a recurrent theme. There is often a witness figure, usually in the form of a dog, by means of which the artist invests his paintings vaguely with the transcendent presence of a moral order— suggesting guilt, conscience or shame. It was at this time, we know, that Boyd was greatly moved by two Renaissance masterpieces: Piero di Cosimo's *Death of Procris*[3] in the National Gallery, London, and the Harewood House *Diana and Actaeon* by Titian. The influence of these two paintings provides the undercurrent of mood, and much of the imagery within which the highly complex metamorphic canvases of the early 1960s were created.

The theme of the star-crossed lovers clinging to one another, like Dante's Paolo and Francesca, was taken up again in another context when Boyd produced his *Romeo and Juliet* ceramic polyptych of 1963—64 on commission for the Shakespeare Exhibition at Stratford-on-Avon, Edinburgh and London. That completed, he moved from ceramic to pastel, and from profane to sacred love, in the *St Francis of Assisi* cycle of twenty-one pastels executed in 1964 and exhibited at the Australian Galleries, Melbourne, in 1965. Boyd subsequently produced sixteen lithographs based on the *St Francis* pastels to illustrate the second edition (the first had appeared in 1936) of T. S. R. Boase's *St Francis of Assisi* (Thames & Hudson, London, 1968).

The *St Francis* series first developed from a visit Boyd made to Umbria with his wife in 1964, when the story of St Francis and the wolf of Gubbio took his interest: the metamorphosis of the soul under the transcendent power of divine love. It was by his continued preoccupation with the Eros theme, in its material and transcendent aspects, that Boyd reaffirmed his deep response, both mystical and humanistic, to the cyclic nature of man and the universe. But in the 1960s the deterministic, evolutionary emphasis, the Lucretian fatalism of the early work of the war years, is transformed into a humanist, if not existentialist, emphasis upon the role of choice in the destiny of man: that man is what man chooses to be.

Indeed some of the later paintings of Arthur Boyd might serve as illustrations to the most famous utterance that has come down to us from the philosophers and mystics of the Renaissance, Pico della Mirandola's *Oration on the Dignity of Man*. In his account of the Creation of Man, Pico tells how the Creator gave to all other creatures, from the archangels to the most lowly, their appointed place and role—to which they were forever bound:

Whereupon the Greatest Artisan ordained that the creature to which he could give no special property should, instead, possess the endowments of every individual being in common with it. He formed ' an according to a general image that contained no particularities, and, setting him in the centre of the world, said to him: 'We have given you Adam, no definite place, no form proper only to you, no special inheritance, so that you may have as your own whatever place, whatever form, whatever gifts you may choose, according to your wish and your judgement. All other beings have received a rigidly determined nature, and will be compelled by us to follow strictly determined laws. You alone are bound by no limit, unless it be one prescribed by your will ... I created you as a being neither heavenly nor earthly, neither mortal nor immortal, so that you may freely make and master yourself, and take any form you choose for yourself. You can degenerate to animality or be reborn towards divinity ... on man the Father conferred, at the moment of birth, the seeds and germs of every form of life. If they are the plant seeds, he will vegetate; if he follows the senses, he will become an animal; if he cultivates the power of reason within him, he will become a celestial creature; if he follows intelligence, he will become an angel and a son of God.[4]

Notes

[1] Franz Philipp, *Arthur Boyd*, Thames & Hudson, London, 1967.

[2] Lucretius, *On the Nature of Things*, tr. L. L. Johnson, Central Press, Horsham, Sussex, 1963.

[3] The identification of the subject-matter of the painting with Procris is however in dispute. It is questioned by Martin Davies but accepted by Irvin Laving and Erwin Panofsky. See National Gallery, *National Gallery Catalogues: The Earlier Italian Schools*, 2nd edn, London, 1961, p. 421.

[4] *Oratio de hominis dignitate*, quoted from Ernst Casirer, *The Individual and the Cosmos in Renaissance Philosophy*, Basil Blackwell, Oxford, 1963, pp. 85–6.

60
Robert Hughes on Australian Art
—1973—

Robert Hughes' *The Art of Australia* (Penguin, Harmondsworth, 1970) was first published in 1965 but, for reasons never fully explained, was suppressed by the author and publisher after a few hundred copies had been released for review. In preparing the present edition the author has removed what he describes as the 'more egregious naïvetés' of the original—the manuscript of which was completed some months before his twenty-fifth birthday. He also points out that the survey does not go much beyond 1964, the year he left Australia to become an art critic in London and later in New York.*

The book is written in a lively, vigorous and transparent style through which the opinions, insights and feeling of the author shine sharply. On his own ground, confronted by the art of his own generation and that which immediately preceded it, Robert Hughes writes with confidence and perception, already the master of a wayward, uneasy, critical brilliance. The unity of this early work of his, however, is flawed by a central weakness: inability to find a point of view which will enable him to get his material into focus. Like a sharpshooter on the run his vulnerability springs not so much from the inaccuracy of his shots as from his inability to establish a base from which to keep the whole ground held by the enemy, that is to say the subject of his discourse, well in view.

Indeed, there is clearly in this book some doubt in the author's mind whether a consistent point of view is even desirable when the work of creative persons like artists is under discussion. In the event three positions have influenced the critical tone and historical perspective. The first position was stated in Hughes'

First published in *Historical Studies*, vol. 15, no. 61, October 1973, pp. 777–80.

highly influential introduction to the Exhibition of Recent
Australian Painting held at the Whitechapel Gallery, London, in
June 1961, where he claimed that its quality was due to its
condition of innocence of the European or any other tradition.
Since then, however, he has come to find this position increas-
ingly untenable, but its presence certainly hovers (like a white
Australian savage, naked and ignoble in the desert air) over
much of this book. As when Hughes writes:

Neither myth nor history is a vital part of Australian awareness yet. The
country is too amiably pragmatic for that, and too little exposed to the
conflict of ideologies, cultures, dreams, fanaticisms which is the seedbed
of great historical painting. One cannot imagine an Australian equivalent
of David's *Death of Marat*, Goya's *Second of May*, or Delacroix's *Liberty
Guiding the People*. The experiences that produce such paintings do not
exist there. Neither does genius.

Well, one can identify the mood of exasperation at the com-
placent philistine pragmatism which has predominated and determined most of Australia's values during this century—and
sympathize with it. But his irritation is here clouding his judgement. If neither myth nor history is a genuine part of the Australian
awareness it follows that artists such as Sidney Nolan and Arthur
Boyd, who have drawn upon myth and legend as a source of
invention, have played a kind of artistic confidence trick upon
the public and made much of something which is not, or in
Hughes' phrase, 'not vitally there'. The integrity of the vision of a
good many Australian artists is called into question in this way.
Such a view ignores the dynamic relationship between art and
myth. Hughes seems to assume that artists of the twentieth century can only operate as the exploiters of created, shall we say
institutionalized, myths.

There is surely much more to it than that. Hegel, and more
recently Robert Graves, have argued that the Greek artists were
the members of Greek society who were really responsible for the
character and activities of the Greek gods as they have come
down to us through history. Gombrich has argued that naturalism
in western art originated from the need to depict the events of
the Homeric epic. If Hughes believes that this condition no longer
holds and that, to state but one of many possible views, the
function of creating myth has been taken over increasingly by the
advertising and public relations people, then it is up to him to
make the case. But to see myth as something that is merely
socially given by the community upon which the artist operates

looks like an exceedingly superficial use of the Marxian notion of superstructure—I do hope that it does not spring from an uncritical reading of my own book, *Place, Taste and Tradition*.

Hughes' second position is a modification of the first. Australian artists, though not entirely cut off from tradition, suffer a situational disability. Their knowledge of tradition is received for the most part second-hand through the highly distorting media of reproductions. This view has become quite fashionable in Australian art circles in recent years, just as Hughes' first position, of the Australian artist as innocent, gained wide currency among London critics in the early 1960s. But as a *sufficient* cause of provincialism it does not amount to much. Until the creation of public galleries in the nineteenth century, engravings were the principal means by which artists gained information about the work of their colleagues and about the art of the past. And they did not do too badly. If it is contemporaneity rather than quality which is the concern it should be recalled that André Malraux has argued cogently that one of the determining characteristics of the art of our day proceeds from the immediacy with which the art of all times and places is made available to artists from the wealth of illustrated art books now available.

No doubt access to great originals is a matter of importance to some artists at a certain stage of their development. Others, however, are intimidated and frustrated by the staggering achievements of the past. This, of course, was at the root of Marinetti's call to the young artists of Italy (and Europe) to burn the museums. To have the Great Tradition constantly breathing down your neck can be a little stifling. Some artists prefer to keep it at arm's length. On this point the experience of Patrick White is, of course, relevant.

The argument, that is to say, is a double-edged one. Artists do need access, many of them, to originals for inspiration and also for knowledge about matters of technique. But a comparative lack of access to originals may also be a positive factor in the growth of a relatively vigorous tradition. I believe, for example, that a fairly convincing case could be made out for the opinion that there were more good paintings produced in Italy before 1520 than after 1520; more good paintings produced in Holland before 1700 than after 1700; more good paintings produced in England before 1820 than after 1820. But the painters of those countries who lived and worked after those dates had, of course, far more good original paintings available to them. It is possible to have too much of a good thing.

In the preface to *The Art of Australia*, Hughes abandons his two former positions and writes:

It now seems to me that the most interesting issue raised by Australian painting is the complex, partly sociological, issue of its pendant relationship to the European Tradition both old and new. A history of Australian art should be written in terms of its overseas prototypes.

So we come full circle: from an innocent art with no discernible prototypes to a provincial art whose main interest is its relationship to its metropolitan sources. Certainly the last position is, from a historical point of view, the more professional approach. But here, too, no interest is expressed in the possibility of such an approach revealing the presence of something a little different from imitation, the presence of a local tradition.

The author's failure to establish a consistent point of view opens a gap between his generalizations and his critical comments on the work of individual artists or, to put it another way, the empirical evidence does not support the conclusions. It is claimed, for example, that 'hardly one good painting' was produced in Australia between the arrival of the First Fleet and the appearance of Tom Roberts. Yet we are also informed that John Glover in Australia (but not in England where so many excellent originals were available to him!) 'consistently painted clear and vivacious pictures'; that Conrad Martens 'co-ordinated sensual verve with inquiry'; and that S. T. Gill's art 'rang as true as a half-crown on a bar counter'. This is not the language which one uses to describe poor or indifferent paintings. It is a case of knocking with the head and appreciating with the eye.

I notice, if I may be permitted to introduce a personal note at this stage, that Hughes has flattered me by making considerable use of my own books on the subject, particularly in his treatment of the art of the nineteenth century. However, I am bound to say that the originality of *The Art of Australia* would have been enhanced had he taken care to ensure that not quite so many of the paintings which he discusses and so many of the quotations from contemporary sources which he uses to illustrate his points had not appeared previously in those books.

And since I have been called to task in the discussion of the Antipodean Manifesto for the 'Marxist stance' that I adopted in *Place, Taste and Tradition*, I am delighted to plead guilty. Marxism provided me with the broad base of a system by means of which I have tried in my own work to bring my material into both a historical and an aesthetic focus. I have no doubt that there have been other, and modifying, influences as well, but Marxism has, I suspect (for who can know in such matters), been the major influence upon my writing of history.

The strength of *The Art of Australia* lies in its value as criticism. In dealing with the artists with whom he was in direct personal contact — Olsen, Perceval, Whiteley, Eric Smith, Albert Tucker, and many others — Hughes always has something challenging, controversial and usually very much to the point to say. His account of the Melbourne and Sydney art scenes during the war and early post-war years is handled in a masterly fashion. One minor pleasure of the book is the freshness of the writing and a kind of undergraduate humour which keeps bubbling through the earnestness of what is, after all, a serious and highly committed work: as when he describes how the romantic painter W. C. Piguenit 'enjoyed a good crag' or compares Sidney Nolan's conquest of London in the 1950s to a handbill description of the Wonderful Kangaroo from Botany Bay, published in 1790.

Notes

*There is little difference between the two editions, apart from rephrasings and some significant omissions. For example, speaking of Donald Friend's work, Hughes writes: 'A negrophile, he has a strong belief in the Noble Savage' (1966 suppressed edition, p. 147); in the 1979 edition (p. 173) this becomes 'He has a strong belief in the Noble Savage'.

61

Max Dimmack on Noel Counihan

—1974—

Those of us who were associated with the first generation of social realist painters in Australia (a second emerged in the 1950s) were drawn to the style, I believe because it was the only style that was radically critical both of the *forms* of painting then practised in Australia and of the *function* which art played in Australian society. The avant-garde styles such as expressionism, futurism, surrealism and constructivism, all of which reached Australia almost simultaneously in the years immediately prior to the Second World War, seemed to us for all their fascination— and they exercised a deep fascination—to be changes in form only, whereas what we were desperately concerned about as political radicals was that art should change its functional role in our society.

This was not the view of the avant-garde of the time. In common with their academic opponents they maintained that the artist had no business with politics or with social concerns. Everybody who was anybody at that time seemed to believe with Clive Bell that 'the only good thing society can do for the artist is to leave him alone'.

By contrast, we were inspired by the work of the Mexican muralists who drew upon the Mexican Revolution and the life of the peasantry for the sources of their art; we read with excitement of the work of the Federal Arts Project (under Roosevelt) in seeking to bring the artists and their work out into public places and make it a popular concern. We were well aware of the close involvement of French painters throughout the nineteenth century with social and political matters, and that at this time French painting led the world; and we were moved by the deep sense of

---

First published in *Overland*, no. 62, Spring 1975, pp. 78–80.

humanity that we found in the work of Brueghel, Rembrandt, Goya and Courbet.

Our position, however, was compromised—almost fatally compromised—by the fact that social realism (in the nineteenth century an art of minority protest) had been adopted by the Communist Party of the USSR as the official style of the party and the state and was being used (for more than a decade before we came to it) to repress by terror, imprisonment and exile all other forms of artistic expression opposed to it.

Small wonder that most Australian artists and critics abjured politics altogether. Yet for a few the conviction remained that the avantgarde protests were a series of palace coups, revolts that left the social function of art unchanged.

In the circumstance a whole spectrum of positions emerged among the artists and intellectuals of the left — hybrid forms of developed realism linked variously with the more acceptable avant-garde forms: expressionism, surrealism, and the like. The moves were largely an honest endeavour to find a way out of the dilemma, that is, to find a way to avoid using realism purely for the purposes of disseminating political propaganda, while developing it as a mode that was capable of expressing personal political involvement and social concern. In this difficult situation Noel Counihan, more single-mindedly and in the end probably more effectively than any other artist in Australia, managed to develop from social realism that sense of conviction that is conveyed by a personal style.

The strength of his art grew from its professionalism grounded in drawing, in cartoon and caricature. Here the comparison with Daumier is close and instructive. For both, drawing was the economic mainstay, and the mode by means of which direct comment on pressing social and political matters might be made. By contrast, painting came slowly. It acted as a reflexive medium by which past events in the artist's life could be transformed into celebrations and records of wrongs done, of evils committed, of the humiliation of the weak and the defenceless: a kind of history painting of the back streets. Counihan in this respect belongs to the revolutionary tradition within romanticism; an art in which emotion is recollected not in tranquillity but with a kind of brooding retrospective sympathy. In this his paintings are quite distinct in tone from the satire and irony of his cartoons. *The Start of the March*, painted in 1944, has as its subject an unemployed procession remembered from 1932; *Woman with Candle* (1972) recalls a childhood experience. True, not all of his paintings were composed in this way. The fine Wonthaggi series, for example, followed fairly soon after the drawings made in the mines. But his best and most memorable paintings possess this retrospective quality.

Max Dimmack's admirable monograph is arranged so that we may gain a better understanding of Counihan's distinctive contributions to the cartoon and caricature, to original print-making, to drawing, to the painting of social genre and to portraiture. He recounts his childhood in a family 'clouded by religious disputes and bitterness' and also by violence; how he first made contact with the arts as a boy chorister for five years in St Paul's Cathedral Choir, Melbourne; his friendship with Eddie Richardson, who widened his appreciation of art and literature. It was Richardson who lent him Merezhkovski's biography of Leonardo, entitled *The Forerunner*, and it was this book, it would seem, that made him decide to become an artist. It was a critical time, with the country's economy tilting into the great Depression of the 1930s. Counihan, after twelve months at Caulfield Grammar, gained a job in a workshop in Flinders Lane, attended night classes at the Gallery School, and met up with the left-wing circle of artists that gathered in the workshop of William Dolphin, the violin-maker, and were associated with the magazine *Stream*. It included Cyril Pearl, Alwyn Lee, Gino Nibbi, Guido Barrachi, Adrian Lawlor and others. Artists closely associated with him at this time included Herbert McLintock, Nutt Buzacott, and Roy Dalgarno.

Counihan became a political activist, and unlike most Australian artists of his generation who were drawn to Marxism in those years, remained so. For example, in protest against the suppression of street meetings in Melbourne, he had himself locked in a cage bolted to a truck, in which he defied the police for twenty-five minutes before being arrested. His successful appeal led to the revision of the existing legislation in a new Act, the Street Meetings Act of 1933.

In the mid-1930s he met Danila Vassilieff, and was impressed by his paintings of Woolloomooloo and the Surry Hills area of Sydney. (The history of urban painting in Australia still needs to be written—it is after all a predominantly urban society—and not all of our artists have hankered after the blue hills and the dead heart.) Later he became intensely involved in the politics associated with the early years of the Contemporary Art Society.

Counihan's passionate political commitment might have destroyed some artists of a different temperament; it provided him with a kind of sheet-anchor to his development. He became the only social realist to pursue his popular—unpopular art from one decade to the next, supported by a few friends and one or two dealers, who recognized in Counihan (whatever they thought of his politics) an artist who was his own man, not a hack in the dealer's stable. Others who painted as well, and often with greater sensitivity to the nuances of paint and personal feeling, lacked his toughness of mind and of spirit to see things through.

One day someone will write the history of realism in Australian painting. It will be a history mostly of defeat. But it will be worth writing. And it should throw a harsh new light on the nature of *successful* achievement in the Australian art world.

62
Merric Boyd
—1975—

In the annals of Australian art Merric Boyd belongs to a generation that has been largely forgotten. The generation before his, that is to say the generation of Tom Roberts and of Arthur Merric Boyd, his father, together with the generation that came after his, that is to say the generation of Sidney Nolan and of his own son, Arthur Boyd, succeeded in tracing out a curve of value around which critical opinion about Australian art as a whole has formed, historical accounts of its development have been written, and the market prices of individual works of art have been largely determined. These two successful generations won for their art a popular audience in their own country, though in many cases acceptance by the community was a long time coming.

For both of the successful generations, once the new vision and the techniques associated with it were grasped, a peak of achievement was reached after a few exciting years of exhilarating activity. Thus Roberts and his companions, armed with hints from *plein air* and impressionist painting, effectively created in the five years between 1885 and 1890 a heroic, pastoral vision of a sunny Australia. Fifty years later, that is immediately before and during the Second World War, the second successful generation, armed with hints predominantly from expressionist painting, created an art which was to some extent a criticism of, and to some extent a reaffirmation of the values of the Heidelberg school.

It is associated with the names of Dobell and Drysdale in Sydney, of Nolan and Arthur Boyd in Melbourne, and their respective circles. Both generations in consequence of their coming to a peak of achievement at a comparatively early age and in gaining popular recognition in their middle years have had to

First published as the preface to Christopher Tadgell's *Merric Boyd Drawings*, Secker & Warburg, London, 1975.

confront and withstand to the best of their ability the populariz-
ation and vulgarization of their vision. (And most of both generations found it easier to 'peak early' than to last the distance.)

In recent times two attempts have been made to reconsider the
validity of the curve of value so deeply and perhaps indelibly
traced by the creative energy of the best Australian artists at
work in the late 1880s and the 1940s. One such attempt has
produced a new interest in the work of colonial artists such as
John Glover and Eugen von Guerard whose achievements were
certainly underestimated by the Heidelberg school and its critical
supporters in its own struggle for recognition. It is unlikely,
however, that this growing interest in colonial art will reverse the
established curve of value; more likely it will score it still more
firmly, viewing the Heidelberg achievement as the culmination
of a century of endeavour to come to terms visually and emotionally with the Antipodean environment. The other attempt at
reconsidering the two-generation model has directed itself towards
a better understanding of the Australian pioneers of modern art
in its abstract and non-figurative, as distinct from its expressionist,
aspects. The principal names associated with this attempt are
Roy de Maistre, Roland Wakelin and Ralph Balson. When seen
within the perspective of the triumph of non-figurative painting
in Australia during the 1960s, this revaluation, like the colonial
revaluation, may also be viewed as a search for appropriate
origins.

Now this second attempt at revaluation is of special relevance
for the serious consideration of the art of Merric Boyd, because
the pioneers of non-figurative art in Australia, like Boyd himself,
belonged to what I have already called the forgotten generation,
lying as it does in a kind of trough of public indifference between
the popular achievements of the successful generations. By what
standards shall we seek to assess the achievements of this generation within the overall context of Australian art? That the successful generations succeeded in contributing creatively to an
understanding of nature and life in Australia is today beyond
serious question. But what, we are bound to ask, did those who
lived out their creative lives in the trough, so to speak, contribute
to Australian experience? The question needs, I believe, to be put
in this way, for those who have sought to rehabilitate the pioneers
of non-figurative art have tended to apply, often implicitly and
unwittingly, but also predictably, purely external criteria such as
the formalist dogmas of modernist painting, in which value is a
function which increases in direct proportion to the degree of

non-figuration. Such criteria are contingent rather than central to the Australian situation. For most of the most creative artists of Merric Boyd's generation pure formalism was but one field for promising experiment among others, not the sole bent and purpose of their art (to Boyd himself it was not an issue) and to assess such art, even implicitly, by the degree to which it approximates to pure abstract form is to misunderstand it; to apply, that is to say, the rituals of our own day to a quite different existential situation. In order then to find a way of approach to the understanding of the art of the forgotten generation, a more elaborate, more detailed and sympathetic examination of the mental, moral, aesthetic and social contexts needs to be undertaken.

In this book Christopher Tadgell makes a splendid beginning towards the reconstruction of such concealed but influential contexts in his perceptive analysis of the moral and spiritual forces, the aesthetic interests and ideals, the national and supra-national motivations that were the setting for the emergence of Merric Boyd's highly personal art. Tadgell lays down a number of guidelines that could be of value not only for the understanding of Boyd's art but also that of his generation. For here we may clearly observe how one member of that generation starting out, in the manner of Morris, with a belief in art as a social healer of mankind's wounds was drawn, by the pressures of life, increasingly towards a belief in art as a personal ritual, an inner necessity. In Merric Boyd's Australia few men survived as creative personalities to the end. None of them can fairly be said to have 'peaked' early; their development was gradual but persistent through life. Their personalities as artists are private when compared with the more public personalities of the successful generations. There is an air about them of the defeated, of ideals unrealized; the austere dignity of lives finely attuned to an aesthetic ideal yet unfulfilled. Merric Boyd certainly failed to implement in Australia the wider social and artistic ambitions of the Arts and Crafts Movement but he and his wife succeeded in the more delicate task of establishing a creative home and workshop for the family in which art was pursued as an essential aspect of moral and spiritual perception. It was very much a case of 'education through art' successfully conducted years before the late Sir Herbert Read coined the phrase. So that it became possible for the tenderness and fear which the father discerned in the paws of the kangaroo and in the melting eye of the koala to be seen by his sons much later in the hands and eyes of Aborigines and survivors from Buchenwald. Art as an unsolved problem in sympathy; in the sacredness of life. Merric Boyd is important, as Tadgell reveals, for an understanding of the persistence of vitalism in Australian art.

But what does appear to have been central to the experience of Merric Boyd's generation was their experience, never to be forgotten, of the unspeakable, unimaginable human carnage of the First World War. For him and for some other artists such as Godfrey Miller, Ian Fairweather, and John Power, all of whom experienced the effects of trench warfare, perhaps the pursuit of art became a personal defence against the innate savagery of humankind, an art used as an inner necessity for the survival of the personality and for whom popular recognition (so necessary to sustain those of the successful generations who were not forced to look down into the pit) was irrelevant.

63
Modern Masters Exhibition—Manet to Matisse
—1975—

Only one other exhibition comparable to the Modern Masters Exhibition at the Art Gallery of New South Wales (April to May 1975) has been shown in Australia: the exhibition of French and British Modern Masters, arranged by Basil Burdett for Sir Keith Murdoch in 1939. And for the ensuing period of thirty-six years an exhibition comparable in quality and scope to that show has been quite beyond Australian resources. It is not possible, therefore, to praise too highly all those who have combined to make Manet to Matisse possible: the International Council of the Museum of Modern Art (the museum, in any case, which has done more than any other overseas museum to keep us in touch during the interim with twentieth-century developments); the Alcoa Foundation; the Australian government; the many private and public lenders of paintings; and in particular Mr William Lieberman, who has lived with the exhibition for many months, devising its form, supervising its assembling, its cataloguing, transport and, most importantly, its security during its exhibition in Sydney and Melbourne.

The exhibition begins with three paintings by Manet. In choosing to begin thus, Mr Lieberman follows the view favoured by many art historians and some highly influential critics, such as Clement Greenberg, that the modern movement may be said to begin with Manet to the extent that it can be said to begin with any one painter (and one must of course begin somewhere!). Much can be said in favour of this view; although it is not, of course, a matter beyond question. There is, for instance, the view coming increasingly into favour that the significant point of departure is to be found in the work of Gustave Courbet.

The question turns on the paradoxical tendency of realism and

First published in *Art in Australia*, vol. 13, no. 1, July–September 1975, pp. 69–79.

naturalism to flatten forms and assert the picture plane. This tendency in Manet's art is revealed in three delightful paintings. The early *A Boy with a Sword*, from the Metropolitan Museum of Art, New York, painted in 1861, reveals Manet's desire to dispense with half-tones, and so contrast lights against darks sharply, to give a greater visual thrust to his image, technical devices he learnt (and developed in his own fashion) from his deep study of Spanish painting, most notably Velasquez; the small painting from Cincinnati, *Women at the Races*, painted four years later, reveals how he applied this flattening of modelled forms to an open-air crowd scene; and the third painting, of Manet's own country house at *Rueil* (1882), from the National Gallery of Victoria, and completed shortly before his death, shows how much he had come to adopt the methods of his impressionist friends.

The three Manets thus present the framework of the first section of the exhibition. Impressionism is represented by a group of exceedingly beautiful paintings, probably the finest impressionist paintings ever shown in Australia, for the Murdoch exhibition of 1939 did not include examples of the impressionist masters. Perhaps the two most notable are the jewel-like painting by Renoir of *Monet Painting in his Garden* (c. 1874) from the Wadsworth Atheneum, and the opalescent Monet, *Still Life with a Basket of Eggs* (c. 1910), from the collection of Mrs Lloyd Bruce Wescott. A slight matter for regret here is the lack of an early Monet, one say prior to 1872, not only because it is in such paintings that we may witness that poignant and tremulous moment when naturalism begins its retreat before the science and the poetry of pure colour, but also because one such painting might have made clear better than any other the distinctions (that were to widen) between French and Australian impressionism. Even so, a careful study of the Renoirs and Monets in this exhibition serves to make abundantly clear how inadequate it is to think of impressionism simply as an application of pure colour by means of divided brushstrokes in the service of optical sensation. Of course impressionists also made use of ground colours, used tones, mixed their colours on the palette and blurred their brushwork where it suited their artistic purpose to do so. What makes their work so different from the work of the Heidelberg school (who around the late 1880s adopted and adapted most if not all of the impressionist techniques) is the objective fact that they were recording their feelings about a different range of colours and different atmospheric effects, and that as a group they were less adventurous and experimental in developing their own personal styles.

Mr Lieberman's selection of impressionist painting is of great value in revealing how in both the late Monet and the late Renoir colour asserts its poetry and its independence. In the Waterlily paintings and the two paintings (Renoir's and Monet's) of the Doge's Palace, Venice (Lieberman's juxtapositions are one of the joys of the exhibition) colour tones begin to transfuse the whole surface of the canvas. In this way they foreshadowed, and helped to inspire, the colour-field painters of the United States such as Mark Rothko.

Paul Cézanne is, and quite justly, one of the painters most strongly represented in the exhibition. Lieberman was able to borrow two absolutely superb Cézannes: the monumental portrait of his wife, *Mme. Cézanne in a Red Armchair* (c. 1877) from the Museum of Fine Arts, Boston (Paine Bequest), and the beautiful *L'Estaque* landscape (1882–85), Museum of Modern Art (Paley Gift). The Boston portrait is as fine a picture as ever Cézanne painted. Colour here asserts its own new freedom while achieving a plastic architecture; and here lies the seed not only of cubism but also the best of Matisse. It is difficult to grasp today what now seems here to be so inevitable in terms of paint, tone and structure; won only by means of a fumbling, patient obstinacy combined with a genius for knowing what was right when it was right. In the *L'Estaque* there is a facet of painting in the lower right mid-distance which reveals something of Cézanne's methods. Here he clearly began with a shape drawn from the large, flat and bare slope of the roof of a country cottage, but in developing his composition he proceeded to paint landscape motifs onto this bare plane without obliterating or disguising the original form. By such means Cézanne permitted contingencies in the process of painting to remain visible in the final result. This is an excellent example of but one of several of the devices he adopted for creating a visual ambiguity (the delight and despair of his successors) between depth and flatness.

Matisse is the most strongly represented painter in the exhibition: no less than eleven splendid paintings, all but one of which are illustrated and discussed in Alfred Barr's classic monograph on the painter (1951). This is not altogether surprising because it would be fair comment, I believe, to say that the exhibition is more tuned to Matisse's kind of excellence than it is to any other major twentieth-century master, Picasso say, or Klee, or Kandinsky, or Pollock. And there is of course the title of the exhibition itself which, as we proceed to viewing, gains in significance; so that we come to realize that the show is centred upon the declaration of those pictorial qualities that are released by Manet and find their fulfilment in Matisse.

Indeed Matisse's *Guitarist* (1903), lent from the Colin Collection, New York, reveals Matisse taking off from Manet's Hispanic style, and then in *The Young Sailor* (1906) from the Gelman Collection, achieving with a profound sense of personal assurance and free colour within swinging arabesques. Here we have demonstrated before our eyes the twentieth-century heritage not of Cézanne but of Gauguin. One of the unquestionable delights of this exhibition, as noted above, has been the points of comparison and contrast Lieberman has succeeded in setting up within his selection; in this case, for example, between Matisse's *Sailor* and Gauguin's *Man with an Axe* (1891) from the Lewyt Collection, New York, especially in the painting of the two heads. Another such instructive comparison is that between the Matisse *Collioure* (1908) (Gelman Collection) and Picasso's *La Rue des Bois* (1908) (David Rockefeller Collection), both painted at about the same time and recording the same view (but the first lying in descent from Cézanne, and the other from Gauguin).

Equally suggestive is Lieberman's choice of portraits. Here the history of modern painting may be traced within the constraints imposed by a traditional category of painting: from Manet's *Boy* (1861) and Cézanne's *Wife* (1877) to Matisse's *Girl with Green Eyes* (1909) from the San Francisco Museum of Art (Levy Bequest), and thence on to the portraits by Jawlensky, Bonnard, Modigliani and Miro and Grosz. One would hope that this splendid range of portraits might give pause to that gaggle of local art critics who have for thirty years (in the name of an intolerant, unlinear, determinist brand of art history) called incessantly for an end to the Archibald Prize because portraiture was no longer, in their view, a viable category of modern painting.

Those artistic kinsmen of Matisse, the Fauves, are well represented, particularly by two excellent Derains: the famous *Henri Matisse* (1905) from the Tate Gallery, London, and that stunning decoration, the *View of Collioure* (1905) from the Musée National d'Art Moderne, Paris.

In contrast to the confident way in which the main line of the tradition from Manet to Matisse is laid down in a series of visually captivating masterpieces, the alternative options available to twentieth-century artists are handled with less certainty. For example, although the two Braques, *Piano and Mandola*, and *Violin and Palette* (both 1909–10) from the Guggenheim Museum, New York, do reveal the radiating, accumulative, 'baroque' aspects of Braque's cubism, I cannot help feeling that the treatment of cubism as a twentieth-century movement is thin. One of its important sources—as Apollinaire made clear—is symbolism. And symbolism, to say the least, gets light treatment in this show. The Ensor *Fireworks* (1887) from the Albright-Knox Art Gallery, Buffalo, is too closely allied to the impressionist-fauve tradition to be typical either of Ensor or of the symbolist movement from which he gained so much. The two Gauguins are both fine paintings, but do not reveal his mastership of painting as the Cézannes and Matisses do. One would not realize from this exhibition that he was the first of the modern masters to become fully conscious of the course that twentieth-century painting was to take from nature towards abstraction. And the representation of Van Gogh by one not particularly distinguished work is disappointing. Basil Burdett, in 1939, did much better by bringing eight very fine paintings by Van Gogh to Australia.

The weakness in the symbolist sources of modernism is revealed also in the lack of any paintings from Pablo Picasso's Blue, Pink or Negro periods; and the cubist Picassos selected do not, in my view, measure up to those by Braque. Juan Gris, with three splendidly representative paintings, comes off much better. But then there is always something of the pedant in Gris' work even at the best of times. For the futurists, one has to turn to their Russian and German followers, to the works by Feininger, Marc and Malevich, rather than to the Italians themselves, because the Balla, though a delight, is just too suavely successful, and the Boccioni, though it reveals the potential strength of the greatest of the futurists, is surely a failure as a painting. By contrast, and perhaps amusingly, Severini, one of the weakest of the Italian futurists, dominates his colleagues with one of his best paintings.

Because of the weight of attention given to the tradition of *la belle peinture* which lies between Manet and Matisse, the contributions of the pure abstractionists, such as Mondrian and Kandinsky, that of the surrealists, and above all the critical edge which gave such nervous volatility to Picasso's genius, all become somewhat contingent on the sumptuous visual delight of the show as a whole. That is not to say that the Kandinsky is not one of his best; or that we should not be thankful for the opportunity to see such a fascinating Picasso as *The Studio* (1927–28) (The Museum of Modern Art, Chrysler Gift), a painting that well repays patient study.

64
Humphrey McQueen on Australian Modernism
—1979—

Humphrey McQueen's *The Black Swan of Trespass: The Emergence of Modernist Painting in Australia to 1944* (Alternative Publishing Cooperative, Sydney, 1979) is a highly important contribution to the literature of Australian art, and will be read and discussed widely. McQueen regards earlier accounts of modernism in Australia as inadequate because it has been treated, he says, primarily in terms of a sequence of arrivals from abroad. 'Modernism arose in Australia from and through identifiably local conditions'. The book sets out to defend that thesis.

McQueen begins with a personal definition of modernism, 'a range of responses to a nexus of social—artistic—scientific problems'; the book is developed around this definition. By responses he is referring to what in more conventional histories would be called movements: surrealism, cubism and so forth. Four problems are chosen to constitute the social—artistic—scientific nexus: class conflict, the unconscious, science and landscape. The nexus, however, McQueen warns us, moves in time and has no fixed centre, resulting in a constant redistribution of the problems. The responses are responses not to the problems themselves, but to the redistribution of the problems. He gives the example: 'Surrealism is not a direct response to the unconscious. Surrealism is a response to a distribution of all the elements such that the unconscious temporarily attains dominance within a nexus'.

The book is laid out around this model. Part One is presented in narrative form—though McQueen makes it clear that he does not much like narrative forms of exposition. But it is not straight narrative art history, for he provides brief narrative accounts of painting, poetry, the novel, and criticism in Australia during the

First published in *Meanjin*, vol. 38, no. 4, 1979, pp. 521–8.

1920s, followed by a narration of the leading events of painting during the 1930s, concluding with an account of the Dobell law suit of 1944. Part Two is taken up with an exemplification of the problems of the nexus; Part Three, with an account of the art, life and work of Margaret Preston, whom McQueen regards as the most important Australian modernist. This last section is also intended as an example of the value of McQueen's model for evaluating critically and historically the work of any artist.

One of the weaknesses of the book is that the author never quite succeeds in delivering what he promises. That is to say he does not reveal the particular distribution of problems within his nexus which produces a given response, for example surrealism, social realism. When he comes to the actual discussion of these matters his approach is much more empirical. This is all to the good, for an attempt to give due weight to the four components of his nexus as an account of surrealism would have become unbearably schematic. But the fact that he does not attempt to use the model with any precision must call its value seriously into question.

That is to be regretted, because the proposition that, in any attempt to understand an art movement, or in McQueen's phrase 'response', a set of relevant components should be isolated and discussed even though they may belong to different levels of discourse and issue from widely different social problems, is soundly based. The trouble is that the number of components are far greater than McQueen can possibly allow for in the space at his disposal, and they differ and vary in weight and relevance not only from movement to movement but from artist to artist. McQueen's approach is superior to a unilinear approach such as the formalist one, which contends that the only problems which affect an artist's work and need to be taken account of are those which emerge within the discipline he practises. Because McQueen's book raises the relevance of contextual studies for understanding a given art movement, the book should be of great value in arousing discussion wherever art and art history are taught in Australia.

One such discussion might turn on the factual question: has McQueen chosen the 'problems' most relevant to an understanding of modernism in Australia? One serious omission is the presence of the tradition of painting itself which is always problematic for any artist who is in any way an innovator. The tradition is there, it produced him as a painter, and he has to contend with it. To say that is not to be a formalist, but simply to state what should be obvious: that the painter as painter can only respond to the nexus of problems which confront him in visual terms; and for the response to take visual form, the techniques and traditions of painting constitute a central problem.

That is a fundamental issue. But there are others of special relevance to an understanding of modernism. Has McQueen omitted some central problems for modernism in Australia? I have long been of the opinion, to take an example, that a thorough account of the history of spiritualism, theosophy and anthroposophy in Australia, as abroad, is much more relevant to an understanding of modernism than, say, Einstein's theories. Einstein's theories may have been advanced as a justification to provide a measure of respectability, but McQueen has not convinced me that they were a problem, or that they acted as a cause within a 'distributed nexus'.

It is quite surprising too that McQueen, being a Marxist—and in my view a percipient and able one—does not include an economic factor among his range of problems. Class conflict, here, obviously is no substitute. One can appreciate his desire not to be trapped in a simplistic base-superstructure account of modernism in Australia, but in neglecting to give due weight to economic factors I suspect that he has overlooked a prime factor leading to the 'emergence'—to keep to his terminology—as distinct from the 'arrival' of modernism in Australia.

The economic factor is to be found in the growth of retail trading and advertising in Sydney in the years after the First World War. Its importance has been examined and assessed by Mary Eagle, where the relation of modernism both to the local and overseas painting of the previous generation is fully considered. Closely connected in Sydney to this economic factor was the opening up of the Northern Suburbs Railway, and the spread of new housing for a younger generation of the middle classes; houses which provided walls and a life-style congenial to modernism both at the level of design and at the level of art. Most of the leading Sydney modernists whose life and work McQueen has occasion to discuss, such as Ethel Anderson, Grace Cossington Smith, Roland Wakelin, dwelt on the north shore—an area which has always been a great fortress of Liberal voters. Ethel Anderson was right, the fears of Lionel Lindsay and his wide circle of anti-Semitic friends were groundless. Modernism was not a Bolshevik conspiracy; it was the grandchildren decorating the new bungalow.

Well, to the extent that it was post-impressionism. This is

where McQueen's concept of modernism as a 'nexus of responses' requires further discussion. There is one great disadvantage in the use of words like 'modern art' 'modernist art', 'modernism'. They are by their nature incapable of naming permanently and substantially any object of enquiry. What they do is to describe the relation of the enquirer to the object of the enquiry as a contemporary or a near-contemporary relationship. There was a time when Gothic art was literally known as modern art. The word was used throughout the nineteenth century on various occasions about quite different things. Consider, for example, Ruskin's *Modern Painters*. By the time we have decided what we are talking about when we talk about modernism, time has passed, and our students or our children are talking about something else. It is a shifting sand upon which to erect a nexus.

This does not apply to the components of 'modernism', as McQueen understands the term: post-impressionism, cubism, surrealism, and so on. Such movements possess a certain specificity, might be shown to have a beginning, a middle and an end; but modernism is at heart a rather nebulous word, and like 'culture shock' a kind of consumer reaction to recent innovation. If it is endowed with a carefully designed and specific meaning it rapidly wears out and becomes obsolete. Clement Greenberg took possession of the word in this way, particularly in its adjectival form, and made it synonymous with his formalist account of twentieth-century art. Its continued use, in my view, only blurs issues both in art criticism and art history.

Let me explain what I mean in relation to McQueen's account. He writes of Australian painting between 1920 and 1944 using the hold-all of modernism; but he fails to point out that post-impressionism and cubism were both from a theoretical and practical viewpoint arts for art's sake, whereas expressionism, surrealism and social realism were, in their own ways, arts of social and political commitment. This is what the struggles in the first years of the Contemporary Art Society were about; but this basic division is glossed over and *no account of expressionism and its influence on Australian art* appears in McQueen's book. I have read the book through carefully twice and cannot recall having come upon the word once. It does not appear in the index. Yet expressionism was the only movement in early twentieth-century art which thoroughly acclimatized itself to the Australian culture and made a substantial contribution to the Australian tradition. It is, for example, by ignoring the impact of expressionism upon the art of Dobell during his last years in England that McQueen is able to present him as an academic painter. Nolan, around whom some basic issues devolved, even well before 1944, is only mentioned in passing.

One of the consequences of McQueen's dislike of narrative accounts is that his substitute, a nexus of problems, lands the reader in a temporal jungle. Although he quotes, at the beginning of Part One, the advice of the King in *Alice in Wonderland* to the White Rabbit, 'Begin at the beginning and go on till you come to the end', throughout the book McQueen himself acts out the role of dissident white rabbit and does nothing of the kind. In consequence, the work of Meldrum, Gruner and Heysen are discussed in the middle sections, long after the discussion about the formation of the Contemporary Art Society, surrealism, social realism. I find it confusing; and I should think it will be even more confusing for art students who might otherwise gain much of value from the book. Indeed the way McQueen has put it all together keeps on reminding me of books by Marshall McLuhan.

McQueen has some flattering comments to make about my own first book, *Place, Taste and Tradition*, but also takes me to task on one or two matters to which I am bound to reply.

The gist of the first is this: my version of social realism and the versions expressed in the work of the artists I supported, Counihan, O'Connor, Bergner, and so forth, contained no view of the future, or of how the future was to be realized; offered, that is to say, no hope for the Australian working class. Now in one sense this is fair comment. To speak for myself, I have never been able to see how a realist can affect the future except by drawing attention to things he considers to be significant in the present. Drawing attention may or may not affect the future, but as realist, he or she can do no more. To incorporate an overt programme of action into a work of art may well be legitimate, but I do not see how it can be called realistic. I should call it idealistic. Much so-called Soviet socialist realism is, in my view, a kind of proletarian idealism. Its parallels are to be found in traditional history painting in which events in the lives of heroes are enacted. Although I have learned to admire masterpieces in these categories, I must confess to a personal distaste for them, whether classical or proletarian, because in my experience the lives of heroes are usually re-enacted, paradoxically, not to encourage heroic action but to encourage conformity.

I do not mean by this that I am opposed to the expression of hope in art—I am only saying that that is not the way realism works. In some of my own paintings, and poems written during the war years, I expressed hope for the future of the Australian working class. The monstrous reality of fascism had to be lived through in order to be understood; it made hope feel like a sentimental indulgence, its expression in art a false rhetoric. Party functionaries who kept on calling for the expression of more hope did not help much.

Should Humphrey McQueen wish to keep playing the tedious 'that isn't Marxist' game, he might like to consider the comparison which the first Marxist, Friedrich Engels, made of the June and February revolutions in Paris, 1848:

The June revolution is the revolution of despair and is fought with the silent anger and the gloomy cold-bloodedness of despair. The workers know that they are involved in a *fight to the death* and in the face of the battle's terrible seriousness, even the cheerful French *esprit* remains silent ...

The unanimity of the February revolution, that poetic unanimity full of dazzling delusions and beautiful lies so appropriately symbolised by that traitor Lamartine, has disappeared. Today the inexorable seriousness of reality tears up all the hypocritical promises of February 25.[1]

There were times during the Second World War when the right to hope would have seemed almost frivolous. Theodor Adorno, for whom McQueen has some respect, has put it as well as anyone:

After Auschwitz
Fear used to be tied to the *principium individuationis* of self-preservation, and that principle, by its own consistency abolishes itself. What the sadists in the camps told their victims, 'Tomorrow you'll be wiggling skyward as smoke from the chimney', bespeaks the indifference of each individual life that is the direction of history. Even in his formal freedom, the individual is as fungible and replaceable as he will be under the liquidators' boots.

But since, in a world whose law is universal individual profit, the individual has nothing but this self that has become indifferent, the performance of the old, familiar tendency is at the same time the most dreadful of things. There is no getting out of this, no more than out of an electrified barbed wire around the camps. Perennial suffering has as much right to expression as a tortured man to scream, hence it may have been wrong to say that after Auschwitz you could no longer write poems. But it is not wrong to raise the less cultural question whether after Auschwitz you can go on living—especially whether one who escaped by accident, one who by rights should have been killed, may go on living. His mere survival calls for the coldness, the basic principle of bourgeois subjectivity, without which there could have been no Auschwitz; this is the drastic guilt of him who was spared. By way of atonement he will be plagued by dreams such as that he is no longer living at all, that he has been sent to the ovens in 1944 and his whole existence has been imaginary, an emanation of the insane wish of a man killed twenty years earlier.[2]

There was not much hope in Australian social realism. It was given to a few of us here to express a great sadness in which hope would have been an impertinence. For the first time Australian art embraced the plight of the Jews, the Aboriginals, and the Australian working class during the Depression. For that extension of range, Australian society being what it is, we are not forgiven.

All of which introduces a larger question: the attitude of McQueen, Terry Smith and others of the New Left to the realist tradition in Australian art. The attack is not only upon the social realists, but the whole tradition of realism in Australia: Gill, Roberts, McCubbin, Dobell. McQueen writes, 'A good number of the paintings in Smith's realist tradition demonstrate, even celebrate, the bourgeoisie's triumph'. Of course they do: however else, in the circumstances, could they do anything else? In a dependent colonial society such as Australia, what class but the local and emergent bourgeoisie were in a position to support a realist tradition? Realism was the historic style by which the bourgeoisie, from J. L. David on, established its ascendancy in France. But there is more to it than that. It is only the realist tradition which holds out the possibility of an independent Australian tradition; when it declines in painting it re-emerges in theatre or in film. If the New Left is bent upon destroying the realist tradition in Australian art, what are they proposing to put in its place: a colonial tradition based upon Eugen von Guerard and J. J. Hilder? Of course it is not difficult to show the relation between Roberts and the pastoral interest. But that is only one part of the story. One must also keep in mind that it was largely the work of the artists around Roberts who fought for the recognition of an independent school of Australian artists in the face of the prevailing preference for European-derived art in the public galleries and private collections.

On one other personal point I must take issue with McQueen. He writes, 'Smith subsequently degutted this work (*Place, Taste and Tradition*) to make two editions of *Australian Painting*, in 1962 and 1971.' Degutted is a rather rugged word. When the first edition of *Australian Painting* appeared the art critic Alan McCulloch said that it was substantially a rewrite of *Place, Taste and Tradition*, or words to that effect. Subsequently he admitted to me personally that he had not had time to read the book before he reviewed it. I suspect that Humphrey McQueen has not read much of *Australian Painting* either.

I must leave it to others to decide whether *Australian Painting* is a degutted version of *Place, Taste and Tradition*. Fortunately, both books are now in print, so the comparison is readily available. Actually they are quite different books, but complement each other. One was written in the darkest days of the Second World War at a time when Hitler's armies had reached their greatest expansion in Europe, Russia and Africa. The other was written at a time when the cultural imperialism of the United States was such that only American-derived forms of modernism were finding unqualified critical approval in the art schools and among the most influential critics of this country.

Humphrey McQueen makes out a brave case for Margaret Preston as the leading painter of the inter-war years. I think that he is probably right so far as the 1920s are concerned. If one considers her work both in terms of its inherent aesthetic achievement and its contribution to an independent Australian tradition, I doubt whether there was anyone at that time to equal her; this is well-argued, and one of the most positive things about the book. I do not, however, think that this can be said of Preston during the later 1930s. This was the time when I got to know her quite well, and came to admire her volatile temperament and tremendous vitality. I opened her last exhibition in 1953. But in those years, as McQueen's analysis bears out, she was no longer certain of her direction. The post-impressionism upon which she had built her style, even when married to her important experiments with Aboriginal design and colour, was not an art to cope with the terrible realities of the war years; and I think she was aware of it. She lived too close in time to the Heidelberg school to grasp its substantial achievements, seeing it only in terms of the chauvinistic image fashioned during the 1920s by critics such as J. S. MacDonald and Lionel Lindsay, rather than its original achievement. Instead, she made a brave foray into the *forms* of Aboriginal art. That may still be of importance for the future. But it was a personal achievement only, not, as she had fondly hoped, a new direction for Australian art. If one wants to find a clue to the reason why that path was not at that time a viable one for Australian artists, the best thing to do is to take a good steady look at Yosl Bergner's paintings of contemporary Aboriginals.

Margaret Preston, *General Post Office, Sydney*, 1942, oil on canvas, 43 × 53 cm. Art Gallery of South Australia

White Australian art, in my view, will only be able to draw a genuine vitality from the Aboriginal tradition when emergent twentieth-century Aboriginal art, literature and theatre are in a position to meet it on something like equal terms. That was not possible in Preston's day; with all the best will in the world and despite herself, her forays into Aboriginal design could not fail to be, in a profound sense, a kind of cultural exploitation. I always had the greatest admiration for her creative energies, but was continually concerned lest her restless search for a national style would land her among the proto-fascist ideologues of Jindyworobak. McQueen is in a position to take a cool look at that group and redress an injustice here and there. Indeed, if one looks carefully at McQueen's revaluations the Right seems, all in all, to do very well indeed. Much, much better than Christopher Caudwell, for example, whose books were an inspiration and who died young in Spain; or Rah Fizelle, who spent a lifetime in the schools of New South Wales working towards a more liberating attitude to art education, and getting on with his own work at night and weekends in the days before the cultural grants; or William Frater, a fine artist, who does not deserve to be dismissed in the way that McQueen dismisses him. This tendency to put up and knock down greatly detracts from the many solid qualities of the book.

The Black Swan of Trespass then is an irritating but thought-provoking book; a most welcome change from that great pile which is threatening to collapse our coffee tables. *Le Style est l'homme même.*

Notes

[1] Marx-Engels, *Collected Works*, Lawrence & Wishart, London, vol. 7, pp. 130−1.

[2] Theodor W. Adorno, *Negative Dialectics*, tr. E. B. Ashton, Seabury Press, New York, 1973, pp. 362−3.

65
Robert Hughes on Modern Painting
—1981—

Robert Hughes' *The Shock of the New* (British Broadcasting Corporation, London, 1980) has been developed from the original BBC television series of that name. Eight themes explore different aspects of modernism: its relation to technology, to the pursuit of power, to personal liberty, to sensory experience, popular culture, and so forth. As befits a popular presentation, no attempt is made to pursue the themes with rigour. Nothing is demonstrated; everything is suggested. The book works by an elaborate interlace of metaphor, anecdote, wit and suggestive allusion, and indeed it works very well, for Hughes is the master of a flexible and sensitive prose style. Perhaps the finest moments are those in which he relates the masterpieces of early modernism to the specific environments which helped to inspire them. To read him on Cézanne and the Provençal landscape, on Van Gogh and the environs of the asylum of Saint Rémy, where that artist spent his last years, is a moving experience. It has never been done better. For this is not only a popular and readable, but also a perceptive and sensitive book. One of its most important achievements is that it places modernism, for those seeking an introduction to the subject, within a much more human context than the rigid strait-jacket of formalism into which New York critics like Clement Greenberg have sought to confine it.

Yet the book possesses serious flaws. It is weak, for one thing, on historical fact. It is misleading, for example, to write that the designs of the French architect Louis Boullée were 'provoked by the early industrial revolution'. Boullée died in 1797 and probably never saw an early industrial factory in his life, and certainly

Not previously published. *The Shock of the New* was reviewed for the Australian Broadcasting Commission in March 1981.

never designed one. In another place Hughes writes, 'The first artist to paint in Tahiti was a Scot, William Hodges, who went there with Cook in 1769. (Unlike Gauguin he cannily gave up painting when he got back to England and became a banker.)'. Now Hodges was not the first artist to paint in Tahiti, he was not a Scot, he did not go to Tahiti with Cook in 1769 and he did not become a banker when he returned from the Pacific in 1775. He continued to paint for another twenty years, becoming the first important English painter to work in India. Other specialists may find Hughes equally vulnerable on fact in their own areas of interest. Such flaws however are not fatal to the strengths of the book; they can be removed in later editions.

But more serious criticism will be mounted. For this is very much an Establishment book. Although a token criticism of modernism is sustained throughout, making it livelier to read than the apologetics of earlier men like Read, Haftmann, and Arnason, there is no attempt made to revalue the avant-garde canon. All the grand old chestnuts of the first-year course in modernism pass through the projector once again, but now with all the authority of the BBC and the art critic of *Time* magazine. There is a paradox here. Modernism, Hughes repeatedly assures us, is finished. He is quite a master of the thumping historical generalization with the flaring apocalyptic edge. The first decade of twentieth-century architects, he assures us, was probably the last that felt itself to be a community of the chosen. Braque was probably the last avant-garde artist to be inspired by the bric-a-brac of his studio, Picasso was the last Mediterranean man. And so on. Yet the thin line of avant-garde masters emerges unscathed and each is awarded his red badge of cultural courage. When even such official organizations as UNESCO are calling for a more diverse, more pluralist, view of international cultural achievement this book emerges as a very old-fashioned one indeed: as a reinforcement of the European—North American cultural ascendancy. Consider Hughes' own position. He grew from Australian soil, as certainly as Cézanne grew from the soil of Provence, yet no Australian artist is mentioned in this survey of the art of the past century. Is this proof of Hughes' now mature critical objectivity or is it a conspicuous example of cultural cringe, the work of a well-trained Janissery at the court of MOMA? It is revealing that the phrase 'cultural cringe' is the only Australian thing to appear in the book.

Nor is it an original book. Important questions are not distinguished from trivial ones. Hughes has not grasped the significance of avant-gardism as a cultural mimicry of high technology, and that both are likely to be around for some time yet. Instead, in keeping with current fashion, he wants to write *finis* to modernism. The end of the book is nostalgic, a premature elegy for modernism. The large questions, such as the relentless secularization of modern man—the Ayatollah Khomeini notwithstanding—are avoided. Certainly it is most pleasing to see the origins of abstract art in the hocus-pocus of theosophy at last appearing in the popular literature. But the penny has not yet dropped. Hughes is not aware that abstract art is a kind of end-phase to the Gothic Revival, a vain attempt to put the ghost back into the machine. And he imagines that he has found a convincing answer to the political art of our time by questioning whether any political work of art ever influenced a political event. As well ask whether holy icons ever converted the pagan. Such questions are unanswerable. What matters in this context is that art traditionally acts as a socializing, bonding process, and that in our time the social space once occupied by the sacred is now being increasingly occupied by the political; the spiritual itself becoming an aesthetic metaphor. Modernism is not dead. But its heroic days are over and we live on in the twilight of its trivialities. Hughes has nothing new to tell us about this decline from heroism to triviality.

66
Patrick McCaughey on Fred Williams
—1981—

Patrick McCaughey's *Fred Williams* (Bay Books, Sydney, 1980) is obviously an important book, the most detailed monograph yet to appear on any Australian artist and in some respects at least the best one. It compares more than favourably, for example, with Franz Philipp's book *Arthur Boyd* in the fluency of its presentation if not in its grasp of context. The plates are keyed to the text, so that one has no difficulty in following the argument. Great care has been expended to achieve an acceptable standard of colour. There is a bibliography, and a useful list of Williams' exhibitions and selected reviews of his work. The index, however, is inadequate. Almost a random affair. The Helena Rubenstein but not the Archibald Prize is listed; Rudy Komon, but not the Joseph Brown Gallery; John Reed, but not William Lieberman. This is regrettable in a book which is more likely to be consulted with a specific purpose in mind than read through.

These are technical matters as much the responsibility of the publisher as the author, but in more basic matters the book must be challenged. Although McCaughey has the deepest admiration for Williams' art, responds warmly to it, and has studied it more thoroughly than anyone, his account of its emergence within the general context of Australian art is, it seems to me, misleading. As one reads the text one gains the uneasy feeling that Williams' art is not being located within its own context of aims and aspirations, of the constraints and opportunities which his life and times have afforded, but is rather being used as a kind of apologia for a lost cause—a cause which was never the artist's, but was once the author's.

The cause, that is to say, of a totally non-figurative art for

First published in *Meanjin*, vol. 40, no. 3, October 1981, pp. 389–94.

Australia which would render other forms obsolete. During the 1950s and 1960s every artist and art student in Australia had to front up, in one way or another, to this new mythology of the avant-garde at once historicist and apocalyptic in its pretensions. It is important to be clear about this. The question was not the validity of abstract art as one art among others, but the claim that it was a new visual language which would render all other forms obsolete. Different generations confronted the challenge in different ways. This is the clue to McCaughey's reading of Williams' art. Williams was born in 1927, McCaughey in 1943. The aspirations of two distinct artistic generations divide them.

McCaughey's deep early commitment to the significance of abstract art in Australia has made it difficult for him to come fully to terms with Williams' equally deep commitment to naturalism. He persistently attempts in his account of the evolution of Williams' style to fit it into the mould of New York mainstream criticism and its hero-figures, a mould fundamentally anti-naturalistic.

In order to come to terms with Williams' art one must first come to terms with the nature of naturalism. Naturalists among painters are out-of-doors men. They hold tenaciously to the view that if their art is to grow, flourish and retain its strength, it must be replenished constantly not only by the observation and experience of nature but also by a kind of intimate communion with it. It is this kind of communion, established by long habit, that one finds in all the great naturalists: in Claude and Jacob Ruisdael, in Constable and Paul Cézanne. And one finds it in Williams, as indeed Patrick McCaughey demonstrates on almost every page of his book. But the full implications of Williams' chosen role of a naturalist painter in the twentieth century, faithfully adhered to through a successful career, are not examined.

This occurs because McCaughey does not distinguish between the reductivist programme of the New York school, which sought to eliminate all references to nature from art and create a pure, non-referential art, from the traditional transformational process, often described as 'abstracting from nature', by which all artists whether classic or romantic, traditional or modern, admit nature to their art. McCaughey writes as if this process were employed only by those kinds of artists for whom the formal qualities of art are consciously held to be pre-eminent, whereas the real division, to the extent that it exists at all between artists, turns upon the degree to which 'abstracting from nature' is regarded as a conscious and deliberate process, a point of view favoured by classicists and formalists, and the degree to which it is held to be an intuitive, if not sub-conscious, process, as favoured by, for example, romantics and expressionists.

Williams received his early training as an artist at a time when it was still possible for artists and their teachers to take the continuous study of nature as an all-important base for the development of a personal style. Williams' own development, as McCaughey notes, was traditionally oriented. In contrast to the generation which preceded him, of Nolan and Tucker, Perceval and Boyd, he made no explicit gestures, characteristic of the avant-garde, of revolt from traditional practice. His individuality was not forced, it emerged slowly. McCaughey stresses how deeply Williams, as a student, was influenced by the work of Hugh Ramsay. George Bell's justification of Ramsay's art, quoted by McCaughey, is not substantially different from Reynolds' justification of the Grand Style. If we keep in mind the many ways in which Williams' art differs from classicism it is helpful to view his method from the standpoint of classical naturalism. In McCaughey's long and detailed, and in this respect, thoroughly convincing account of Williams' style we may see him evolving for himself personal schemas of an ever-increasing generality. Schemas both firm and flexible, capable of containing and expressing the variety of his experience and emotional response to the Australian landscape, yet within the matrix of a personal and yet evolving style. This is not far removed from the traditional methods of classical naturalism.

But the visual results are, as might be expected, far different. For Williams in the twentieth century, even more than for Cézanne in the nineteenth, the effort to hold to a naturalist position has been subjected to considerable duress, so that one might almost read, were one pessimistic about the future of naturalism, Williams' naturalism as a naturalism *in extremis*.

The crux of the question lies in the interpretation of Williams' *Australian Landscapes* of 1969–70, where his art reaches close to the minimal concerns of Australian chromatic abstraction of the 1960s. Are we to read the development of his style up to this point as that of the work of a sound but somewhat old-fashioned artist who, under the pressure of superior aesthetic ideas, was gradually catching up with all that was new and vital in twentieth-century painting, or are we to view it as an elaborate strategy by which an artist, who was already well aware of where the true strength of his art lay, sought to absorb whatever was valuable to him in the new minimal modes without sacrificing the internal integrity of his own art? McCaughey calls the *Australian Landscapes* of 1969–70 Williams' 'most distinctive series'. 'They sum up so much of his development through the sixties and so much of what was new and important in that decade generally'. But he also writes, 'Neither then nor later did Williams ever think of becoming an abstract painter—the term is meaningless to him'; and also 'they did not give full scope to Williams' great painterly gift'.

There is a real sense of strain here between McCaughey's framework of interpretation and the evidence of the work. In justice to McCaughey it must be said that his sensitivity to the nuances of Williams' art does not permit him to ignore the evidence of Williams' deep commitment to naturalism. If the *Australian Landscapes* do indeed sum up so much that was new and important in Williams' art, how precisely are we to interpret his return to a much more patently representational mode during the 1970s? Have we here the potential recruit to abstraction who failed, at the critical moment in his career, to take the great plunge? Or is Williams' gift simply an eclectic one responding elastically to the differing pressures of each decade without any internal logic of its own? Neither model surely can provide a coherent and stable account of the stylistic development and the sustained quality of Williams' art.

There is another but related aspect of McCaughey's reading of Williams' art that must be challenged. His highly formalist account of Williams' development, deriving from New York mainstream methodology, severely isolates Williams from the influence of his Australian contemporaries. A highly selective use of influences is crucial to this approach. Williams is presented as a kind of avant-garde hero. All true heroes are descended from the gods. So it is only the great and dead among artists who are permitted to exercise an influence upon the emergence of Williams' style: Daumier, Matisse, Courbet, Goya, Monet, Picasso and for the English episode, Sickert. The index, despite its limitations, is most revealing in this regard. Yet one has only to leaf through the book looking at the illustrations to see how often Williams' work reveals close and quite exciting affinities with the work of many of his Australian friends and contemporaries. To take an obvious example: the link between his work and that of John Perceval during the early 1970s. This subordination of colleagues to the depiction of the hero is, of course, in the best epic tradition, but it does not make for good history.

Heroes do not only trace their descent from the gods. They also suffer rejection. Fred came unto his own but his own received him not. McCaughey explains how Williams was 'excluded' from the Antipodean Exhibition and Manifesto of 1959, and how it acted as a kind of stimulus to his future development. The case is put convincingly by McCaughey, and there is no good reason to doubt it. But a word of explanation is necessary.

The Antipodean group was formed quickly. The first discussions which led to its formation were held on Sunday, 15 and Monday, 16 February 1959 and the full group, with the exception of Bob Dickerson of Sydney who had already agreed to become a member, met for the first time on the following Thursday. At that meeting it was agreed not only that a manifesto should be written to accompany the exhibition, but that membership should be limited to those present. The reason for that decision was pre-eminently practical. It was recognized that the greater the number in the group the more difficult it would be to come to an agreed and coherent statement. As it was, the manifesto went through two drafts, much informal discussion between meetings, and was not agreed upon until the fourth meeting of the group, held on 3 May. But before the decision to limit membership to those present was taken at the first meeting several names, including that of Fred Williams, were discussed. A few, most notably John Brack, favoured his inclusion. I was one of those opposed to it. Not upon grounds of quality, but because from the little that I had seen of Fred Williams' art at that time—and I had only seen two exhibitions and did not know him personally—I came to the conclusion that it was teetering upon the edge of a total abstraction. It could hardly be expected that any self-respecting artist in those circumstances would be prepared to give his support to a manifesto which was quite stridently opposed to non-figurative art.

This is not the place to discuss the Antipodean affair in any detail; what it achieved and failed to achieve. The conventional wisdom of our avant-garde establishment long ago decided that it was a 'phoney' dispute, a 'non-question', one which aroused an 'acrimonious' but unnecessary division within the cosy Australian art world. It has never been considered from an international point of view as, for example, one of the early signs of the impending crack-up of avant-garde mythology, or in the context of the cold war, during which the American styles of abstraction had ceased to be the preserve of a creative minority and become a vehicle of cultural imperialism. No real thought has ever been given by Australian art historians or art critics to the whole context of the affair. Nor will it be possible until they liberate themselves from the mystifications of the avant-garde methodology for writing criticism and writing history. Those who are interested in liberating themselves could not do better than read, or reread, Max Kozloff's seminal article, 'American Painting during the Cold War' (*Art Forum*, May 1973) and the trenchant criticism of modernist historical method recently written by Fred Orton and Griselda Pollock, 'Les Données Bretonnantes: La Prairie de Répresentation' in *Art History*, September 1980. (The article, incidentally, unlike the title, is wholly in English!)

I have been discussing questions about which there may be legitimate differences of opinion, but there is an aspect of the book which is disturbing. In the preface Patrick McCaughey, in distributing his acknowledgements, writes that 'Rudy Komon administered just the right balance of carrots and sticks to get the manuscript out of me'. Apart from this enigmatic statement we are given no information as to the part which Komon, Williams' dealer, played in the production of the book. Of course Komon has just as much right to publicize the goods he has to sell as Bryant and May have to advertise their matches. But as readers we are also entitled to know whether the author has joined Komon's advertising agency, because it would be bound to make some difference to the way we assess his opinions. Up to the present Australian art history and art criticism has, on the whole, been able to maintain a decent distance and independence from the promotion mechanisms of the art market. That is not, of course, to assume that it can ever hope to be entirely neutral in its stance. But it can at least aspire to objectivity. If art criticism and art history in Australia are to maintain their credibility as serious intellectual disciplines, then it is a matter of the first importance that their independence is not only maintained but is seen to be maintained.

Two things linger in the memory as one puts the book down. The first is the profound affinity between the art of Fred Williams and that of Paul Cézanne—an affinity which reaches far beyond influence. Beside it the influence of Matisse, Monet, cubism and all the other tokens of legitimation employed by mainstream modernism pale into insignificance. It is as if Williams decided to go on 'realizing the motif' come what may, letting each wave of fashion roll across his vision as best it could, knowing that all the others—I hope I shall not be accused of racism—were only intent upon producing, in Cézanne's words, 'Chinese images'.

The other thing is his Australianness. That is why Lieberman chose him for the Museum of Modern Art, New York. That is why Clement Greenberg preferred the work of the Antipodeans to the work of those colonial exponents of chromatic abstraction which for a moment dominated the scene here in the 1960s: in their Australianness lay their quality. Greenberg of course had no interest in regionalism, but he had a good eye though his theories creak with rigidity. For his part Williams from the beginning has retained a clear grasp of the aesthetic imperatives which history and geography place upon an Australian artist. His *Stump* (1976), to name but one of his many compelling paintings is as thoroughly 'Antipodean'—in the now popularized sense of the term—as any image ever painted by that brief, turbulent, and much misunderstood brotherhood.

67

Richard Haese on Australian Modernism

—1981—

Richard Haese's book *Rebels and Precursors: the Revolutionary Years of Australian Art* (Allen Lane, Ringwood, 1981) is a book that everyone seriously interested in Australian culture should read. During the 1940s, Haese claims, modernism in all its diversity was grasped and assimilated by a revolutionary generation and resolved into forms which accorded with their own living experience as Australians. They brought a new radical vitality to Australian art which surpassed that of previous generations.

The members of this rebellious generation ... created a movement of revolt more volatile than anything hitherto seen in Australia. They were revolutionaries both in step and out of step with the times, men of the 20th century struggling to come to terms with the modern world and its history.

The problem at the core of the book turns on the relationship between the art of that time and the involvement, of so many who participated, with communism. For not only were social realist painters such as Counihan, Bergner and O'Connor members, for longer or shorter periods, of the Australian Communist Party, but so also were several of their leading opponents within the Contemporary Art Society, such as Albert Tucker, Max Harris and Danila Vassilieff. Close friendships existed between artists and writers who were party members and others who were not. The political question is central to the art of the time.

Why was it that so many became communists or communist sympathizers during the 1940s? The social impact of the Depression of the 1930s first alerted many to the profound moral vacuities of capitalism, which become so obvious whenever it is under stress. But it was the march to power of Hitler, the destruction of the

First published in the *Age Monthly Review*, vol. 1, no. 6, October 1981.

Spanish Republic and the programmed extermination of Europe's Jews and political radicals which convinced so many artists, writers and intellectuals that the western democracies possessed neither the will nor the capacity to defeat Hitler, and led to their joining the Communist Party. They were not entirely mistaken. Hitler was eventually defeated largely by the armed might of the Soviet Union. Communists were not the only, nor the most consistent, anti-fascists during the war, but their record was a highly creditable one. Picasso joined the French Communist Party as a personal tribute to the bravery of the French Communist Party during the Occupation. When an American critic told him in an interview that many of his admirers would be happy to hear that he had resigned from the party, Picasso replied: 'Look. I am no politician. I am not technically proficient in these matters. But communism stands for certain ideals I believe in. I believe that communism is working towards the realisation of those ideals'.

Although Haese strives hard to preserve a historical balance in his discussion of the central debate between the Angry Penguins group and the Melbourne social realists, the debate that largely determined the tone of the art of the decade, his sympathies clearly lie with former. This does at least give the book a force and consistency that it would not have achieved had a less engaged stance been adopted. And it is timely that John and Sunday Reed and the artists to whom they gave hospitality at Heide, apart from the publicity ventures of the group, are placed in a proper framework of recognition. It was probably the most creative act of patronage in the history of our culture.

But when Haese turns to the other side of the political debate, sympathetic insight all too often gives way to slogan and cliché and, in one sad case, to a gross misreading of sources. To describe *Australian New Writing*, the small wartime literary journal which I edited in company with George Farwell and Katharine Susannah Prichard, as Stalinist is grossly inaccurate. If support of the war is to be described as Stalinist then Roosevelt and Churchill must be described as Stalinist. *Australian New Writing* was never intended to be an organ for élitist discussions in aesthetics; it was essentially populist in intention, seeking poems and short stories from workers and soldiers. There was no desire to stifle opposing views, but our real interest lay in discovering literary talent among workers and soldiers. In some ways, in its advocacy of independent Australian attitudes, it was a wartime forerunner of *Overland*. Its best tribute, published in the American literary journal *Direction* (Autumn 1945) came from an American serviceman:

As a seaman who has been active since before this war, I have had the chance to get around. Recently I was in Australia, a country which by its own admission is 'culturally backward'. Yet they have just put out the third issue of a little book called *Australian New Writing*. It was hailed by the Press, all of them, as a great effort ... the main thing is that, despite a certain clumsiness, it is a dynamic publication which has sold like hot cakes and owes everything to the fact that its writers are not sage pundits who sit in the Sydney equivalent of the Village and peer at the world from behind glass.

In an endeavour to prove that I was publicly intolerant of other views Haese sadly misreads his sources. He quotes from a copy of a letter which I wrote to Max Harris in July 1943:

The claims of *Australian New Writing* were not, Smith replied, based on claims for any new artistic tendency or impetus since this would suggest equally valid rival claims. 'There is no rival. It is'. The artist had one choice and one choice only: to be progressive or to be reactionary.

My letter stated the exact reverse of this position. The words 'There is no rival. It is' are not mine, they are Max Harris's, and I was reminding him that he had written them. My letter reads:

Frankly, your letter does not make sense. ANW makes no claim to being 'the true art'. Surely you read the wrong editorial; it was not we who said, 'Like it or not, such work as this IS valid and valuable art here and now. *There is no rival to it.* It is.'

This was quoted from the *Angry Penguins* no. 2 editorial. Later in the letter I wrote:

There is room for controversy. There is room for discussion. We don't want 'Lines' but we do want artists and writers to have sufficient vigour to present their own attitudes and beliefs as forcefully as possible. There is room for ANW and AP and *Meanjin* and *Southerly*. There is room for a hell of a lot more as well. Talk about sabotage! Do you want us all to be symbolists; worship at the feet of Baudelaire and Rilke; watch the seaweed from the whale's transparent belly?

Slogans like Stalinism applied to the Australian social realism of the war years obscures the real situation, which is immensely complex. I always advocated a pluralist position but also supported a political unity of artists against fascism while recognizing their right to individual aesthetic positions. I had not only read a good deal of Marx but had absorbed Anderson's views on pluralism, and I did not find the two as incompatible as many more conservative Andersonians did. An understanding of the art of the 1940s demands a close examination of the political and aesthetic expectations and perceptions of each of the leading participants. I joined the party early in 1939 and was an active member for about five years. During that period I did not find, in Sydney at least, any attempt on the part of the party hierarchy to lay down a line on art. Indeed I recall my decision to test the matter by giving J. B. Miles, who was the party secretary at that time, a draft copy of *Place, Taste and Tradition*. I had earlier strongly supported Dobell's art, which had caused some consternation among some communists, and Reed, I recall, did not approve of Dobell. Surrealism was a delicate issue. Although I had attacked surrealism in general James Gleeson's work was dealt with at greater length than any other contemporary artist, and on the whole sympathetically. So I wasn't at all certain about JB's reactions. As it turned out he accepted it as it stood, and he read the book carefully and made some very useful editorial corrections. I always found him a decent human being whose inclination was to respect other people's opinions.

But all that changed drastically when the Australian Communist Party decided that it had to promote the Zhdanov version of Soviet socialist realism. It had dominated Soviet art since 1934 but until Miles pronounced it with all the authoritarian certainty that a Communist Party hierarchy can muster when it feels it must, socialist realism of the Soviet kind was only one, and one of the least important, of the influences contributing to our thinking. Politics was a different matter: the Soviet influence dominated there. I regarded socialist realism of the Soviet kind as a debased form of neo-classicism. We respected the work of the Mexican muralists, of the graphic artists of the American 'new masses' and the great realists of the European tradition, Brueghel, Rembrandt, Daumier, Courbet, and German expressionists such as Grosz and Kollwitz. But such general sympathies do not explain the stylistic formations of Australian social realist painting, for which one must also turn to the state of Australian contemporary art, and a growing respect for the work of the Heidelberg school.

In Melbourne, as in Sydney, relations between the party hierarchy and artists and writers were often tense, and usually difficult. I lived in Sydney throughout the period, and had no personal knowledge of those intricacies. But it was in Melbourne that an authentically Australian social realism developed around social and political experiences. In the event it turned out to be quite distinct from Soviet socialist realism, even if at times the theoretical justifications advanced to support it were not.

The whole issue turns on the philosophical role of hope in Marxist theory. Hope is central to Marxist thought since it posits an ultimate future of earthly happiness for mankind. It is an extremely powerful social myth of great appeal—especially when one examines available alternatives. But Melbourne social realism was not centred upon hope, nor was it about the optimistic aspirations of the working class. Both attitudes are central to the Zhdanov pronouncements on realism. While it is true that personal distinctions have to be made, as with all artists, between the art of Counihan, Bergner and O'Connor, taken as a whole Melbourne social realism was a sombre art, not defeatist but almost elegiac in its mood and temper, and concerned with the artists' individual perceptions of suffering, privation, endurance and survival. It was an art possessed of great human dignity. When it is still practised it still is—as Counihan's recent exhibition of work depicting the peasants of Opoul testified to all those who saw it.

If there is an expression of hope in Melbourne social realism it emerges obliquely as a rather bitter and resigned awareness that human beings can suffer all kinds of hardship, barbarity and atrocity, and still endure. Although the Melbourne realists could have had little if any knowledge of French existentialism during the war years, Sartre's conviction that the modern secular artist creates in a metaphysical situation of anguish, abandonment and despair provides a better entry to the understanding of the Melbourne realism of the 1940s than the assumption that it fits into the mental strait-jacket of the Stalinist model.

I have long held that the work of these artists was the finest achievement in art of the war years in Australia. By contrast, the wartime art of Nolan, Perceval and Arthur Boyd—stimulated by that great formal initiator Vassilieff—remained immature and unfocused; they were all still very young men, obsessed by the personal problems and predicaments with which war confronted them, and their art lacked the distancing and objectifying structures that they achieved later. Their great works were painted in the immediate post-war years when they succeeded in creating a group of paintings which are among the masterpieces not only of the 1940s but of Australian contemporary art in general.

For both parties in the debate, the liberation of their art— whether from the limitations of personal fears and obsessions on the one side, or of submission to party demands for slogans and banners on the other—lay in their capacity to reach out and make use of the mythic elements in their personal experience of reality. This is where Albert Tucker, in his crucial article 'Art, Myths and Society' in *Angry Penguins*, no. 4, was, on all the crucial issues, so right, and where, in my somewhat dismissive reply in *Place, Taste and Tradition*, I was so wrong. A preoccupation with the ways in which the Nazis had used myth for their own purpose had led me to discount the significance of myth in artistic creation. Tucker's article provided a theoretical base for the later creation, out of national myth, of Nolan's Eureka, Kelly, Burke and Wills and Mrs Fraser paintings, and for the great cycle of Arthur Boyd's paintings which are structured upon Biblical history and myth.

The objective correlatives, however, which lay behind the paintings of the Melbourne social realists and of Albert Tucker himself at this time proceeded neither from nationalism nor from religion but from the historical world view of communism and the mythical elements implicit in it.

What I am driving at may be explained best by a quotation from George Steiner, who is certainly no Marxist, but is only too well aware of Marxism's implacable and potent historical presence. For Steiner, Hellenism and Christianity have been the two central mythologies of European man. But towards the end of his *The Death of Tragedy* he writes:

Marxism is the third principal mythology to have taken root in western consciousness . . . it is as articulate and comprehensive as any mythology ever devised to order the complex chaos of reality . . . It stands as one of the three major configurations of belief and symbolic form available to the poet when he seeks a public context for his art.

Steiner has much to say that is highly critical of Marxism as well, but my point here is that the Melbourne social realists were able to crystallize a dignified and solemn humanism from the structures of their political beliefs; that those beliefs were an inspiration and challenge to them, not, as is so often assumed, an impediment.

The argument is similar when we turn to the wartime paintings of Albert Tucker. And here it is most important to let the paintings speak for themselves rather than to classify them according to the rhetoric between the two groups. Tucker's Images of Evil series of paintings based upon his perception of wartime Melbourne as a city of moral corruption owes the emotional space it inhabits to Marx's classic indictment of capitalism. The series affords a startling parallel with Bertolt Brecht's love—hate relationship with Berlin: 'The vast pile of stone, concrete, and asphalt so many of his poems speak of, where man is lost in a jungle; the seething cauldron of lust, greed, and corruption that for him summed up the 20th-century world: dreadful, doomed—and magnificent'. Martin Esslin's words describe Tucker's relation to Melbourne in creating his Images of Evil paintings.

It is misleading then to present the debate within the Contemporary Art Society in the dualistic form of a confrontation between what Haese calls 'radical liberalism' and Stalinism. The term 'radical liberalism' was never used by either side, and Stalinism was used only in the form of abuse. It was a real debate concerning the relation of art to politics in which both sides acted in accord with their own judgements and not at the dictates of others. It determined the character of the best of the decade.

Then the cold war closed in. Under cultural pressure from Britain, the USA and the Soviet Union, Australia returned to its normal condition of neo-colonial genuflection. The Antipodean affair was a defensive rearguard action to protect what was best and most vital in the art of the 1940s. But its potential was diluted by our imperial connections and the affluence of the 1960s. As the capital gains of the old revolutionaries of the 1940s grew greater their aesthetic relevance grew less. But what they achieved as young men will stand.

One thing for the record. When I heard J. B. Miles trumpeting the Zhdanov line in 1947 I knew that my days in the Communist Party were numbered. But I did not make the final decision until the summer of 1949 when I stood one day in the studio of a Czech sculptor in Prague. He had once produced competent bronzes rather in the manner of Rodin but he was then producing countless effigies of Gottwald, the Czech communist premier of the time. I resigned from the party shortly afterwards. But I did not place the responsibility for the sculptor's unhappiness or my disenchantment upon a god that failed. Marxism possesses an enormous potential both for liberation and for tyranny. And having, like Christianity and Islam, arrived, it is bound to be around for a long, long time.

68
Gary Catalano on the 1950s
—1981—

Gary Catalano's extended essay, *The Years of Hope: Australian Art and Criticism 1959—1968* (Oxford University Press, Melbourne, 1981), arises from a grant awarded by the Visual Arts Board to the author to write a study of contemporary Australian art. Catalano argues that the mid-1950s were a time of cultural re-awakening when Australian writers and artists began to take a new interest in the development of indigenous forms of expression. He traces the descending curve of these aspirations from the time of the Antipodean Exhibition of 1959, which he sees as a high point of national confidence, to the time of the Field Exhibition of 1968, one of the shows arranged to mark the opening of the new building housing the National Gallery of Victoria. At the end of his book Catalano concludes that the artists of the 1960s betrayed the hopes of the previous decade. It is not that the author is a simple-minded nationalist. He obviously has much sympathy with the point of view of the artists of the 1960s. Many, he says, 'were simply not interested in a national artistic tradition and took delight in spurning an unwanted legacy'. But he does, nevertheless, feel some unease about an enterprise which sought to cut away so completely from local roots and local allegiances. 'No culture,' he concludes, 'grows from indifference... Apart from a few isolated and largely unrepresentative figures such as Mike Brown and Richard Larter, few of the younger artists gave signs of any deep feelings about the society to which they belonged. As far as one can determine most of them hardly thought about it at all'.

Yet after making that quite challenging and it seems to me valid statement Catalano concludes lamely and pessimistically: it

First published in *Island Magazine*, no. 8, November 1981, pp. 35—6, under the title 'Affluence and Art'.

was all probably inevitable, and argues that the reason for the indifference to the development of an indigenous art was 'a by-product of the rising affluence of the times—and therefore susceptible to the indifference which affluence breeds'.

The assumption—and it is crucial to Catalano's essay—that affluence breeds indifference to national forms of expression must be questioned. In the case of mature and independent nations affluence almost invariably brings stronger and finer expressions of the indigenous culture. Consider the case of England in the eighteenth century, France in the second half of the nineteenth, the United States in our own century. In all such cases affluence brought with it a more confident and easeful expression of the indigenous culture. In order to appreciate why increasing affluence in the 1960s worked against indigenous forms of expression requires a socio-cultural examination of the case upon which the author reveals little inclination to embark. The rapid increase of foreign capital investment in Australia during the 1960s is of the first significance for an understanding of the problem. One local advertising group in Australia informed the Senate Select Committee on Foreign Ownership and Control in 1972 that 'fifteen large foreign-controlled advertising agencies now account for over half the annual advertising turnover handled' and that if present trends continued 'all significant locally-controlled agencies will disappear'. The importance of such changes in advertising control for the formation of taste in high art cannot be overlooked. Mary Eagle has recently drawn our attention to the crucial role which the arts of retail advertising and design played in winning an Australian public for the modern movement itself in Australia. Gary Catalano does note the fact that the group of young artists who created and established Central Street in Sydney and promoted an art which ruthlessly denied all national associations were all trained in the advertising business. The dealer whose gallery took the lead in supporting non-figuration, Max Hutchison of Gallery A, eventually moved to New York to continue his business. If one is seriously seeking to understand why so-called 'international' values increasingly prevailed over indigenous forms of expression in the visual arts in Australia during the 1960s one cannot ignore the determinate role of greatly increased foreign capital investment in this country and its social and cultural ramifications.

It is because he does ignore such basic socio-cultural factors in his essay that Catalano misreads, it seems to me, what he describes as 'a cultural re-awakening and coming of age' in the mid-1950s.

Most of the artists and writers whom he cites in justification, whose reputations were being 'consolidated'—Hope, McCauley, Wright, Dobell, Drysdale, Passmore, Miller, Fairweather—were associated with a much earlier and far stronger expression of an Australian cultural awakening: that which occurred during the later 1930s and the war years. The only artist who is mentioned as having come to the fore in the mid-1950s for the first time is Ross Morrow, and his work was not regarded as important enough to be given a plate in the book.

It is not until towards the end of this basic background chapter that Catalano stumbles almost by accident upon the real significance of what was occurring in the mid-1950s. This was essentially a structural change in the marketing of art, changes from the older dependence upon artists' societies and the older kind of private gallery, to the development of highly professional dealers and new modes of art promotion. Any serious study of the conflict and interaction of the claims for an indigenous art and the claims for an international art would need to examine in some detail the policies, social and political backgrounds, entrepreneurial affiliations and capital bases of the professional dealers active in Australia during the 1960s and the links they possessed with the media and with those empowered to advise for state galleries in the matter of purchases; the kinds of persons appointed to state gallery trusts, their social, religious and political backgrounds. In other words a full sociological study. It is, of course, quite unfair to expect that Mr Catalano could have undertaken such a study, given his interests and the comparatively short scope of his book. But it is well to remember that until such studies are undertaken all our answers to such complex questions as the role and relationship of an indigenous art and the claims of an international art are likely to remain superficial.

Gary Catalano, however, is a poet not a sociologist. We might well have expected, therefore, if not a penetrating study of art system structures, some personal and revealing identifications between at least some of the artists he discusses and his own view of the world. One thinks of the exciting and creative relationship which developed between Apollinaire and the young Picasso, between Blaise Cendrars and the Delaunays. But in this the book is disappointing. There are in places some sensitive reconsiderations of artists' work—a particularly fine one is his reconsideration of the work of David Strachan. And one of the good things about this book is that the author does seek to do critical justice to a number of good artists who he believes have been overlooked: John Molvig, Edwin Tanner, Michael Shannon, and others. The pity is that he did not give himself more space to express more of his own opinions about such artists. But in this he was greatly hindered by the rather cumbersome method which he adopts throughout. That is to say, instead of confronting the art and work directly he prefers to come at both in an oblique way, citing, first, in most cases, what other contemporary critics have said, sometimes with approval but more frequently to reveal their shortcomings, and then cap the discussion with a 'Gary knows best' comment. The trouble about this rather irritating one-upmanship is that, as he is never in a position to provide the full context from which a particular critic was writing at the time, he cannot, as a competent historian might have done, recreate the point of view that might have given the comment its validity. Catalano assessing work in retrospect comes to the situation with values quite different from those of contemporary critics. To treat them all as if they operated at the same time and level with the same force is one of the cardinal fallacies of a historical formalist criticism. But in a much more practical way it distances the poetic critic from his subject, since so much of the space of the book is being taken up with quotations from other critics.

To the obliquity of thus seeing work first through the eyes of other critics Catalano adds the hesitancies of his own judgements. These are so often qualified almost out of existence with 'some-whats', 'perhapses' and 'maybes' that it is often difficult to discover his point of view. Quite typical for example is:

Of all the generalisations made about the two main centres of Australian art, the most common has surely been that Sydney artists, unlike those of Melbourne, are hedonistic in spirit. There may well be some justification for this attitude, but if we compare the work of Laycock with that of Leonard Hessing then the opposite may well be true.

Hessing may or may not be less hedonistic than Laycock, Sydney may or may not be more hedonistic than Melbourne. Such uncertainties make it exceedingly difficult at times to assess the weight of the author's own personal judgements. For this reason alone it becomes a confused and confusing book. Much of it is talk about talk about art.

Predictably, Catalano diverts at some length on the Antipodean Exhibition and Manifesto. While his approach cannot be said to be wholly dismissive his criticisms of that enterprise raise few issues that have not already been raised before. A review is no place to deal with them in detail. Like most previous critics of the Antipodean Manifesto, Catalano refuses to come to terms with the central issues involved simply by asserting that the real concerns were not aesthetic concerns but some other concern that the critic presents to his or her own satisfaction. It is all reduced to motive hunting, instead of a discussion of the issues as raised in the manifesto.

Despite Catalano's attempt to reduce the issues to social issues and for a whole generation of critics to repeat mechanically that the whole matter was a 'phoney' or a 'no' question, the manifesto did raise real aesthetic issues for Australian artists and for artists in general. That is no doubt why the smouldering debate continues. Apart from that of course Catalano knows so little about what occurred. He is in no position to appreciate, for example, the close relationship between the Antipodean Exhibition and the later Australian exhibition organized by Brian Robinson at the Whitechapel Gallery. That story remains to be told. The documents were available to Catalano, with many interesting facts that would have thrown a lot of light on some of the issues with which he deals. But at no time did he approach me to consult them. Perhaps he might have felt that the facts would have influenced his opinions.

The book is quite well produced and well illustrated. There are two chapters on sculpture, out of thirteen. Which is about right, though Catalano himself once again expresses the usual whinge that Australian sculptors are neglected. What he does not appear to appreciate is that Australian sculptors have never developed a sense of their own tradition, nor have they been interested in developing one. Each generation has kept its eye upon the metropolitan fashion-makers of the time. There was nothing in their own country to interest or excite them. And this is the reason why they have been largely ignored by the Australian public—ignored or resented. Sculpture suffers from the inherent weakness of an inherently avant-garde tradition attempting to function effectively in an inherently colonial situation.

Occasionally Catalano gets onto some interesting themes such as the use of childhood among the figurative painters of the period, but even in this case the discussion peters out into vague historical generalizations. The greatest value of the book is the sense of enjoyment one sometimes catches from the discussion of the works of a number of artists whom the author enjoys, such as Dick Watkins, who certainly emerges as the most talented of the non-figurative artists of his generation, in my view. But for the most part it is a confused and confusing book, never penetrating deeply into the historical problems it raises nor developing new and illuminating critical insights into the work of individual artists. Yet Catalano writes well and easily enough and never resorts to jargon, which is a great relief. It is strange that it is not a better book than it is.

69
Murray Bail on Ian Fairweather
—1982—

I suspect that the life and art of Ian Fairweather will continue to be discussed when many of the better-publicised names of twentieth-century Australian painting are locked away securely in their period pigeon-holes. Not only because he created an enduring legend of himself in his own lifetime but because both his life and art raise sharp issues concerning the course of modernism in Australia. Fairweather's was a life of intractable honesty and consistency lived entirely for his art. So those who would criticize a life lived for art's sake must come to terms with Fairweather's achievement. And this is no easy question. For we are not here in the presence of an artist who begins as a picturesque radical and ends his life with Royal Birthday honours, a fat bank balance, an appropriate shrine of remembrance, and his name on every journalist's lips. Fairweather was for real. Towards the end of his life he made a revealing comment worth quoting: 'Painting the way in which I have done all my life is a selfish inverted thing. It is self-consuming. It takes all one has to offer and leaves no room for anything else'.[1]

Fairweather's art has always been appreciated in Australia by other artists and by critics. It does not fall into the easy journalist's stereotype of neglect. But it may take some time before its full significance for modernism in Australia is grasped and understood. Meanwhile we are well served by two valuable studies of the man and his work: Nourma Abbott-Smith's excellent little profile of the artist (*Ian Fairweather*, University of Queensland Press, St Lucia, 1978) and now Murray Bail's close study of the paintings, *Ian Fairweather* (Bay Books, Sydney, 1981).

First published in *Island Magazine*, no. 12, September 1982, under the title 'Ian Fairweather and the Problem of Total Abstraction'.

Although I have some reservations about Bail's interpretation of Fairweather's art that I shall return to later, the first thing that must be said is that the book is a very considerable achievement. It makes it possible for us to consider Fairweather's *oeuvre* fully in retrospect. It is closely analysed and perceptively commented upon both with respect to its stylistic development and its aesthetic achievement. To get the material in some kind of chronological order is, for an artist like Fairweather careless about dating, in itself a considerable achievement. Bail furthermore, though skilled in its use, does not bring the imaginative discc urse of fiction to his task. What he has to say is usually said clearly and unambiguously and well supported by the visual evidence of the paintings. Though obviously tempted on occasion he suppresses poetic language: the prose is in the service of the paintings. It is only on the rarest of occasions that a metaphor will seduce him with its very felicity, as when he describes Fairweather's memorable self-portrait as 'a mangrove of misunderstandings'.[2] Clever, but it does not ring true either from what we know of Fairweather's life as he has recorded it through Abbott-Smith, from his letters, or from Bail's considered discussion of his art. Fairweather himself may well have suffered at times, if not through most of his life, from a severe persecution complex—we have no serious pyschological study of the man—but his art, that is another matter, that surely was a long effort in understanding and the self-portrait bears the evidence of it.

But lapses of this kind are rare; Bail's prose is normally at the service of the paintings and helps us to understand them. The book moreover has been designed to support a close reading, with the illustrations always near the relevant text, and a wealth of admirable colour plates on which the Japanese printers seem to have expended great care, so that the book is a delight to read. The layout has been criticized for the printing of some large paintings across the spine but it is an acceptable compromise when the only alternatives would have been either a much smaller illustration or those awful broad-shaped formats which raise more problems than they solve.

Nor is it only a handsome production; it has been assembled with a real sense of responsibility to the needs of the scholar and the connoisseur. Although Bail has not set out to provide a catalogue *raisonné* of Fairweather's known 500-odd works—a daunting task that lies ahead for someone—the cataloguing of the 204 works illustrated is presented with the care and precision that we normally associate only with the best gallery catalogues (such as those produced in recent years by the Art Gallery of South Australia) than with monographs published with half an eye on the luxury collector's market. Bail provides us with the variant forms of Fairweather's signature, a chronology of his life, an inventory of exhibitions and reviews, a comprehensive bibliography and an index. Again Bail's literary manners are exemplary; he rarely quotes a critic merely to disagree, but quotes criticism in order to provide an account of the ways in which Fairweather's art has been evaluated over the years in the effort to understand it. All those who enjoy and respect Fairweather's art will be deeply indebted to the author and Bay Books for a beautiful and scholarly book handsomely presented.

Bail mercifully avoids that all-too-familiar cliché adopted at the beginning of the typical monograph on an Australian artist produced for the popular market. The artist hero, such books invariably inform us, whose achievements will now for the first time be made clear to the world, has been shamefully neglected by art historians (nameless) and art critics (nameless) and where he or she has been mentioned at all has been totally misunderstood. The monograph, the assumption is, will now set all to rights. Bail is not only too sophisticated in his approach to fall for that one, he also knows that it could never be made to fit the Fairweather case.

Australia can take some pride in the way it treated Fairweather. Perhaps he was just lucky to meet the kinds of people who could respond sensitively and creatively to his extremely difficult and complicated personality. But it is really amazing. From the beginning, where Fairweather was concerned, the Australian art world seemed to be on its best behaviour. The list is quite a long one: Jock Frater, Lyna Bryans, Cynthia Nolan, George Bell, Laurie Thomas, Lucy Swanton and Treania Smith of the Macquarie Galleries, Robert Smith, Lord and Lady (Maie) Casey. Despite his difficult personality Fairweather seemed to bring out the best in people. Perhaps they sensed that they were in the presence of the real thing. The record may not be quite as good as I suggest, but if not it has not yet come to light. All things considered, Australia treated Fairweather well. Shortly after he arrived in Melbourne he wrote to his friend and patron H. S. Ede, 'here for the first time I feel I am not a criminal, trying to make a living by painting. They have been very kind'. And as it began, so it remained.

Australia assisted Fairweather to achieve the best that was in him. It did not corrupt him. In this the time of his arrival—

1934—was important. We are still in the phase of early modernism with its moral rigour and genuine experimental vitality, the passing of which Suzi Gablik, in a passionate and lucid but somewhat tiresome article, laments: 'What has happened is that modernism became successful, gained power, succumbed to its opponent, the world of business and money'.[3] Though he came to it rather late in the day Fairweather, we must remember, belonged to this primary, heroic phase of modernism. He held within himself the rigorous aesthetic morality of a Cézanne, a Van Gogh, a Gauguin. But he could not have left it much later. For the post-war generation of modernists was confronted by the triumph in art, as in sport, of the cash-nexus and the quality of their art was deeply affected by it. But by that time he was an old man and had said what he had to say. The triumph of power and money in art could not affect him much and he was able to relax a little.

At Bribie Island in the years shortly before his death Fairweather began to accept visitors more frequently, artists and professionals alike. One was the dealer Rudy Komon. 'I welcomed Komon. He was such good company even without the fine wine he would bring with him', Fairweather recorded. And Rudy Komon informs us:

Fairweather being a Scot was a whisky drinker. I remember visiting him one day in his hut when he had been bitten by a rat. He kept rats which he fed regularly. The rogue rat was an outsider. To console Fairweather I took him out for a drink and introduced him to red wine. After that I would send him selected reds which he immensely enjoyed.[4]

It would be quite useless to surmise the course that Fairweather's art might have taken had he been introduced to Rudy's selected reds earlier in life. But Redfern Gallery, Macquarie Gallery style was different from Komon style. They kept their distance; it is perhaps the distance between early modernism and late modernism, between art and the cash-nexus. Patrick McCaughey, in a perceptive article, 'The Artist in Extremis: Arthur Boyd 1972–73', has been one of the few to touch upon this problem, albeit obliquely.[5]

At the beginning of his book Murray Bail makes an important point about Fairweather: 'His art does not fit the local boundaries'. And he shows also that it cannot readily be contained within the period styles of modernism. Post-impressionism, expressionism, cubism, abstract art feel like the uncomfortably tight-fitting garments of Parisian *haute couture* when we try them on Fairweather's art. Bail himself does, quite conscientiously, like any well-trained critic or historian. But they really do not fit, as he discovers, and he says so.

We have to look elsewhere for the stylistic genesis of Fairweather's art. And when we do this he emerges again at a heroic level as one of the last of the first ones. In these late days when modernism is being attacked on all sides for its submission to corporate capitalism—that perspective which reveals modernism as a cultural imperialism—it is usually forgotten that there is an international aspect of modernism which will stand the test of time, an aspect first clearly stated, so far as I know, by one of the United States' finest art historian, Meyer Schapiro, in an article on modern art (written years ago) in which he observed that modernism was creating for the first time an art the historical origins of which were no longer Europo-centric but which reached back to the art of all peoples, places and times—an art diacritically international. This has been modernism's great challenge to the classical and post-classical traditions of the European cultural hegemony and will in the end be seen to be of much greater importance than those periodic signs of Angst and ageing which have appeared inevitably upon the face of modernism as its energies gradually weakened and flagged: post-impressionism, cubism, expressionism, surrealism, total abstraction etc, etc. What inspired Fairweather's art and life reaches to this central energy of modernism, a desire for the convergence of traditional styles and a sympathetic awareness of their historical independence and value. It is manifest in his lifelong endeavour to assimilate within his own personal style something of the traditional arts of the East and the art of the Australian Aborigines. It is indeed indistinguishable from Gauguin's programme—the first truly self-conscious modernist.

This desire for a convergence, this hope for a genuinely international culture was not for Fairweather merely an intellectual or aesthetic concern. He knew that if he was to assimilate these exotic arts—exotic to him—into his own he had to live as Asians, as Aborigines live, to bring his own life-style closer to theirs. So he was prepared to cross not only geographical boundaries, but the boundaries of class and western home comforts also. It has been said that Fairweather was unpolitical. Indeed he said so himself, but he was referring to a politically directed art. It was his supreme scorn of the *dolce vita* as a life suited to the aesthetic sensibility, of art married to the cash-nexus, that was Fairweather's politics and he played it out for over eighty years with what can only be described as heroic courage.

It was surely because he learned how to live a simple life devoid of all but his absolute necessities that he was able to assimilate into his own art something of the style and aesthetic quality of Aboriginal art without any great feeling of conscious strain. So that he succeeded where Margaret Preston, as Bail in my view correctly points out, failed. Margaret Preston played an invaluable role in pointing for the first time to the importance and relevance of Aboriginal art for all Australian art. But her own art was caught on the horns of an enormous dilemma. As an early modernist she championed, like the Italian futurists, the delights of the industrial modernity—utopia with the Electrolux. Then in the second half of her life she turned to a traditional art which was being destroyed by the Electrolux and all that it stood for. Her art reveals the evidence of that self-conscious strain and the tension of the contradiction.

In the end, however, Murray Bail just misses out on demonstrating the reasons for the deep originality of Fairweather's art, in its search for a diacritical internationalism, because he attempts to evaluate its achievement by means of that hierarchy of aesthetic values established by late modernism. A mistake in many respects similar to that made by Patrick McCaughey in assessing Fred Williams' art,[6] the mistake of imposing one's own aesthetic system upon an art which was generated by a quite different system. To say in such cases that one can only use one's own system is the defence of the insensitive, a dangerous line to take in the presence of artists as original as Williams and Fairweather. It is in the presence of original art (perhaps only in its presence) that we possess an opportunity of broadening the categories of our own understanding.

As so often happens, the warning signal that Murray Bail is preparing to ride his own high aesthetic horse across Fairweather's paintings is revealed in a change of language on p. 161 when a personal preference is asserted as an incontrovertible fact. Speaking of what he describes as Fairweather's 'total abstractions' of 1960, a brief but important phase of the artist's work, he writes in opposition to the contemporary views of Robert Hughes and others, who expressed qualifications about this phase of Fairweather's art: 'In fact, they remain among Australia's finest paintings—certainly the finest abstract paintings—and fine enough to be shown without equation to the rest of the world'.

Now there need be no question about the high quality of these abstracts, and expressed as a personal preference none could take objection to Bail's opinion. *De gustibus non disputandum.* But Bail wants this personal preference to stand as a judgement in all its authority, objectivity and universality. The problem here, for those who are prepared to take the specificity of context seriously, is that Bail is not only seeking to contradict the opinions of contemporary critics such as Hughes and others, but that his is an opinion framed in the face of Fairweather's own deep distrust of a totally abstract art.

Bail, perhaps unwittingly, tends to suppress this aspect of Fairweather's sensibility: crucial statements are presented in ambiguous contexts; are not investigated for their bearing upon Fairweather's most deeply held opinions. Thus he quotes as an epigraph to chapter 4 a sentence from a 1934 letter from Fairweather to his English friend H. S. Ede: 'If I stay (in Australia) I will have to work in abstractions—it would be too irreverent to represent such wholiness'. The last word was a punning comment on the depression he felt after experiencing a Melbourne Sunday (as the full quote in Abbott-Smith, p. 54 makes clear). The significant point is that Fairweather does not want to work in abstractions; Australia might compel him to, so he leaves.

Then, at a much later phase of the artist's life, Bail presents the artist propelled, despite his own deep misgivings, towards a totally abstract art and in the process producing what is, for Bail, his best art. Such an explanation of course is determinist and historicist: the artist's work gets better because it is impelled by forces over which he has little control. At his best, Fairweather was a great artist despite himself.

Since this question is crucial for an understanding and appreciation of Fairweather's art within its own specific areas of fulfilment and achievement it is essential that we appreciate the strength of Fairweather's resistance to a totally abstract art.

Commenting on *Ave Maria* (1957) after it was purchased by the Art Gallery of Western Australia, Fairweather wrote: 'the title was an afterthought and had little to do with the intention of the painting—However I don't feel I am a complete abstractionist—I still like—perhaps mistakenly in this age of collectivism—to retain some relic of subjective reality'.

Bail then comments that 'Such a stand against the inevitable would survive scarcely eighteen months'. Bail's critical strategy required him not only to assert the inevitability and aesthetic supremacy of total abstraction but to diminish the significance of the brevity of Fairweather's involvement and the quality of the works which Fairweather began to paint as he moved away from this total involvement towards a more figured style, such as *Monastery* (1961), *Epiphany* (1962) and *Marriage at Cana* (1963), paintings which have generally been accepted as representing the high point of his achievement. It required too that he suppress in a very large measure Fairweather's deep distrust of a totally abstract style. To appreciate the level of this distrust we must turn to Abbott-Smith's book, which was written largely from interviews with the artist during the last two years of his life.

On one occasion Fairweather recorded:

I am conscious of the figure. Maybe it is one of the reasons why I cannot be a completely abstract painter. I was brought up in a civilized landscape, the European background teeming with the history of man, and I never feel interested in painting a thing unless there is some evidence of this, buildings or human beings or some action going on in relation to them.

I think you simply have to include the figure, it's basic and you can't do vigorous work without it, the Old European influence, truth to nature—it's hard to eradicate and, indeed, why should one try to.

One another occasion he recorded his opposition, *pace* Murray Bail, to those who 'pinned the label of abstraction on his work'.

My paintings are not abstract. I was trained as a traditionalist and thence proceeded under my own steam towards the abstract; but never completely. Abstract does not suit me and I will always put into my painting some representation. It is hard to live in two worlds. In any case I loathe such labels.

With these two quite explicit statements from the artist himself to guide and warn us we should turn again to that short burst of paintings of the 1960s which Bail describes as totally abstract *and* his best work. They certainly reached a high level of abstraction and Fairweather recognized this. 'They are mostly without titles—for they refer (mostly) to nothing in particular—sort of soliloquies—I suppose will have to come under the heading of abstracts', Fairweather wrote to Treania Smith of the Macquarie Galleries.

Now it would seem to me that to argue that these paintings of the 1960s are totally abstract and Fairweather's best involves a strong and distorting commitment to the ideology of a total abstract art. What they do seem to represent is the high point of Fairweather's movement towards abstraction (and we may accept Bail's quote from Eliot as apt: 'Old men ought to be explorers'), but which nevertheless contain representative elements which, as Fairweather tells us, are never entirely absent from his work.

The difference between a high point of abstracting from figuration and a totally abstract art may appear to some today to be a question of merely academic interest. But grave issues were at stake. A process of abstraction lies at the base of all aesthetic creation. It was the attempt to erect this process as the whole of the art process and place it at the highest aesthetic level and the art of the future that disturbed painters, like Picasso and Fairweather, trained in the humanist tradition. A total abstraction has always been present in the artistic tradition of European and non-European art: from neolithic basketry and pottery to the great achievements of Islamic art. But it was one tradition among others. Where it has achieved a complete supremacy, as in the iconoclastic controversies and Islamic art, it has operated as a form of visual censorship suppressing (for centuries) the specificity, particularity and individualistic forms of expression possible in figurative art. It has become increasingly clear even to American artists themselves how well the total abstraction championed by the New York school and its critical prophets came to serve the power structures of American corporate capitalism. It was the tendency within total abstraction to reduce art to an anonymous collectivism which obviously distressed Fairweather.

Fairweather's art, we may conclude, just as it does not fit readily into the period styles from post-impressionism to cubism so it cannot be fitted readily into the strait-jacket of total abstraction. He carries on into his abstractions the figurative elements, the evidence of 'buildings or human beings or some action' which are at the root of this humanist but diacritical international art.

If Fairweather's abstracts of 1960 are separated from the rest of his *oeuvre*, and read as total abstractions, something of their aesthetic quality will survive but they lose much of their quality and meaning in a kind of collective anonymity of impersonal values which Fairweather dreaded.

Bail's bizarre attempt, then, to present Fairweather as Australia's greatest abstract artist despite his own intentions fails to be convincing. The enterprise could never have been undertaken had Bail not confined his attentions largely to the 'study of the paintings'. The art is not sufficiently well related to the artist's personal aspiration, his anxieties and ambitions. For this we have to go to Abbott-Smith. This may sound rather churlish criticism of a book which is technically so sound in many respects. It reveals perhaps the weakness of the *study* of an artist's art pursued apart from his life as an art historical genre, inadequate attention being given to the personal aspects of an artist's life. It is a point which Jack Lindsay has stressed repeatedly in his important biographical studies of artists from Hogarth to Cézanne, in which the lives are treated as seriously as the art.

Notes

1 Nourma Abbott-Smith, *Ian Fairweather*, University of Queensland Press, St Lucia, 1978, p. 151.
2 M. Bail, *Ian Fairweather*, Bay Books, Sydney, 1981, p. 180.
3 *Art and Text*, Melbourne, January 1981.
4 Abbott-Smith, p. 124.
5 A. Bradley and T. Smith (eds), *Australian Art and Architecture*, Oxford University Press, Melbourne, 1980, pp. 210–20.
6 See my article in *Meanjin*, no. 3, 1981.

70
Felicity St John Moore on Vassilieff
—1982—

Books on Australian artists appear almost every week these days. Most have grave weaknesses.

If the artist is still living they tend to be abject hymns of praise. No faults are found; informed criticism is absent; the artist's name becomes a brand name to extol the product. Dealers adore them for they help the trade.

If the artist is dead, his or her life, and all its personal problems, tend to be ignored in favour of the art. A powerful aesthetic theory supports this approach. Art, it claims springs from former art; the best thing you can do with life, if you are an artist or a critic, is to keep it at a distance. One of the many dangers of this approach is that the aesthetic theories and assumptions of the writer can be slapped upon the creative struggles of the artist like a strait-jacket, to impose an order upon it that is the writer's and not the artist's.

By contrast with such books, Felicity St John Moore's *Vassilieff and His Art* (Oxford University Press, Melbourne, 1982) is a little masterpiece of its kind. We now possess a lucid and challenging account of the life and work of an artist whose influence upon the development of Australian painting was second to none. Ignorance concerning the main facts of Vassilieff's life, difficulty of access to his works — not readily available in the public galleries, because they did not buy them, and held largely in the private collections of close friends or possessive relatives — has meant that Vassilieff has remained a shadowy figure to those not admitted to the circles in which the artist moved; that is to say, to the Australian art world at large.

First published in the *Sydney Morning Herald*, 27 November 1982.

Vassilieff was not a great painter. He was an uncontrollable fountain of pictorial energy. He was also the greatest art teacher that Australia has ever had, and lucky enough to deeply influence some of the most promising pupils. It was teaching, of course, of an entirely informal kind. His immediate, free-flowing art acted as a kind of liberation, at a crucial formative period, upon the work of a group of young artists, most notably Sidney Nolan, Albert Tucker, Arther Boyd, John Perceval and Charles Blackman. They went on to paint, at their best, pictures of greater aesthetic merit than anything he did; but without the example of his art and his life the liberation might never have occurred. If it had it would certainly have taken quite different forms.

It is not at all pejorative to compare Vassilieff's art with child art. It possesses the vitalism, the assertive urgency of good child art. Form emerges intuitively. Vassilieff, and many of his generation, went to child art for their inspiration. It taught them much; that is why they became such good teachers of art to children. For them, as for their pupils, art and life were indivisible.

It is not only a question of style. Just how well Vassilieff could enter sympathetically into the imagination of childhood is to be seen in his wonderful illustrations to *Peter and the Wolf* recently published by the Australian National Gallery, Canberra. It is a superb example of his unique capacity to combine timeless qualities of folk art with his own radiant and insouciant expressionism.

What is rarely to be found in Vassilieff's paintings, in all their tumbling urgency, is a due sense of the importance of accent, of the relation between major and minor, in the articulation of pictorial space. His paintings pay little respect to consciously articulated form. So that in order to enjoy his pictures most fully, and the effort is worth it, we must suppress our own intuitions of form.

There is a sense in which his paintings complement those of Norman Lindsay—modernist and anti-modernist converge in the vitalist mainstream of Australian painting. A similar rumbustious energy, a similar impatience with all perceived constraints. It is difficult to say why this vitalistic stream should leap across the styles and generations in this way; but the simplest explanation might be the best one: that for a young, emergent society, it was better for artists capable of identifying and articulating personal feeling to put their trust in life rather than in aesthetic systems, however venerable or convincing, derived from the metropolitan centres of the northern hemisphere.

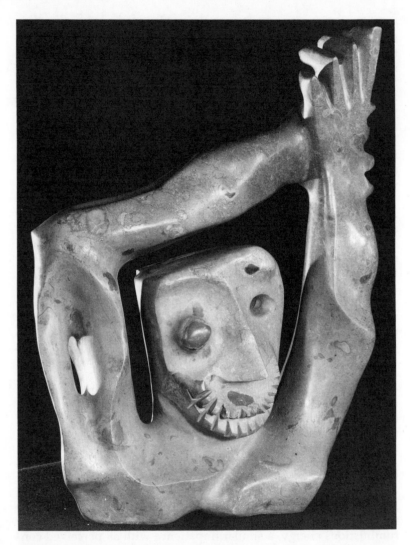

Danila Vassilieff, *Stenka Razin*, 1953, Lilydale limestone, 51.0 × 40.0 × 13.5 cm.
Australian National Gallery, Canberra.

Yet, paradoxically, as Felicity St John Moore convincingly
demonstrates, Vassilieff brought a highly developed aesthetic to
Australia—and a modernist one to boot. It was the aesthetic
developed by Diaghilev and the great circle of dancers, musicians,

choreographers and composers that he brought together in the creation of the modern ballet. Vassilieff absorbed the Diaghilev aesthetic largely through Polunin, who had worked for seven years as a scene painter for Diaghilev. At the time Vassilieff met him he was head of the Decorative and Stage Painting Departments at the Slade—the only artist, Vassilieff acknowledged privately, ever to influence him.

It was the Diaghilev aesthetic that became the mode of modernism which acclimatized itself during the late 1930s and early 1940s, more successfully than any other, to the Australian cultural condition. Diaghilev's heady mixture of Russian folk components with modernism, of life with art, met with a ready response in Australia, as the overwhelming enthusiasm which greeted the successive tours of Colonel de Basil's company testified.

The Diaghilev aesthetic affected the art of Sydney and Melbourne in quite different ways. In Sydney it was the decorative component as revealed in the work of Loudon Sainthill and the Merioola Group that triumphed. But Sydney rejected Vassilieff, though he had absorbed the aesthetic during his years in London more profoundly than anyone in Australia. It was in Melbourne that Vassilieff was able to develop the expressive component of the Diaghilev aesthetic and influence a generation of Australian artists.

This was made possible by the sympathetic criticism of Vance Palmer, Basil Burdett and George Bell; the encouragement of John and Sunday Reed; the receptive interest of Nolan, Arthur Boyd, Albert Tucker and other young painters. So Vassilieff's painting inspired a mode of modernism, figural and expressionist (in a broad sense) that came to constitute the mainstream of Australian contemporary art.

By contrast, Sydney, albeit uneasily and uncertainly, settled for a different kind of modernism, one that sought its inspiration in dynamic symmetry and an art-school variant of cubism devised by André Lhote. It appears to have possessed theosophical underpinnings and chose to distance itself from the vulgarities of life. It was this aesthetic that prepared the ground for the reception of those provincial modes of abstraction that came to dominate the Sydney art scene during the late 1950s and 1960s.

But they were modes that, because of their provinciality, never became widely popular either in Australia or abroad. There was always the smell of the studio lamp about them: textbook modernism, not life. The break did not begin to come until the time of John Olsen and Brett Whiteley, though signs were already present in the paintings of John Passmore. There was a time in the early 1960s when Olsen and his circle of so-called 'abstract' artists thought that they were opposing the figurative vitalism that Vassilieff had seeded in Melbourne. But it is clear in retrospect that they were accommodating their art to vitalism and developing their own modes of it.

Vassilieff may not have been a great painter but he certainly was a great sculptor. Arguably, despite the smallness of the scale in which he worked, the greatest the country has ever had; undoubtedly the most personal. Felicity Moore's discussion of his sculpture is one of the great strengths of her book; indeed it was pieces like *Stenka Razin* that first drew her attention to his work. It was in his sculpture that Vassilieff's enormous creative energy met a sufficiently resistant material, and the results, again and again, are sculptural forms that are wholly satisfying as structures as well as symbols—something that can rarely be said of his paintings.

It was a loss to Australian art that he came to sculpture so late in his life. If he had been able to influence a generation of sculptors in the way he influenced a generation of painters, Australian sculpture might by this have possessed a tradition instead of being a discontinuous history of hesitant beginnings.

71

Robert Smith on Counihan's Prints

—1982—

No other Australian artist of his generation has explored the complex problems of realism more persistently than Noel Counihan.

For that reason his name is unlikely to be found in future New Year or Queen's Birthday Honours lists. No one to my knowledge ever gave Rembrandt, Hogarth, Goya, Daumier or Courbet an Order of the British Empire, or the equivalent. Which is understandable. For Counihan's art, like all good realist art, seeks to subvert the class distinctions and social pretensions perpetuated by such baubles. His loyalties reside in the aspirations of common people for a better world containing less inequality, hypocrisy, inhumanity. It is made clear in his art. To work as he has done for over fifty years is an honour requiring no decorations.

It is now possible for the first time to appreciate the full range and quality of Counihan's graphic art, in the outstanding catalogue by Robert Smith, *Noel Counihan Prints 1931–1981: A Catalogue Raisonné* (Hale & Iremonger, Sydney, 1981). Each print is illustrated, each state described sufficiently to identify it. The types of paper used are given; the place and nature of the printings; significant identification marks; the known holdings in public collections; in short, all the information a specialist will require, whether a discriminating private collector or a museum curator. The introduction is excellent, providing an admirably clear account of the artist's working processes from initial drawing to finished print. It provides also the best discussion of Counihan's realism as a pictorial process.

In his introduction Robert Smith makes an important point. Artists do not always proclaim themselves in their large-scale

First published in the *Sydney Morning Herald*, 23 January 1982.

works. Their more intimate, more deeply felt perceptions are often realized in prints and drawings. This is true of some of the most renowned artists: Dürer, Rembrandt, Goya, Picasso. It is a characteristic Counihan shares with them. Smith explores in detail how the artist has evolved some of his most memorable images by progressively abstracting and generalizing from a highly particularized drawing or group of drawings. He reveals in the process the complexity of realism as a creative activity.

It is a complexity in which the pathos of individual life is sustained and transformed into more general truth. Not a nostalgic love affair with tradition in the nature of classicism, nor an obsession with form in the nature of modernism, but by a continuing commitment to the heroism and tragedy of contemporary life.

Consider the print *The Cough-Stone Dust*. It began with drawings of a miner whom the artist met at Wonthaggi in 1947; an Italian called Big Chris who had contracted silicosis and talked about his illness with Counihan. What resulted was not an illustration of one man but a secular icon embodying a general truth about the life of a miner in the twentieth century, whether he lives in Wonthaggi in 1947 or Silesia in 1982.

Or consider his image of the Australian Aboriginal artist Namatjira as the crucified Christ. It towers above the city and its spired cathedral, an image perhaps of St Paul's, Melbourne, where the young Counihan sang as a choirboy under the baton of a famous choirmaster, the late Dr A. E. Floyd. How vividly it brings to mind that other memorable Australian image of crucifixion: Norman Lindsay's *Pollice Verso*. In Lindsay's etching Christ crucified gets a lusty thumbs down from a group of young life-be-in-it white Australians as they dance their way to the double-fronted bungalow, two-car garage, and two-tier beer gut. Counihan's *Namatjira* might be read as a riposte to Lindsay's etching, reminding us that Norman's guilt-free society may not be so quickly achieved.

Such uses of traditional imagery are not uncharacteristic of Counihan's graphic art. His image of the *Laughing Christ* was evolved from a memory of Polish folk carvings, but transformed into a brilliant metaphor. It joins the image of Christ in torment with the image of the crowing cock that announced Christ's denial by Peter to the common people. Oddly enough no national or state gallery yet appears to have included this powerful but disconcerting image in its print collection.

Hale and Iremonger have produced a handsome book at a modest price with assistance from the Australiam Academy of the Humanities, Flinders University and the Visual Arts Board of the Australia Council. It is a catalogue that should become a model of its kind.

72
Lou Klepac on Drysdale
—1984—

His genius sets him apart from the very people he belongs to and mixes
with so well. They have the permanence, the sense of belonging, denied
to him, and when he paints them the loneliness of his own deprivation
as well as the strength of his identification comes through.

So wrote Geoffrey Dutton with shrewd insight of the work of
Sir Russell Drysdale in his excellent book on the artist published
twenty years ago. Drysdale was a little irritated by people like
Dutton who read loneliness, as he said, into his landscape. For
him there was no loneliness. The Australian landscape, he assured Dutton, was not lonely nor need it evoke fear. In the
interior one always had the company of birds; the ground was
full of insects and life. There were no savage animals, no endemic
fevers, nothing a 'normal healthy man' could not combat.

This was typical of Drysdale. There was a certain touchiness.
Suggest an influence, a parallel, the presence of a mood or a
possible interpretation for his paintings and he would be ready
with his rebuttals. He not only painted the pictures, he was
confident that he knew what they meant. But on such questions
as loneliness the paintings give one a greater feeling of conviction than the artist.

Yet we certainly run a risk if we ignore his readings of his own
work. For no Australian artist worked more deliberately towards
his intentions, nor more self-consciously. Even when he makes
use of the devices of surrealism—that art of chance and the
irrational—it is always for a premeditated effect; and he wants to
tell us, he insists, that the characters who inhabit his paintings
do not suffer from loneliness, nor are they filled with fear or

First published in the *Age Monthly Review*, June 1984, pp. 6–7.

melancholy. They do not suffer from such weaknesses. They are sticking it out. The land tests them but cannot destroy them. His vision is stoical. Heroes inhabit the Australian landscape, quaint heroes, positively surreal. You have to laugh perhaps. But not in their faces. He memorizes every stance and gesture as he drinks with them in a country pub. Then goes away and draws the images stowed in his memory: Rocky McCormick, Tom Finch, Greenhide Jack, Big Edna, Old Tom, The Drover's Wife. A gallery of real Australians. All bush types.

In his new and comprehensive book, *The Life and Work of Russell Drysdale* (Bay Books, Sydney, 1984), Lou Klepac tells how the artist and his wife lived for a time shortly after marriage at Eaglemont, a well-known haunt of Roberts, Streeton and Conder. Yet he did not respond, Klepac adds, 'to the pastoral tradition these painters had glorified'. In a technical sense this is true. His early training, first under George Bell, then in Paris, told against that kind of painting, the blue and gold palette, the *alla prima* methods. But Drysdale was born on both sides of his family into a long historic association with the pastoral industry, and it is in the particular nature of his response to the challenge that the pastoral tradition of the Heidelberg school presented him with, that Drysdale's great importance as an Australian artist lies: perhaps the most influential artist (I am not talking about style) of the early twentieth century in Australia.

Not, it goes surely without saying, the most aesthetically gratifying. A host of others: Godfrey Miller, Ian Fairweather, Dick Watkins even, come to mind. Drysdale's paintings have become highly treasured possessions not because of their beauty—although the colour is usually resonant and attractive—but because of their iconic significance. Before work of this kind the distinction between élitist and popular art, often made at the moment, becomes irrelevant. What begins as a highly radical move both in technique and imagery, understood and enjoyed only by an élite and professional audience, gradually achieves the character of popular imagery accepted throughout the nation. As Klepac notes, you can run into reproductions of Drysdale's paintings in just about every other pub in the country. A few other painters in Australia such as Roberts, Streeton and Heysen have achieved a similar distinction.

As an art student in Paris, Drysdale absorbed the lessons of post-impressionism, and its influence may be discerned clearly enough in his work. But to dwell on his European sources is to misunderstand profoundly the whole thrust of his work. The exhibition which he held in the Macquarie Galleries, Sydney, in 1941 is a landmark in the history of Australian painting. It revealed that he had developed from an art-student with a European message to an artist deeply concerned with contributing to an Australian tradition. The exhibition was the first to challenge the landscape stereotypes of Heidelberg painting and he devoted the rest of his life to the establishment of an alternative tradition of landscape. But he did not dislodge the pastoral tradition itself from its dominant position in Australian art. Instead he gave it a new twist.

People were painted back into the landscape, from which they had virtually disappeared since McCubbin's time, and a greater range of bush types, both male and female, white and eventually black, begin to make their appearance, expressed in terms of a pastoral myth which he had internalized, so that it could be said that he repainted the Australian legend before Russel Ward wrote its history. But whereas Ward was interested in tracing the radical, democratic roots of the legend, in Drysdale's hands it comes to serve an increasingly conservative purpose. Although bizarre and convivial characters confront us within his country towns, the isolated figures or family groups that battle it out in the country itself take on a heroic mould, living monuments to the pioneering virtues of endurance and survival. This legend of the pioneer, as J. B. Hirst has convincingly argued, elided the class division and self-interest that accompanied the pastoral occupation of Australia. Class relationships, inter-personal relationships even, play little part in his work. His characters stare out at us with a kind of glazed stoical vacancy, monuments of survival. The overall effect of his art was to recast the pastoral tradition from an arcadian into a heroic mould and thus reinforce landscape painting itself as the dominant genre of Australian art. So that today masters of Australian art (as distinct from those messengers of modernism and post-modernism who return from time to time from the northern hemisphere) are measured by their contribution to landscape painting. The apotheosis of the late Fred Williams as Australia's most recent old master is a case in point. Even the abstract expressionists of the 1950s who once rejected any kind of regional association are now legitimated by stressing those aspects of their art that evoke the spirit of the Australian landscape.

Drysdale's art would never have gained its widespread recognition had it not revealed a deep affinity for Australian country life that was closed to most Australian artists, born and bred in cities. It sprang initially from his strong populist sympathies. In an article Drysdale published in the *Society of Artists Book 1942*, he wrote:

this is the very time to encourage and foster our cultural movements so that from this period of trial and sacrifice we shall be able to build a new and vigorous growth with its roots firmly planted in the interests and expression of the common people ... it gives me little satisfaction to know that a picture I may paint in which I may strive to express and formulate an attitude to life becomes the property of one individual and thus practically a personal document for him alone.

For Drysdale, however, although he lived for most of his life in cities, the 'common people' are invariably inhabitants of the bush; types built out of his own keen observations and commitment, and the ubiquitous national legend that legitimated them. City workers, the industrial proletariat, play no part in Drysdale's art. He thus reinforced the pastoral myth and with it the predominance of landscape painting as a genre in Australian art. With the steady passing of time both have created a kind of Australian false consciousness.

It all began honestly enough. In the work of colonial landscape painters such as Martens, Glover, von Guerard and Gill a sense of identification with Australian experience begins to emerge; but with the growth of the cities landscape painting and the bush legend began to encourage compensatory fantasies that comforted but were far removed from the living experience of most Australians. During the post-war years this gap between city life and the popular rural imagery with which Australians have identified has become increasingly apparent.

It is just conceivable that it might have happened differently. During the war years images of the city of a highly personal kind arose in the work of a generation of young artists born and bred in cities. They were Drysdale's contemporaries: Tucker and Counihan, Nolan and Bergner, Arthur Boyd and Victor O'Connor were the principal ones. It was for the most part (although Nolan here was an exception) an image of an oppressive and corrupt city. So that in a sense it complemented the bush legend: the city was a good place to escape from. That is what many of them did as they grew more affluent, setting up their studios in picturesque landscape and turning increasingly to Australia's favoured genre, landscape painting.

Those historians who have attempted to bury Russel Ward's 'Australian legend' have shown little capacity to understand the protean nature of myth, from which both radical and conservative legends have emerged to serve the emotional needs of city and country people alike. The city as a promise to be fulfilled, especially Hugh Stretton's paradisal image of the suburb, has played little part in Australia's high visual culture. Yet it was the suburbs that made most of our artists—whatever they are.

The real fear was that city-based images would arouse political associations. Sali Herman was criticized for painting Sydney slums when he was in fact reacting to picturesque beauty that had been forgotten. To paint bush workers was to evoke a hallowed legend but there was no Australian cultural precedent for painting an urban proletariat. Those who during the Second World War painted memories of the Depression, mine-workers, refugees from Nazi terror, the conditions of urban Aborigines, were not seen as enlarging and liberalizing an extremely narrow iconographic tradition. They were indulging, most of the Australian art world agreed, in politics.

This was a fear that worried Drysdale. He did not want to be thought political. He concluded his article on 'Art and the People' with the comment: 'This may read, I feel, like a political diatribe, an impression I am anxious to avoid, as I have no political standpoint, only a sympathy for humanity which has made me a painter'. He was speaking for many, and as the 1940s came to an end and the cold war intensified most traces of a figurative, urban-based imagery began to disappear from Australian painting. Only a few courageous ones, like Counihan, persisted. But the high tradition in painting, from which Drysdale's popular imagery descended to 'the common people' remained steadfastly rural as it had been in colonial times; and landscape painting retained its hegemonic role.

Lou Klepac does not address these wider contextual concerns of Drysdale's art. Instead, quoting Sir Joseph Burke, the author of the first book on Drysdale, as his model, he structures his book around biographical detail into which he sprinkles general aesthetic comments somewhat haphazardly. Our knowledge of the influences bearing upon Drysdale's work is certainly deepened, and Klepac is particularly good on technical matters, such as Drysdale's use of black oil as a medium and his method of drawing from memory.

Yet I found it a disappointing book. The now considerable body of Drysdale criticism is not seriously engaged—although the customary acknowledgements are made. This third book on

Drysdale provided an admirable opportunity to revalue that criticism in the light of the artist's achievement. Nor does Klepac show any desire to penetrate beneath the public front of the artist in searching for a deeper understanding of his work. What are we to make of a boy, for example, reared in England who can remember 'virtually nothing' of two years spent in tropical Queensland between the age of seven and ten? A strange case indeed of prolonged infantile amnesia for an artist who was later to make so much of the bush. A discreet veil is drawn across the suicides of both Drysdale's son and wife. Perhaps that is as it should be. Friends like Donald Friend have been unstinting with their assistance, but one has the feeling at times that a curtain is being drawn across the inner life of the artist and that in place of understanding we are being presented with a cosy hagiography. Drysdale did not paint his own portrait. Perhaps that was the way he wanted it to be.

73
Fred Williams
—1988—

Fred Williams died of lung cancer at the age of fifty-five in 1982. Whether he was the most original Australian landscape painter of the twentieth century is best left to a later generation to decide, but it has become increasingly clear during the past twenty years that he was the most creative artist working in Australia within the aesthetic constraints of late modernism.[1]

Born in 1927, he was considerably younger than those other three artists. Russell Drysdale (born 1912), Sidney Nolan (born 1917) and Arthur Boyd (born 1920) who have transformed the public perception of the Australian landscape during recent years. Despite their debts to early modernism, expressionism and, especially, surrealism, those three retained the human figure as a major component of their pictorial imagination and continued to work in large measure within traditional pictorial categories: heroic, picturesque, sublime, and so on, though often in highly inventive ways. Williams in his search for an original mode virtually abolished the figure from the landscape and worked beyond traditional categories. Was it possible to absorb into one's own art the successive innovations of late modernism and retain a hold of one's personal perceptions both of the world and of picture-making? That was largely Williams' problem.

For the most original art produced in Australia has possessed a deeply conservative component, and has been radical in its conservatism, reaching back to European roots that present themselves as a broken and divergent tradition. On the one hand there is a local component that constantly asserts itself as an imperative of place. It has been present as a painting tradition since the 1880s and (though ultimately European in origin) has acclimatized itself to the local physical and social environment.

First published in *Modern Painters*, vol. 1, no. 1, February 1988.

There is also that other imperative, the continuing awareness of those avant-garde movements, also European and metropolitan, that Australian art students encounter in the schools, the galleries, the journals, and their visits to Europe and the United States. Being an original Australian artist is to a large extent a problem of coming to terms with this broken, diverging tradition.

Williams' conservatism is revealed in his training: an art student who was not a romantic rebel. He spent four years (1943–47) at the National Gallery School in Melbourne where he preferred the most conservative of teachers, William Dargie. He sought an adequate training in his craft. But the modern movement could not be ignored. From 1946 to 1950 he studied with George Bell, who taught a somewhat academic version of post-impressionism in his socially fashionable Melbourne school. He then spent five years (1951–56) in London taking classes at the Chelsea Art School under John Berger (he painted his portrait) and studying at the Central School of Arts and Crafts.

The comprehensive Williams retrospective mounted at the Australian National Gallery, Canberra, from 7 November 1987 to 31 January 1988, by its director James Mollison, documents fully these apprenticeship years. It reveals high skills in drawing and painting the nude, in portraiture; an artist equally at home in the varied techniques of water-colour, gouache and oil, and a highly competent etcher. As a student Williams was profoundly influenced by that realism which suddenly emerged in the western art world during the Second World War and continued into the early post-war years. It cut across and confounded the battle lines drawn between academic art and modernism during the 1930s. Williams' sympathetic response to the art of Daumier, apparent in his paintings, and to Goya, apparent in his etchings, is best understood as a personal response to the intellectual climate of those times. In this matter his work affords an interesting parallel with that of another Australian artist, William Dobell (1899–1970). Like Dobell, Williams spent a significant formative period of his later training in London living in conditions of austerity and occasional poverty: Dobell for ten years during the 1930s, William for five, during the early 1950s. Not surprisingly both responded to the life of London they experienced in the terms of a distanced, a voyeur's humanism, lightened occasionally by visual wit. But the similarity ends there. Dobell returned to Sydney in 1939 and during the war years painted some of the greatest examples of expressive realism in the history of Australian art. Williams returned to Melbourne in 1955 and, apart from an occasional portrait of a personal friend or a highly-placed academic dignitary, the human figure virtually disappeared from his art. What he did achieve, and it was considerable, was achieved within the constraints of the formal aesthetic that dominated Australian art during the 1960s, and the associated conditions of the patronage characteristic of the cold war.

Within the climate of that time he was able to find a creative space for himself by burying himself in the craft specifics of painting while maintaining a tenuous but firm grasp upon the natural world. As Patrick McCaughey has put it, 'His chief efforts as a painter are spent clarifying and elaborating the pictorial structure suggested to him in that direct contact and experience of nature... What he makes not what he sees is the centre and focus of his activity—although what he makes always proceeds from what he sees'.[2]

The aesthetic and craft foundations of his work are to be found in his study of the nineteenth-century masters, Daumier, Manet and Courbet, and the early moderns, Matisse, Monet and finally Cézanne. There was also a great admiration for the work of Turner, though his influence on Williams' work is much more difficult to assess. His art is grounded in the craft of these masters. There need be no doubt that he was aware of them but in his formative years there is no attempt to emulate the contemporary avant-garde artists of Europe, Britain or the United States. It is another example of his conservatism.

Following his return to Australia, Williams experienced some years of uncertainty and personal anxiety, unsure as to the direction his art should take. Set on a professional career, he avoided teaching and continued to work as a framer. In July 1957 he held an exhibition of paintings at the Australian Galleries, Melbourne, and exhibited a series of his London music hall etchings at John Reid's Gallery of Contemporary Art. Apart from a few English landscapes both exhibitions were figurative in their general emphasis and were well received by the critics. But there were few sales. Williams turned away from the human figure of his student years and devoted himself to landscape.

For him that also meant coming to terms with modernism. Avoiding perspective formats and flattening out the picture space, he experimented for a time with the early cubist manner of Braque. But the influence of cubism on Williams is easily exaggerated. The progressive reduction of illusory pictorial depth, for example, was not a cubist innovation, though it is often assumed to be. It is a traditional characteristic of the decor-

Fred Williams, *Portrall of Harry Rosengrave*, oil on canvas, 120.3 × 76.0 cm. Private collection.

ative arts. What became crucial to Williams' subsequent development was his involvement with Cézanne. It became a highly creative involvement. For whereas most artists, following Emile Bernard's example, have used Cézanne's art to legitimate a rejection of naturalism, Williams adopted Cézanne's methods rather than his manner. To the end of his life he made a practice of working regularly out of doors before the motif, from which he later developed and elaborated his pictorial metaphors of nature in the studio.

In so doing, Williams was assisted by the tensions ceaselessly obtaining between the broken, diverging traditions of Australian art. As a student in Melbourne he had been deeply impressed by the firm plastic construction present in the academic portraiture of Hugh Ramsay (1877—1906). The local tradition always meant a good deal to him. Whether he was aware of it or not it was unquestionably the conditions of patronage prevailing during the cold war that caused him to jettison the human figure from his practice; but he was not encumbered by that modernist tunnel vision which sees the past as a load of old junk. He sought both metropolitan and regional correlatives as he edged towards his own kind of originality. While experimenting in 1958—59 with cubist ways of organizing pictorial space he worked in Sherbrooke Forest, Victoria; that was where Tom Roberts (1856—1931), the founder of the Heidelberg school, produced during the 1920s some of the finest of his late landscapes. Responding to the impact of cubism Williams continued the visual exploration of Australian landscape where Roberts had left off. He reduced his palette, cut out horizons and skies, and turned his forest landscapes into a severe succession of verticals—the sort of thing that Edmund Burke would have called the artificial infinite. It was not possible for a viewer of those landscapes in those years, and probably not possible for Williams either, to know whether the reductivist moves into which his art was taking him would lead to a complete rejection of landscape and the emergence of a totally non-representational manner.

It was at this point that my own life intersected with Williams' and affected it in some ways. Around 1957—58 it had become increasingly clear to me that the local pressures on all sides, both in criticism and practice, towards a wholly non-representational, autonomous art, whatever merits might flow from it ultimately, would have the effect of erecting a powerful *aesthetic* censorship that would block the production of *new* figurative art. The Antipodean Manifesto of 1959 gave strident voice to that concern.

But as it happened, six of the seven artists who participated in the Antipodean Exhibition—Charles Blackman, Arthur and David Boyd, John Brack, John Perceval and Clifton Pugh—were all personal friends of Williams. At the outset he had been considered as a possible member of the group but largely on my advice he was not included. He later made it known that he felt that exclusion keenly. My own view was that inclusion would have placed him in an impossible position. An artist whose work then seemed to be on the verge of abstraction—Victor Pasmore's dramatic conversion to abstract art in 1947 and its subsequent effect on British painting had exercised a powerful influence on my own thinking—could hardly be expected to sign a strident attack on non-representational art.

The clamour that ensued in the Australian art world induced Williams to take stock of his own position. For a short time he experimented with abstract art. Then he began to feel his way forward towards a highly creative solution to his landscape problems.

Williams always stressed that he was not in love with the Australian landscape. He wanted to use it to make paintings. Like most colonial settlers he found the forested bushland monotonous. It possessed no focal centre. So he sought ways to create his own foci: ways that avoided the overarching categories of sublime and picturesque. Horizons, skies, people and, to a large extent, water, tended to disappear from his paintings. The gum tree, *fons et origo* of the Australian bushland, became his central concern. He sought new metaphors for the eucalypt and the eucalypt forest. The achievement was not an exercise in self-expression. He created a vision of the Australian landscape that has come to be accepted increasingly in recent years as being not only aesthetically but also culturally valid.

The new visual metaphors for landscape were first fully realized in the You Yangs and Upwey landscapes (1963—66). The space between objects becomes ambiguous: foliage, trunks and branching are interwoven into a single but dynamic spatial continuum. Yet the links with nature are not abandoned. His palette recalls colours long associated with the landscape: ochres, russets, pale olive greens, pale blues and dull brick reds. His surface textures are often rich and opulent, ranging through thin, scumbled transparent stains to creamy, impasted accents, or the colour is modulated and grained as if seen bleached by veils of dust or heat haze.

Sketching constantly before the motif was the true source of

Williams' originality, but an awareness of Cézanne's methods of composing in water-colour, and accidents arising in the translation of paintings into aquatint, with its curiously suggestive granulated surfaces probably assisted the process.

Not to have exhibited in the Antipodean Exhibition of 1959 in the long term assisted Williams as an artist and in the advancement of his reputation. The debate that the manifesto inaugurated created an aesthetic space between abstract art and figuration that remained open long enough for him to exploit in his own terms. On the other hand he did not have to confront the obloquy faced by the Antipodean group for their uncompromising critique of the limitations of abstract art. It is not surprising that none of the Antipodean group have ever been invited to exhibit their work in the Museum of Modern Art (MOMA), New York, despite the now recognized quality of their work. For all its championship of aesthetic freedom, those who challenge the theoretical basis of 'American type' painting are not welcome at MOMA. Yet by the 1970s many were seeking a middle way. MOMA was certainly not interested in exhibiting Australia's 1960s acolytes of the New York school. When Clement Greenberg arrived in Australia in 1968 he realized how derivative they were and preferred Antipodean type work. Not that such work could ever, in the light of the manifesto, be shown in New York. But the art of the United States' loyal little ally in the Pacific deserved some kind of recognition. William Lieberman solved the problem when he saw something of Williams' work on a visit in the early 1970s, and his *Landscapes of a Continent* was shown at MOMA in March 1977. Williams' art had been well received by virtually all of Australia's art critics following his breakthrough in the 1960s, but after the MOMA show, man, he had really made it. It was roses all the way!

Williams' work in the 1970s built on his creative breakthrough of the previous decade. A greater interest in pure colour emerged and a greater diversity of textures, but his work did not change radically. To some extent it became more naturalistic. Working on location with friends, such as John Perceval, his work was often subtly influenced by them. It is an aspect of his work that has not been studied.

Williams kept in touch with the younger generation, the colour-field painters of the 1960s, and was influenced by their work also. In his Australian Landscape series (1960–70) he reached the most minimal point in his *oeuvre*. They were, as Patrick McCaughey has written, 'works that appeared to contemporaries (still appear to some) to be the epitome of sixties painting... paintings which come out of other paintings and form part of a continuing progress to a logical conclusion'.[3]

But the Australian Landscape series is not Williams at his best. It reveals an element of eclectic uncertainty under the pressure of fashion, a kind of homage to young men who felt certain they had History on their side; confetti thrown across Australian desert sand to celebrate a marriage that never took place. During the 1970s Williams wisely moved back to a style of painting more in keeping with his genius. The best of his work, however, is to be found in its first flowering, in the Upwey landscapes of the mid-1960s.

Williams created a new naturalistic vision of Australian bushland landscape when naturalism was *in extremis*, a vision now increasingly winning public acceptance. His success with the Australian desert landscape is more problematic. True, there are some, such as James Mollison, who consider his Pilbara paintings, produced during the last years of his life, as summarizing 'his life's work as a landscape painter'.[4] That judgement is an almost irresistible topos with which to celebrate the death of the artist as hero. But I doubt whether there is much truth in it.

I doubt whether Williams had time to come to terms with the desert landscape. Looking at the paintings one is reminded of his predecessors, Heysen, Namatjira, Nolan, rather than Williams' own personal vision, even when the hieroglyphs of his vision are invoked. I doubt whether he felt spiritually comfortable with the Australian desert. There had been the case of those gouaches of Aboriginal graves that he had made at Tibooburra, in New South Wales, back in 1967–68. Though he tried, as Patrick McCaughey explains, to develop them, he could not:

Deep within Williams there was a resistance to mythmaking even when so pregnant an image presented itself. The mythos of the interior died before Williams's tough 'positivism', painting proceeded from the observed and not from romantic inspiration.[5]

But the Aboriginal graves were not myths; they were as much a part of Williams' contemporary reality as the trees from which the graves were constructed. There were regrettably some kinds of reality that neither Williams nor the minimal aesthetic were equipped to face. So the painting of the Pilbara series became the painting of a *terra nullius*, of spaces without a history. Like so many European travellers before him, the road to Tibooburra and the Pilbara had taken Williams far from the sacred country of Daumier and Goya.[6]

From 1963 on Williams kept a diary, at first for technical and professional reasons, but later developed into a full daily account of his life. I conclude with his entry for 5 June 1979 when he was painting in the Pilbara as a guest of CRA, the mining corporation:

Leave here at 8. There is more than a lack of reality about the place—because of a total shut-down of the mine. Today I hope to really get into things by having a full day of painting. Lyn gets me down to the road leading to the airport. I find a 'suitable' spot straight at the side of Mt Nameless. I work behind some small shrubs—but I collect a fair amount of dust. I have a lot of difficulty getting started—at one stage damn near give up.

I work on until the light has gone on 8 gouaches with mixed fortunes—but at least I have a fair-to-good look at it ... I am trying to work out a kind of symbol for the fascinating white trunked small gum (with a tubular base). Tomorrow I will have another go at it. Weather is quite perfect on around 21 each day. We eat steak and onions for dinner.[7]

Notes

[1] Patrick McCaughey, *Fred Williams*, Bay Books, Sydney, London, 1980, is the definitive monograph. See also James Mollison, *Fred Williams: A Souvenir Book of the Artist's Work in the Australian National Gallery*, Australian National Gallery, Canberra, 1987. For my own earlier comments on Williams, see the *Age*, Melbourne, 1 April 1964; *Australian Painting*, Oxford University Press, Melbourne, 1972, pp. 413–14; and 'Framing Fred Williams', *Meanjin*, vol. 3, 1981, pp. 389–94.

[2] McCaughey, p. 16.

[3] ibid., pp. 216–17.

[4] Mollison, p. 44.

[5] McCaughey, p. 196.

[6] On this particular point Lyn Williams, the artist's widow, has assured me that 'Fred was deeply moved by the contrast between the two graveyards at Tibooburra, particularly the humble and transient nature of the Aboriginal graves', and that 'he painted a number of oils from the gouaches made of the Aboriginal graves' (letter dated 20 May 1988). Yet the fact that McCaughey in his definitive study chose to ignore this aspect of Williams' work, and that the artist himself, for reasons unknown, apparently never exhibited the oil paintings of the Aboriginal graves, lends further point to my contention that Williams was working within the non-humanist constraints of late modernism.

[7] I wish to thank Lyn Williams for permission to quote this extract from Fred Williams' diary and for showing me many of the gouache paintings from the Pilbara.

74
Concerning Donald Brook's 'New Theory of Art'
—1988—

In his letter to *Meanjin* (no. 4, 1987), Professor Donald Brook assumes that I hold him responsible for what he describes as 'the poverty of the Aboriginal collections in the National Gallery of Victoria'. He misconstrues what I said. In fact, the National Gallery of Victoria possesses a small but interesting collection of Aboriginal art. What I did say (*Meanjin*, no. 2, 1987) was that Dr Ann Galbally's survey of the collection ignored its existence. Since I wrote, Dr Galbally has assured me that she was dissuaded from including a section on Aboriginal art by the former Director, Patrick McCaughey, who warned her that it might 'open a can of worms'. I went on to argue that the Gallery had been slow to recognize the existence of Aboriginal art, and cited its exclusion from Galbally's book as an instance. Obviously Professor Brook cannot be held solely responsible for this lack of recognition. I simply mentioned his theory as typical of an attitude that had prevailed for over a century and had deterred curators from including Aboriginal art in Australian collections.

Professor Brook has published his theory in several versions on different occasions. I shall confine myself to his article, 'A New Theory of Art' (*British Journal of Aesthetics*, Autumn 1980). Here, Brook begins by claiming that all definitions of art constructed in terms of a single necessary and sufficient condition (art as imitation, revelation, communication, expression, etc.) have failed. He proceeds to criticize Tolstoy and Clive Bell for rejecting the sonatas of Beethoven and most of the painting from Giotto to Cézanne respectively, in order to retain their essentialist definitions. Yet he obviously retains a lingering respect for their

First published in *Meanjin*, no. 1, 1988. (Professor Brook's rejoinder will be found in *Meanjin*, no. 2, 1988, pp. 165–70.)

capacity·to exclude works categorically: 'There were giants in those days', he comments. And well he might, for if we take his theory seriously we shall have to reject many more traditionally accepted masterpieces than ever Tolstoy or Bell did.

Brook's theory derives its gargantuan capacity for rejection in part from taking words too seriously. Under its guidance we enter a blind desert of cognition in which words are the only touchstones. We are confidently informed that, because the Ancient Greeks possessed no word clearly translatable into the English word 'art', they produced no art; *ergo*, Sophocles' *Antigone, The Odyssey*, the Parthenon and its marbles, the bronze Zeus from Cape Artemision, are not art. Nor did the Middle Ages possess a word for art after the manner that Brook defines it. Most medieval work, in his view, would be an exhibition of craft skill. So out with Chartres, out with the *Book of Kells*, out with the *Très Riches Heures*. It is open to doubt whether the *Mona Lisa* is a work of art, even though Leonardo might possibly have known what art was. There is no lack of intellectual courage here. Let's outdo Marinetti, here, now and in Adelaide, before modernism utters its last gasp.

Like the Greeks, traditional Australian Aboriginal cultures possessed no word that is translatable into 'art'. Therefore, Brook informs us, they cannot be said to produce art. On similar grounds, it might be argued that, because no Aboriginal languages possess words for the clavicle and scapula, it would be wrong to give these names to bones found in Aboriginal skeletons. And to the objection that bones are one thing and art another, it must be pointed out that Brook's theory provides for bones to be named as art simply by stipulation, as Duchamp transformed a urinal into an (artistic) fountain.

Brook distinguishes between art objects and art works. An art object is 'anything subjected to the kind of attention and given the use appropriate and peculiar to art', a definition about as circular as the music of the spheres. But the important point is that art objects are established by a voluntary act—attention. Whether an object is an art object or not will depend upon its being available for public appraisal by persons competent to decide whether it contributes to the 'process of discovery and invention in the very region of epistemological and linguistic uncertainty where what is, or what might be, individuated by a competent person is *not* yet apparent or clearly settled'. Now, to say all that is apparently to say a good deal. To simplify and, I trust, not to distort the meaning, an analogy with scientific invention is being suggested here but with an important qualification. Scientific invention arises within an institution—the institution of science—and thus serves a particular, a scientific interest. Art, on the other hand, transcends institutions, serving no particular interest but capable of performing a service to 'any and all institutions'.

It is difficult to grasp what Brook means here. How is it possible to serve any and all interests but no particular interest? If I asked my daughter to help serve all and everyone with a drink at a cocktail party but serve no particular person, I suspect she might think I was going ga-ga. Or is Brook thinking of the model of the benevolent terrorist, who will dispose of particular persons in order to serve all and any of the interests of humanity? Or does he mean, if I may use conventional language, that the *interpretation* of an art work is available to any point of view, any interest? If this is what he means, I would agree with him. But in that case, surely if the interpretation of a work is available to all interests it may come to serve a *particular* interest.

Brook's theory is a version, perhaps an inversion, of Kant's theory of art. Whereas for Kant, taste—aesthetic judgement—is characterized by disinterest, for Brook art is characterized by its service to all interests. But his theory is similar to Kant's in being a consumer's theory. It is the competent and voluntary judgement of critical appraisers that brings objects of art into existence.

How do they perform this task? By a process Brook calls modelling (again, the recourse to scientific analogy; there is a good deal of technological triumphalism at the heart of Brook's theory). What he seems to be saying is rather like Baudelaire's metaphor of the world as a forest of symbols. Obviously anything in the world may be made to serve as a sign for something else; that is the nature of language. Brook tends to collapse art into language. But the interesting idea is that the competent appraisers, these art makers who wander about the world's great forest of symbols, are licensed by his theory to spot, either in the form of artefacts or natural objects, *new* things emerging in the total symbolic forest. If it is an artefact it is entitled to be called a work of art. There are three possible grades of art works. An art work is *relative* if it does no more than extend the language of the artist. It is an *absolute* work if it also extends the language of his or her society. It is possible, too, that it may be a *super-absolute* art work if it extends the language of all existing societies. The fact that, on

Brook's account of the matter, all existing human societies will then need to possess a word for 'super-absolute' art fills me with no sense of joy.

You might well ask at this point, how does the artist get into the act? On this Brook is perfectly clear. Artists cannot produce works of art in the way that the appraisers of art objects identify them. Artists produce art by the production of 'non-voluntary concomitants' from their voluntary acts. To distinguish: voluntary acts, such as priming a canvas, are of course intentional; involuntary acts, such as stomach rumbling, unintentional. Non-voluntary concomitants are neither intentional nor unintentional; they arise as the uncontrollable consequences of voluntary activity. As an example, Brook cites the case of striking the floor a resounding blow with the hand when breaking a fall. The intent is to break the fall, the resounding blow a non-voluntary concomitant of the intention. Of course, non-voluntary concomitants are necessary but not sufficient conditions for the production of a work of art. Brook's notion raises interesting possibilities. Consider the case of a woman who desires a child and does not want to become involved in IVF technology. She must voluntarily engage in sexual intercourse in the hope that a non-voluntary concomitant will be pregnancy. That does not in itself make her child a work of art. But if the child were, say, Picasso, he could be rightly appraised as apt 'for use as a new ... prescriptive model' of a part of the world (Brook's functional requirement for an art work)—in Picasso's case, a model of the artist for the conditions of modernity. Would the mother then have produced a work of art or a work of nature?

Other difficulties arise in using the voluntary/non-voluntary distinction. There are logical problems. On one occasion Brook tells us that 'art works are things that have been made (wrought, constructed, even merely selected) explicitly to serve as art objects'. (Incidentally, this distinction, as Brook is aware, would reduce enormously the number of items in most of our art museums.) On this description, all the artist needs do is to make it and name it art. Brook, however, then proceeds to tell us that 'the success or failure' of an art work will depend upon its non-voluntary content. Non-voluntary content presumably gives the work a chance of being a good art work. But it is unclear here whether he means that a work that consists of nothing but voluntary activity is a poor art work or not an art work at all; whether the voluntary/non-voluntary distinction is a principle for grading or one for exclusion. Yet I should have thought that to make works of art that serve explicitly as art objects is a voluntary activity and to engage explicitly in non-voluntary activity is incomprehensible. That Brook intends the distinction to serve as a principle of exclusion seems clear from his statement that 'the manifestations of voluntary actions are considered to be works of design, craft or skillful performance'. These, being institutional in character and serving particular interests, cannot be admitted into the Brook realm of art.

The distinction also involves Brook in a functional problem, that of describing how a work of art comes into existence. On his account, the non-voluntary is never more than a concomitant of voluntary action. So the artist must engage in voluntary action and hope for the best. Nor is it the artist who distinguishes between his or her voluntary and non-voluntary goings on, but Brook's competent appraiser, who must decide whether a relative, absolute or super-absolute work of art has emerged or not. The artist is like the woman who must go to her doctor to be told whether she is pregnant. Here, as with Kant, art emerges as a function of judgement.

I think that this is a sound view, indeed an inescapable view, if the artist is allowed a place in the act. Brook overlooks the fact that art is a process before it is a thing. To understand art, we need to direct our attention more to its verbal than to its nominal implications. Those voluntary and non-voluntary components of which Brook speaks, by means of which a work of art is eventually constituted, come into play, and into interplay, before the work of art is named as such. Furthermore, the voluntary and non-voluntary activity may be interrupted, and in part, though not entirely, controlled by a sequence of attendant decisions. Some of the decisions may be concerned with the modification or adaptation of the non-voluntary concomitants of actions in order to produce a result that was not initially planned. Or, to use plain English, in the very process of production we may learn from our mistakes. Further, it must be said that the decision to stop process, to say that it is finished, or it works, is a voluntary one. But if artistry consists entirely of non-voluntary concomitants, how can the artist prevent himself or herself becoming committed, like the sorcerer's apprentice, to an endless process of non-voluntary activity? For stopping, short of dying from exhaustion, is surely a voluntary act.

In my view, Brook is correct in asserting that an art work is a mix of voluntary and non-voluntary activity. But in practice, in art practice and critical practice, it is not possible to separate them. Art is always produced and perceived within a matrix of craft.

A major weakness of Brook's theory is his lack of attention to the relationship between art and craft. He appears to view craft as little more than the routine application of acquired skill. He overlooks the fact that in human production outcomes are not to be identified with plans. This is true even of industrial art, another kind of art about which Brook has little to say. Here John Ruskin's insight is relevant: 'Men were not intended to work with the accuracy of tools, to be precise and perfect in all their actions'. Or, in less teleological language, human beings *cannot* work with the accuracy of tools nor, for that matter, can they invent tools that do not ultimately break down. As Eliot put it, 'between the conception and the creation falls the shadow'. It is in such shadows of the productive process, where skills fail and non-voluntary concomitants suggest either new possibility or total abandonment, that the metamorphoses take place. They occur in the *process* before the *work* has come into existence. And since crucial decisions are made in process, they are not readily reconstructed by a retrospective critical analysis. The artist and the craftsperson cover their tracks in the very act of moving towards completion.

For this process is as true for craft as it is for art. Craft incorporates non-voluntary concomitants just as fine art does. The birth of a skill is preceded by 'playful' experiment, by hunches, by tentative hypotheses, by trials and errors, by the voluntary and the non-voluntary. Craft skill inherits and embodies these components. So craft is the means by which the innovations of art are transmitted from artist to artist and from generation to generation. Craft is art's conservation as a dynamic process. And in practice it is rarely only that. As in fine art, at any given point in a craft process traditional skills may fail and the unforeseen appear at the point of engagement between action and material. Here, a decision may have to be made to adopt or adapt the non-voluntary concomitants of craft skills. To do so is not to cease to be craftsmanly and assume the role of fine artist; it is simply to accept, in Ruskin's terms, the nature of human production.

This does not mean that there is no valid distinction between the craft and the fine art processes; it is to say that craft and fine art are distinct modes of artistry. In my own view, the basic difference is that the craftsperson seeks quality in the sequence. A craftsperson does not make a good chair; he or she makes good chairs. A fine artist *qua* artist seeks quality in the unit; each work is expected to be somewhat different from or better than the preceding one. In practice, however, there is always a component of craft skill in fine art, and non-voluntary concomitants constantly arise in craft processes, sometimes in residual, sometimes in novel forms.

Because Brook's theory is neo-Kantian and gives the crucial role for naming art to an act of judgement, it rests uneasily with his contention that art can only be produced by societies like our own, which have given a name to it. If art issues from critics' judgements rather than artists' processes, one would have thought it necessary only for the critics to belong to a society that has a name for art. If they should find, in the artefacts of a society with no name for art, things that comply with all their requirements for art, why should they shrink from accepting such artefacts into their world of art? The significance Brook gives to 'non-voluntary concomitants' as a necessary condition of art indicates that he believes artists are never quite sure just what it is they are producing, whether in tribal or modern societies. On his account it is not necessary for the artist to *know* what art is in order to produce it.

It seems that Brook's reluctance to accept tribal artefacts as art is due to the fact that he believes them incapable of providing '*new* hypothetical or prescriptive models of the world or some part of it', models that may contribute to personal, societal or universal discovery, according to whether they are assessed as relative, absolute or super-absolute art. In Brook's view, tribal 'art' only 'reaffirms an already received understanding of the world'. This is to accept at face value the discredited view that tribal societies are closed, static entities in which so-called 'art' only serves to reinforce a mindless recurrence of custom and ritual. Now, apart from its reactionary, Eurocentric assumptions, this is not the question that Brook should be asking, on his own account of the matter. The relevant question for western appraisers is the aptness of tribal art for a better understanding of modernity. This is precisely the question that the early modernists began to ask themselves towards the end of the nineteenth century. In so doing they greatly enlarged our understanding of art, and of western society itself. The so-called 'primitive' art became, to put it in Brook's words, 'a *new* prescriptive model ... of how things might be ... in the world'.

75
Realist Art in Wartime Melbourne
—1988—

I am glad to say that I have never considered painting simply as a pleasure-giving art, a distraction; I have wanted, by drawing and by colour since these were my weapons, to penetrate always further forward into the consciousness of the world and of men, so that this understanding may liberate us further each day . . . These years of terrible oppression have proved to me that I should struggle not only for my art but with my whole being.[1]

Seriously threatened from the north by Japan and with the greater part of its armed forces deployed in the Near East, Australia was extremely fortunate to escape invasion and the destruction of its cities. Although most of them were mobilized either in the armed or civilian forces, Australian artists found ways of continuing their personal work. The traumatic wartime experience produced a new art in Australia of great power and originality that is still little known beyond its shores.

There are parallels with the United States but Australia did not become an asylum for modernism. No world-famous expressionists or surrealists, running from Hitler, imported their *Angst* to Australia. To a very large extent we were left to cultivate and cope with our own. Whereas the United States became the principal theatre of late modernism in its least creative and most doctrinaire phase, Australian artists during the war clung desperately to the humanist components of early modernism and succeeded in developing an art with a public presence; one that did not, however personal its sources, seek to privatize the emotions completely.

Since the publication of Richard Haese's *Rebels and Precursors*

First published in the catalogue to Angry Penguins and Realist Painting in Melbourne in the 1940s, Hayward Gallery, London, 19 May to 14 August 1988, pp. 55–61.

(1981) the view has gained ground that the emergence of this new radical wartime art resulted from the triumph of an open-minded liberalism championed by John Reed and the group of artists associated with the journal *Angry Penguins* over the rigid 'Stalinist' views maintained by the group of social realists centred upon the work and activities of Noel Counihan and Victor O'Connor. In this respect the book has given an air of historical legitimacy to an implicit attitude that has marginalized realist art from the contemporary art market and the curatorial art world since the late 1940s. The book is thus best viewed, despite its documentary value, as a product of aesthetic values generated by the cold war.[2]

For those who lived through it the wartime art situation was far more complex. During the war realism found favour among a wide range of artists and its influence affected many of the current styles. It was present in the work of artists who professed little or no interest in politics, such as William Dobell, Russell Drysdale and Ivor Hele. Artists were in search of a mode that could relate their personal experience to the wartime situation and many found it in some form of realism, a realism that in the search for personal expression often drew upon expressionism, surrealism, and even constructivism.

Clive Bell had insisted that 'the one good thing a society could do for an artist is to leave him alone. Give him liberty'. Such views rapidly fell out of favour with many young radical artists after the outbreak of war. Mouthing the sacred nature of one's personal right to do one's own thing had not saved a generation of German modernists. What was the role of the artist—citizen in a society engaged in a war universally considered to be just? That was the overarching question that at first united and then divided the young radical artists of Melbourne who, led by John Reed, took over the Contemporary Art Society from George Bell, the founder of the society, and his artist associates within one year of the society's foundation.

They were all radicals either in their art or their politics, and usually in both. Many, such as Tucker, Harris and Vassilieff, were members of the Communist Party of Australia (CPA) during the early years of the war, and others, such as John Reed, maintained a friendly fellow-travelling relationship with it by assisting in the party's election campaigns and in other ways.

The union of avant-garde art and radical politics that developed at this time was expressed in the constitution of the Contemporary Art Society:

By the expression 'contemporary art' is meant all contemporary painting, sculpture and other visual art forms which is or are original and creative or which strive to give expression to progressive contemporary thought and life as opposed to work which is reactionary or retrogressive, including work which has no other aim than representation.

So long as Hitler continued to triumph in Europe and the threat of invasion by Japan remained, the uneasy truce between the apolitical avant-garde and the politically committed artists was sustained. But in 1944, with an Allied victory in sight, a prolonged debate, initiated by an exchange between Tucker and Counihan, erupted. The fact that for months this debate was carried on in the *Communist Review*, the CPA's theoretical journal (with party and non-party people including John Reed participating) is itself an indication that the party had no programmatic cultural programme. It is true that there were intemperate views and dogmatic opinions expressed by individuals on both sides. But it is a falsification of the situation to construct it as a contest between liberals and programmatic realists. There is a sense in which, so far as the Australian art world was concerned, Counihan and O'Connor, in seeking an alliance between conservative and progressive artists in the united front against fascism, were more liberal than the circle associated with *Angry Penguins*.

What has not been sufficiently understood is that the upsurge of wartime realism challenged some of the central assumptions of the modernist aesthetic. The Contemporary Art Society constitution accepted all art except that with no other aim than 'representation'; what the avant-garde of the time did not grasp was that all art is a representation. In practice being modernist in the early 1940s meant gaining your inspiration from child art, primitive art, literature, psychoanalysis or sacred geometry. But those who went *directly* to their own life experience were suspect—that was 'representational' art.

There was nothing at all programmatic about the realism, if that is the word for it, of O'Connor, Bergner and Counihan. What they sought to do, and succeeded brilliantly in doing, was to delve into their own inner feelings and experiences and create works that would stand as a witness to those times, and in so doing share their feelings with others. The fact that such art drew upon many of the traditional skills of the academy and of naturalism meant that it rested uneasily with the de-skilling propensities of modernism. So long as Hitler remained undefeated this odd-man-out modernism was tolerated. But as soon as victory was in sight the tensions engendered erupted in conflict. The realist

Albert Tucker, *Victory Girl*, 1945, oil on canvas, 120.3 × 76.0 cm. Australian National Gallery, Canberra.

threat to the modernist aesthetic, however, remained hidden; the debate was conducted at the level of art politics. The realists had committed the unforgivable sin of placing their public responsibility as citizens before their traditional role as artists; had blasphemed the enduring romantic icon, that of the alienated artist creating in isolation and splendour, apart from his own society. Their wartime act was to haunt them for the rest of their lives. Whenever they held an exhibition during the long years of the cold war, critics, however laudatory, would feel bound to preface their comments with a caveat recalling that they had once in youth subscribed to the socialist heresy of realism. It served, whatever its intention, as sufficient warning to collectors and curators. The artists experienced difficulty in selling their work, it was rarely bought by public galleries, and never included in major overseas exhibitions of Australian art. They were marginalized. Realist art was unspeakable.

Yet a fair-minded assessment will reveal that their wartime work was just as personal and passionate, as much involved with the terror and contradictions of those times, as that of their colleagues who turned for inspiration to French literature, child and primitive art, psychoanalysis, sacred geometry and the archetypes of Jung, and then went on to become the heroes of the post-war Australian art establishment. So that after the passage of forty years one begins to wonder at times, perhaps a little cynically, who then was in it for real and who for personal advancement?

Consider the case of Victor O'Connor, one of the most sensitive painters of mood and place to emerge during the war years. One of his earliest works, *The Acrobats*, shown in the 1941 Contemporary Art Society Exhibition, was singled out by Paul Haefliger, the distinguished art critic of the *Sydney Morning Herald*, as 'one of the most outstanding works in the show'. It shared the society's prize with Donald Friend. O'Connor was not then and never has been a programmatic realist, and deeply resents being stereotyped as a painter with solely political interests. His paintings arose, in those early traumatic war years, from a deep sense of outrage, of inner spiritual loss, that the civilization of Europe which we had all been taught to admire since childhood seemed on the brink of total destruction:

Recollections which I was just old enough to have of the hardship and deprivation of the depression years and their injustices began to give me figures and themes to provide some equivalent of the flight and dispossession of the oppressed minorities of Europe and I painted them against the only landscape I knew, the inner city and my view of it.[3]

It was as a result of winning the Contemporary Art Society 1941 prize that O'Connor came into touch with Bergner and Counihan.

Yosl Bergner grew up in Warsaw, a member of a distinguished family of musicians, writers, poets, painters and dancers. His father, the well-known Yiddish poet known as Melech Ravitch, had visited Australia in 1934 in search of a homeland for Jews in the Kimberley district of northern Australia, but the search came to nothing. Yosl arrived in Melbourne at the age of seventeen. He had intended to be a painter from the beginning and had already taken lessons in painting from the artists Altman and Friedman in Warsaw. In Melbourne, though living in conditions of dire poverty, he quickly established relations with the young radical artists of the time, and during the early years of the war, as personal knowledge came through to him of the fall of Warsaw and the destruction of the ghetto, he painted a profoundly moving and powerful series of paintings that for their sustained intensity and melancholy grandeur are without parallel in the art of wartime Australia. Wartime Melbourne, its markets and working people, the urban Aborigines of Fitzroy, were mirrored in his personal experience of loss. To associate such work with the atrocities of Stalin is an obscenity. But it is only during the 1980s that his wartime work has received a measure of rehabilitation in Australia. Fortunately for his development as an artist he left Australia in 1948 to begin a new life in Israel.

It was the intellectual leadership of Noel Counihan that in large measure, though not entirely, held the small Melbourne realist group together, and it is because of his opposition to the views expressed by the ex-Communist painter Albert Tucker that his reputation has had to bear the guilt-by-association smear of Stalinism. Counihan, a little older than the others, had joined the CPA in 1931; he developed his great natural skills as a draughts-man in graphic art and caricature, and was actively involved in the desperate free speech struggles of the unemployed in Melbourne during the Depression years.

Counihan turned from graphics to painting, partly inspired by Yosl Bergner, while convalescing from tuberculosis for a year in a sanatorium in Victoria. His approach to painting was highly personal, but his socialist beliefs led him to search for a personal art he could readily share with others. He was deeply convinced that art was a sharing of the emotions and distrusted highly individualistic positions. In 1943, when I was writing my first book, *Place, Taste and Tradition* (1945), I asked Counihan if he would outline for me the intentions of the realist Melbourne group, so far as they could be expressed in words. At that time I had not met any of them but had been deeply impressed, in the Sydney exhibitions of the Contemporary Art Society (1941–43), with the passionate intensity and sincerity of their work. He replied, 'Our trend at present is to endeavour to reach the most important, most suggestive social subject matter by digging into the depths of our intimate individual *experience*—that is, the *indirect* approach, to reveal the social relations involved in our most intimate experience'. Their 'realism' required the recol-lection and invocation of past memories, of former experience, by means of which they constituted their own identities as artists.

John and Sunday Reed bought Noel Counihan's first painting, *The pregnant woman*, painted shortly after coming out of the sanatorium and exhibited in the Contemporary Art Society show of 1941 with a price tag of fifteen guineas. The Reeds offered him ten (or it may have been eight) guineas for it, which he was pleased to accept. But it did not make him over-enthusiastic about the nature of their patronage. Nevertheless it must be said that in the end they put together a most admirable collection. It is now part of the Australian national heritage. Selected young radicals artists associated with the Contemporary Art Society in the early 1940s received invitations from time to time from John and Sunday Reed to their house Heide, on the river Yarra in the outskirts of Melbourne, where they maintained a kind of salon, somewhat reminiscent of Lady Ottoline Morrell's at Garsington, and patronized aspiring young artists of talent. Neither Counihan nor O'Connor ever received an invitation to Heide. Perhaps the Reeds felt, being highly sensitive people, that these two had acquired radical views that might last them a lifetime. Bergner was invited once, but after being accused of stealing he never went again.

Perhaps such small, petty things should not be allowed to disturb the calm waters of today's heritage histories. There were faults of dogmatism on both sides, faults more readily forgiven had the realist artists been given some place in the high art of the 1950s and 1960s. But late modernism developed its own peculiar modes of aesthetic censorship. The realists were marginalized almost to extinction and today only their wartime art is much sought after by collectors and curators. Yet their achievement was formidable. They were the first to depict in Australia's 'high art' the frightful conditions of present day Aboriginal society, and the conditions of working-class life during the great Depression; and they foreshadowed, in paintings of prophetic solemnity, the great horror of the Holocaust. Their work deserves to be better known and given a fair go.

Notes

[1] Picasso to Pol Gaillard, October 1944, quoted in Roland Penrose, *Picasso*, Victor Gollancz, London, 1958.

[2] The book may be compared in this regard with Donald D. Egbert's *Social Radicalism and the Arts*, Alfred A. Knopf, New York, 1970, but Egbert attempts to present a more objective perspective on a world scale.

[3] Letter dated January 1988.

Index